First World War
and Army of Occupation
War Diary
France, Belgium and Germany

2 DIVISION
Divisional Troops
Royal Army Medical Corps
6 Field Ambulance
5 August 1914 - 31 August 1919

WO95/1338

The Naval & Military Press Ltd
www.nmarchive.com
Published in association with The National Archives

Published by

The Naval & Military Press Ltd

Unit 10 Ridgewood Industrial Park,

Uckfield, East Sussex,

TN22 5QE England

Tel: +44 (0) 1825 749494

www.naval-military-press.com

www.nmarchive.com

This diary has been reprinted in facsimile from the original. Any imperfections are inevitably reproduced and the quality may fall short of modern type and cartographic standards.

© Crown Copyright
Images reproduced by permission of The National Archives, London, England, 2015.

Contents

Document type	Place/Title	Date From	Date To
Heading	2nd. Division 6th. Field Ambulance Aug-Dec 1914		
Heading	6th. Field Ambulance Volume I Aug 1914		
Heading	2 Division Troops 6 Field Ambulance 1914 Aug To 1919 Aug		
Miscellaneous	O.C. 6th. Field Ambulance	12/10/1914	12/10/1914
War Diary	Redan Hill Camp Aldershot	05/08/1914	09/08/1914
War Diary	Nursery Camp Nr Farnborough	10/08/1914	11/08/1914
War Diary	Nursery Camp	11/08/1914	17/08/1914
War Diary	Southampton Docks	18/08/1914	18/08/1914
War Diary	Mouth Of Seine "S.S Honorius"	19/08/1914	19/08/1914
War Diary	Bruyres-Camp	20/08/1914	20/08/1914
War Diary	Train To Aul-Noye	21/08/1914	21/08/1914
War Diary	Aul Noye	22/08/1914	22/08/1914
War Diary	Bonnet	23/08/1914	23/08/1914
War Diary	Pont Sur Sambre	24/08/1914	24/08/1914
War Diary	Maroille	25/08/1914	25/08/1914
War Diary	La Carte	26/08/1914	26/08/1914
War Diary	La Groise	27/08/1914	27/08/1914
War Diary	Amrigny	28/08/1914	28/08/1914
War Diary	Servais-Armigny	29/08/1914	29/08/1914
War Diary	Three Kilos From Soisson	30/08/1914	30/08/1914
War Diary	St. Dandry 1 Kilo Off	31/08/1914	31/08/1914
Heading	6th. Field Ambulance Vol II Sept 1914		
War Diary	Ambleney	01/09/1914	01/09/1914
War Diary	Boursone	02/09/1914	02/09/1914
War Diary	Oiuse	02/09/1914	02/09/1914
War Diary	Pierrie-Levee	03/09/1914	03/09/1914
War Diary	Moroux	04/09/1914	04/09/1914
War Diary	Chaumes	05/09/1914	05/09/1914
War Diary	Place ?	06/09/1914	06/09/1914
War Diary	Chailly	07/09/1914	07/09/1914
War Diary	Relais	08/09/1914	08/09/1914
War Diary	Charly	09/09/1914	09/09/1914
War Diary	Cheillon	10/09/1914	10/09/1914
War Diary	Ouchly-Chateau	11/09/1914	11/09/1914
War Diary	Braisne	12/09/1914	12/09/1914
War Diary	North Of Vieil Arcy	13/09/1914	13/09/1914
War Diary	Verneuil (Chatea Bourg-Et-Corisin)	14/09/1914	14/09/1914
War Diary	Chateau	15/09/1914	17/09/1914
War Diary	(L'Hopital) Vieil-Arcy	18/09/1914	20/09/1914
War Diary	Vieil Arcy	21/09/1914	30/09/1914
Heading	6th. Field Ambulance VolII Oct 1914		
War Diary	Vieil Arcy	01/10/1914	14/10/1914
War Diary	Bazoches	15/10/1914	15/10/1914
War Diary	On France	16/10/1914	16/10/1914
War Diary	Hazebrouck	17/10/1914	31/10/1914
Heading	6th. Field Ambulance Vol IV Nov 1914		
War Diary	Ypres	01/11/1914	04/11/1914
War Diary	Billetts	05/11/1914	08/11/1914
War Diary	Same Billets	09/11/1914	26/11/1914

War Diary	In Billets	27/11/1914	30/11/1914
Heading	6th. Field Ambulance Vol V Dec 1914		
War Diary	In Billets At Caestre	01/12/1914	01/12/1914
War Diary	In Billets	02/12/1914	05/12/1914
War Diary	Billets	06/12/1914	21/12/1914
War Diary	On Line Of March	22/12/1914	22/12/1914
War Diary	Billet At Bethune College Des Jeones Filles Rue Marcellin Bertuelot Bouleuard Victor Hugo	23/12/1914	23/12/1914
War Diary	Same Billets	24/12/1914	28/12/1914
War Diary	Ecole Paul Bert Rue Du Marais Bethune	29/12/1914	29/12/1914
War Diary	Same Billets	30/12/1914	31/12/1914
Heading	2nd Division No. 6 Field Ambulance Jan-Dec 1915		
Heading	No. 6 Field Ambulance Vol VI Jan 1915		
War Diary	Ecole Paul Bert Rue Du Marais Bethune	01/01/1915	01/01/1915
War Diary	Same Billets	02/01/1915	24/01/1915
War Diary	Farm Belonging To M Cantrainne Robecq	25/01/1915	25/01/1915
War Diary	Same Billets	26/01/1915	31/01/1915
Heading	No. 6 Field Ambulance Vol VII Feb 1915		
War Diary	Ecole De Qarcons Vendin-Lez-Bethune	01/02/1915	01/02/1915
War Diary	College St. Vaast Bethune	02/02/1915	02/02/1915
War Diary	Same Billet	03/02/1915	28/02/1915
Heading	No. 6 Field Ambulance Vol VIII March 1915		
War Diary	Seminaire St. Vaast Bethune	01/03/1915	01/03/1915
War Diary	Same Billet	02/03/1915	31/03/1915
Heading	No. 6 Field Ambulance Vol IX April 1915		
War Diary	Same Billet	01/04/1915	30/04/1915
Heading	No. 6 Field Ambulance Vol X May 1915		
War Diary	College St. Vaast Bethune	01/05/1915	01/05/1915
War Diary	Same Billet	02/05/1915	21/05/1915
War Diary	Burbure Boys School	22/05/1915	22/05/1915
War Diary	Same Billets	23/05/1915	30/05/1915
War Diary	Chateau Le Mont Evenic D.19.6 France Sheet 36C 1.40,000	31/05/1915	31/05/1915
Heading	No. 6 Field Ambulance Vol XI June 1915		
War Diary	Chateau Le Mont Evenic D.19.6	01/06/1915	01/06/1915
War Diary	Same Billet	02/06/1915	10/06/1915
War Diary	Ecole Verquin E.29.C.	11/06/1915	11/06/1915
War Diary	Same Billet	12/06/1915	23/06/1915
War Diary	College St. Vaast Bethune	24/06/1915	24/06/1915
War Diary	Same Billet	25/06/1915	30/06/1915
Heading	2nd Division No. 6 Field Ambulance Vol XII July 1915		
War Diary	Same Billet	01/07/1915	31/07/1915
Heading	2nd Division No. 6 7A Aug 1915		
War Diary	Seminaire St. Vaast Bethune	01/08/1915	01/08/1915
War Diary	Same Billet	02/08/1915	31/08/1915
Heading	2nd Division 6th. Field Ambulance Vol XIII Sept To Oct 15		
War Diary	Same Billet	01/09/1915	30/09/1915
Heading	No. 6 F.A. Oct 1915		
War Diary	Same Billet	01/10/1915	31/10/1915
Heading	2nd Division No. 6 F.Amb Nov Vol XIV		
War Diary	Same Billet	01/11/1915	10/11/1915
Heading	2nd Div 6th. Field. Amb Dec XV Dec 1915		
War Diary	Same Billet	01/12/1915	31/12/1915
Heading	2nd Division Medical No. 6 Field Ambulance Jan-Dec 1916		

Type	Description	From	To
Heading	2nd Division 6 Fd. Ambulance Vol XVI Jan 1916		
War Diary	20 Rue De Lillers Bethune	01/01/1916	01/01/1916
War Diary	Same Billet	02/01/1916	31/01/1916
Heading	2nd Division No. 6 Fld Amb Feb To Mar 1916		
Miscellaneous	D.A.G. Base	29/02/1916	29/02/1916
War Diary	Same Billet	01/02/1916	02/02/1916
War Diary	W.2.A.8.2 Bethune Map 1/40000	03/02/1916	03/02/1916
War Diary	Same Billet	04/02/1916	14/02/1916
War Diary	Busnes	15/02/1916	15/02/1916
War Diary	Same Billet	16/02/1916	27/02/1916
War Diary	Chamboro Barrack Bethune	28/02/1916	28/02/1916
War Diary	Bruay France 36B Third Echelon J.15.B.5.4	29/02/1916	29/02/1916
Heading	6 Fd Amb Vol XVIII		
War Diary	J.11.B.4.5 France Map 36B 3rd Echelon	01/03/1916	01/03/1916
War Diary	Same Billet	02/03/1916	09/03/1916
War Diary	J.36.D.1.7 Sheet 38B	10/03/1916	10/03/1916
War Diary	Same Billet	11/03/1916	17/03/1916
War Diary	J.22.A.2.8 36B Sheet 6th. Echelon	18/03/1916	18/03/1916
War Diary	Same Billet	19/03/1916	31/03/1916
Heading	2nd Div. No. 6 Field. Amb April 1916		
Heading	6 Fd. Amb Vol XIX		
War Diary	J.22.A.2.8	01/04/1916	01/04/1916
War Diary	Same Billet	02/04/1916	16/04/1916
War Diary	R.8 Central Map 36B "Josse Jen"	17/04/1916	17/04/1916
War Diary	Same Billet	18/04/1916	30/04/1916
Heading	2nd Division No. 6 Field. Amb May 1916		
War Diary	Josse Jen R.8 Central Map 36B	01/05/1916	01/05/1916
War Diary	Same Billet	02/05/1916	19/05/1916
War Diary	Maisnil Les Ruitz J.36.C.8.6 36B	19/05/1916	19/05/1916
War Diary	Monneville N.5.A.4.7 36B	21/05/1916	21/05/1916
War Diary	Same Billet	22/05/1916	22/05/1916
War Diary	Fresnicourt Q.19.D.4.3 Sheet 36B	23/05/1916	23/05/1916
War Diary	Same Billet	24/05/1916	25/05/1916
War Diary	Estree-Cauchie W. 2.A.4.6	26/05/1916	26/05/1916
War Diary	Same Billet	27/05/1916	31/05/1916
Heading	2nd Division No. 6 Field Ambulance June 1916		
War Diary	Les Quatre Beuts W9 Central Sheet 36B	01/06/1916	01/06/1916
War Diary	Same Billet	02/06/1916	30/06/1916
Heading	2nd Division No. 6 Field Ambulance July 1916		
War Diary	Quatre Vents	01/07/1916	17/07/1916
War Diary	Q.19.D.7.1 Fresnicourt	18/07/1916	18/07/1916
War Diary	Ferme D'estrayelle	19/07/1916	20/07/1916
War Diary	Saleux	21/07/1916	21/07/1916
War Diary	Corbie	22/07/1916	22/07/1916
War Diary	Main Dressing Stn Dive. Copse J.24.B Sheet 62D	23/07/1916	26/07/1916
War Diary	Main Dressing Station	27/07/1916	30/07/1916
War Diary	Dive Copse	31/07/1916	31/07/1916
Heading	2nd Division No. 6 Field Ambulance Aug 1916		
Heading	A.D.M.S. 2nd Division		
War Diary	Dive Copse	01/08/1916	11/08/1916
War Diary	Ville-Sur-Ancre	12/08/1916	13/08/1916
War Diary	Picquigny	14/08/1916	16/08/1916
War Diary	Fresselles	17/08/1916	17/08/1916
War Diary	Gorges	18/08/1916	18/08/1916
War Diary	Bus Les Artois	19/08/1916	28/08/1916
War Diary	Coigneux	29/08/1916	31/08/1916

Heading	No. 6 F.A. 2nd Division Sept To Oct 1916		
Heading	A.D.M.S.		
War Diary	Coigneux	01/09/1916	10/09/1916
War Diary	Same Billet	10/09/1916	20/09/1916
War Diary	Coigneux	21/09/1916	30/09/1916
Heading	A.D.M.S.		
War Diary	Coigneux	01/10/1916	11/10/1916
War Diary	Varennes	12/10/1916	17/10/1916
War Diary	Bertrancourt J.33.A.5.3	18/10/1916	19/10/1916
War Diary	Bertrancourt	20/10/1916	31/10/1916
Heading	2nd Division No. 6 Field Ambulance Nov 1916		
Heading	A.D.M.S.		
War Diary	Bertrancourt	01/11/1916	18/11/1916
War Diary	Bretel	19/11/1916	20/11/1916
War Diary	Le Meillard	21/11/1916	22/11/1916
War Diary	Ribeaucourt	23/11/1916	23/11/1916
War Diary	Froyelles	24/11/1916	24/11/1916
War Diary	Neuilly L'Hopital	25/11/1916	26/11/1916
War Diary	Yvrencheux	27/11/1916	27/11/1916
War Diary	Maison Rolland	28/11/1916	30/11/1916
Heading	2nd Div No. 6 Field Ambulance Dec 1916		
Heading	A.D.M.S.		
War Diary	Maison Rolland	01/12/1916	31/12/1916
Heading	2nd Division War Diary 6th. Field Ambulance January To 31st. December 1917		
War Diary	Maison Rolland	01/01/1917	08/01/1917
War Diary	Vacquerie	09/01/1917	10/01/1917
War Diary	Val-De-Maison	11/01/1917	11/01/1917
War Diary	Senlis	12/01/1917	12/01/1917
War Diary	Ovilliers Huts	13/01/1917	28/01/1917
War Diary	Ovillers	29/01/1917	30/01/1917
Heading	No. 6 Field Ambulance		
Miscellaneous	A.D.M.S.	06/02/1917	06/02/1917
Heading	War Diary No. 6 Field Ambulance Vol 31 February 1917		
War Diary	Ovilliers Huts	01/02/1917	20/02/1917
War Diary	Albert W.28.C.5.6	22/02/1917	23/02/1917
War Diary	Albert	25/02/1917	28/02/1917
War Diary	Albert Ecole Des Jeans Gens	01/03/1917	09/03/1917
War Diary	Albert	10/03/1917	23/03/1917
War Diary	Vadencourt	25/03/1917	25/03/1917
War Diary	Doullens	26/03/1917	26/03/1917
War Diary	Beauvois	27/03/1917	27/03/1917
War Diary	Blangermont	28/03/1917	29/03/1917
War Diary	Sachin	30/03/1917	31/03/1917
Miscellaneous	B.E.F. Summary Of Medical War Diaries For 6th. F.A. 2nd. Divn 13th. Corps 1st Army		
War Diary	Headquarters		
War Diary	Operations R.A.M.C.	01/04/1917	06/04/1917
War Diary	Moves	07/04/1917	10/04/1917
War Diary	Transfer	10/04/1917	10/04/1917
War Diary	Moves	12/04/1917	12/04/1917
War Diary	Moves Detachment	12/04/1917	12/04/1917
War Diary	Transfer	13/04/1917	13/04/1917
War Diary	Operations R.A.M.C.	16/04/1917	16/04/1917
War Diary	Casualties	16/04/1917	16/04/1917

War Diary	Moves Detachment	27/04/1917	27/04/1917
War Diary	Operations R.A.M.C. Health Of Troops	30/04/1917	30/04/1917
War Diary	Headquarters		
War Diary	Operations R.A.M.C.	01/04/1917	06/04/1917
War Diary	Moves	07/04/1917	10/04/1917
War Diary	Transfer	10/04/1917	10/04/1917
War Diary	Moves To Maronuil	12/04/1917	12/04/1917
War Diary	Moves To Detachment	12/04/1917	12/04/1917
War Diary	Transfer	13/04/1917	13/04/1917
War Diary	Moves	14/04/1917	14/04/1917
War Diary	Operations R.A.M.C.	16/04/1917	16/04/1917
War Diary	Casualties	16/04/1917	16/04/1917
War Diary	Moves Detachment	27/04/1917	27/04/1917
War Diary	Operations R.A.M.C. Health Of Troops	30/04/1917	30/04/1917
War Diary	Sachin	01/04/1917	06/04/1917
War Diary	Rocourt En L'Eau	07/04/1917	09/04/1917
War Diary	Y Huts M Duisans	10/04/1917	11/04/1917
War Diary	Maroeuil	12/04/1917	13/04/1917
War Diary	Ecoivres	14/04/1917	30/04/1917
Miscellaneous	B.E.F. Summary Of Medical War Diaries For 6th F.A. 2nd. Divin 13th. 1st Army		
War Diary	Moves Operations R.A.M.C.	03/05/1917	03/05/1917
War Diary	Casualties	04/05/1917	04/05/1917
War Diary	Moves Detachment	16/05/1917	16/05/1917
War Diary	Health Of Troops	21/05/1917	31/05/1917
War Diary	Moves Operations R.A.M.C.	03/05/1917	03/05/1917
War Diary	Casualties	04/05/1917	04/05/1917
War Diary	Moves Detachment	16/05/1917	16/05/1917
War Diary	Health Of Troops	21/05/1917	31/05/1917
Heading	Vol 35 No. 6 Field Ambulance May 1917 Vol 31		
War Diary	Ecoivres	01/05/1917	20/06/1917
War Diary	Bede Catorive Bethune	21/06/1917	21/06/1917
War Diary	Annezin-Les-Bethune	22/06/1917	29/06/1917
Heading	War Diary For July 1917 "Vol 36" No. 6 Field Ambulance Vol 33		
War Diary	Annezin	02/07/1917	04/11/1917
War Diary	Pecquere	05/11/1917	05/11/1917
War Diary	S. Sylvestre Capelle [Sheet 27 P17D	06/11/1917	06/11/1917
War Diary	Sheet 27 E.19.A.0.8.	07/11/1917	11/11/1917
War Diary	Sheet 27 E.19.A.0 8 Near Houtkerk	12/11/1917	23/11/1917
War Diary	In The Train	24/11/1917	24/11/1917
War Diary	Rocquigny	25/11/1917	27/11/1917
War Diary	Lechelle	28/11/1917	28/11/1917
War Diary	Barastre	29/11/1917	07/12/1917
Map	2nd Division Nov 30 1917		
War Diary	Barastre	09/12/1917	14/12/1917
War Diary	N.4.A	16/12/1917	16/12/1917
War Diary	Beaulencourt N.11	17/12/1917	25/12/1917
War Diary	N11 Central	27/12/1917	30/12/1917
Heading	2nd Division Medical No. 6 Field Ambulance Jan-Dec 1918		
Heading	War Diary No. 6 Field Ambce Vol XLII Jan 1918		
War Diary	Beaulencourt N11	01/01/1918	15/01/1918
War Diary	Beaulencourt N11 Central Sheet 57C	16/01/1918	26/01/1918
War Diary	Beaulencourt	27/01/1918	31/01/1918
Heading	No. 6 F.A. Feb. 1918 Feb 1918		

Heading	War Diary No. 6 Field Ambce February 1918 Vol XLII		
War Diary	Beaulencourt N11 Central 57C	01/02/1918	12/02/1918
War Diary	Beaulencourt	13/02/1918	28/02/1918
Heading	War Diary Month Of March 1918 Vol XLIV March/18		
War Diary	Beaulencourt	01/03/1918	22/03/1918
War Diary	Near Lesars	23/03/1918	23/03/1918
War Diary	Beaumont Hamel	24/03/1918	24/03/1918
War Diary	Louvencourt	25/03/1918	25/03/1918
War Diary	Arquevres	26/03/1918	28/03/1918
War Diary	Hedauville	29/03/1918	31/03/1918
Heading	War Diary No. 6 Field Ambce April 1918 Vol XLIV		
War Diary	Hedauville	01/04/1918	02/04/1918
War Diary	Clairfaye	03/04/1918	03/04/1918
War Diary	Famechon	04/04/1918	04/04/1918
War Diary	Ivergny	05/04/1918	05/04/1918
War Diary	Canettemont	06/04/1918	09/04/1918
War Diary	Oppy	10/04/1918	10/04/1918
War Diary	Pommera	11/04/1918	11/04/1918
War Diary	Saulty	12/04/1918	13/04/1918
War Diary	Blairville	14/04/1918	30/04/1918
Heading	War Diary No. 6 Field Ambce May 1918 Vol XLV		
War Diary	Blairville	01/05/1918	11/05/1918
War Diary	Barly	12/05/1918	31/05/1918
Heading	War Diary No. 6 Field Ambulance For June 1918 Vol XLVI		
War Diary	Barly	01/06/1918	06/06/1918
War Diary	La Cauchie	07/06/1918	16/06/1918
War Diary	Warlincourt	17/06/1918	30/06/1918
Heading	War Diary No. 6 Field Ambulance For July 1918 Vol XLVIII		
War Diary	Warlincourt	01/07/1918	31/07/1918
Heading	War Diary No. 6 Field Ambulance August 1918 Vol XLIX		
War Diary	Warlincourt	01/08/1918	31/08/1918
Heading	War Diary No. 6 Field Ambulance For September 1918 Vol L		
War Diary	Warlincourt-Lez-Pas	01/09/1918	06/09/1918
War Diary	Ervillers	07/09/1918	09/09/1918
War Diary	Mory-Vraucourt Road B.23.B.3.8 (57C)	10/09/1918	12/09/1918
War Diary	Mory-Vraucourt Rd	13/09/1918	26/09/1918
War Diary	Beugny-Vaux Rd I.9.D.4.5 (57C)	27/09/1918	27/09/1918
War Diary	Moeuvres Demicourt Rd K.1.C.5.0 (57C)	28/09/1918	30/09/1918
Heading	War Diary No. 6 Field Ambulance Month Of October 1918 Vol LI		
War Diary	Near Demicourt	01/10/1918	06/10/1918
War Diary	E Track Demicourt	07/10/1918	09/10/1918
War Diary	Demicourt	10/10/1918	12/10/1918
War Diary	Forenville	13/10/1918	21/10/1918
War Diary	St. Hilaire	22/10/1918	22/10/1918
War Diary	St. Python	23/10/1918	23/10/1918
War Diary	Vertain	24/10/1918	30/10/1918
War Diary	Escarmain	31/10/1918	31/10/1918
Heading	War Diary No. 6 Field Ambulance Month Of November 1918 Vol LII		
War Diary	Escarmain	01/11/1918	01/11/1918
War Diary	St. Hilaire	02/11/1918	07/11/1918

War Diary	Escarmain	08/11/1918	13/11/1918
War Diary	Preux Au Sart	14/11/1918	15/11/1918
War Diary	Mecquignies	16/11/1918	17/11/1918
War Diary	Maubeuge	18/11/1918	19/11/1918
War Diary	Fauroeulx	20/11/1918	23/11/1918
War Diary	Anderlues	24/11/1918	24/11/1918
War Diary	Montignies Sur Sambre	25/11/1918	27/11/1918
War Diary	Sart St. Laurent	28/11/1918	28/11/1918
War Diary	Malonne	29/11/1918	30/11/1918
Heading	War Diary For December 1918 Vol LIII No. 6 F. No. 6 F.A.		
War Diary	Malonne	01/12/1918	03/12/1918
War Diary	Sclayn	04/12/1918	04/12/1918
War Diary	Huy	05/12/1918	05/12/1918
War Diary	Ouffet	06/12/1918	06/12/1918
War Diary	Rouvreux-Les-Aywaille	07/12/1918	07/12/1918
War Diary	Vert Boisson	08/12/1918	08/12/1918
War Diary	Andrimont	09/12/1918	10/12/1918
War Diary	Elsenborn-Truppen Lager	11/12/1918	11/12/1918
War Diary	Witterath	12/12/1918	12/12/1918
War Diary	Thuin	13/12/1918	13/12/1918
War Diary	Duren	14/12/1918	31/12/1918
Heading	BEF 2 Div Troops 6 Fld Amb 1919 Jan To 1919 Aug		
Heading	2nd Div War Diary For January 1919 Vol LIV No. 6 F.A.		
War Diary	Duren	01/01/1919	31/01/1919
Heading	War Diary No. 6 Field Ambce February 1919 Vol LV		
War Diary	Duren	01/02/1919	10/02/1919
War Diary	Monheim	11/02/1919	28/02/1919
Heading	War Diary No. 6 Field Ambulance March 1919 Vol LVI		
War Diary	Monheim	01/03/1919	31/03/1919
Heading	No.6 Field Ambulance War Diary April 1919 Vol LVII		
War Diary	Monheim	01/04/1919	08/04/1919
War Diary	Caster	09/04/1919	30/04/1919
Heading	War Diary No. 6 Field Ambulance May 1919 Vol LVIII		
War Diary	Caster	01/05/1919	31/05/1919
Heading	No. 6 Field Ambulance June 1919		
Heading	War Diary 1st. Lowland Field Ambulance 52nd (Lowland) Division 8th. Corps-Helles June 1915-March 1916		
War Diary	Kaster	01/06/1919	16/06/1919
War Diary	Huchelhoven	18/06/1919	18/06/1919
War Diary	Bocklemund	19/06/1919	29/06/1919
War Diary	Kaster	30/06/1919	30/06/1919
Heading	No. 6 Field Ambulance July 1919		
War Diary	Kaster	01/07/1919	08/07/1919
War Diary	Hilden	08/07/1919	08/07/1919
War Diary	Ohligs	09/07/1919	31/07/1919
Heading	No. 6 Field Ambulance Aug 1919		
War Diary	Ohligs	01/08/1919	31/08/1919
Heading	2 Division Troops 6 Field Ambulance 1914 Aug To 1919 Aug		

2ND DIVISION
MEDICAL

6TH FIELD AMBULANCE
AUG - DEC 1914

6th Field Ambulance.

Volume I

2 DIVISION. TROOPS.

6 FIELD AMBULANCE.

1914 AUG TO 1919 AUG.

From:
 O.C. 6th Field Ambulance
To:
 A.G.
  The Base

August/14

 With reference to the enclosed DIARY, will you please note that the delay has been caused by the "Original" being lost during the retreat.

 This one has been compiled partly from my own private diary also those of the Serjt Major & Clerk. All places & dates are accurate.

      J.J. Potter

12 — 10 — 14.
      Major Rowe
     O.C. 6 Field Ambulance

Army Form C. 2118.

WAR DIARY
or
INTELLIGENCE SUMMARY.
(Erase heading not required.)

Instructions regarding War Diaries and Intelligence Summaries are contained in F. S. Regs., Part II. and the Staff Manual respectively. Title pages will be prepared in manuscript.

Hour, Date, Place	Summary of Events and Information	Remarks and references to Appendices
REDAN HILL CAMP ALDERSHOT 5.8/14. 9pm.	The No 6 Field Ambulance commenced mobilization	J.N.N. Winter Major
REDAN HILL CAMP ALDERSHOT 6. 8/14. 8pm	Mobilization progress satisfactory. Personnel arriving lovely. Nothing of note to record	J.N.W.
REDAN HILL CAMP ALDERSHOT 7. 8/14. 8pm	Mobilization progress satisfactory. Personnel still arriving lovely and medical equipment drawn from stores	J.N.W.
REDAN HILL CAMP ALDERSHOT 8. 8/14. 7pm	Mobilization progress satisfactory. Vehicles & equipment drawn from Ordnance Stores.	J.N.W.
REDAN HILL CAMP ALDERSHOT 9. 8/14. 8pm	Day spent in checking equipment. In the afternoon camp evacuated by D.A.Dms 2nd Division. Telephone message received, authority for the removal of the unit from Redan Hill to Rushmoor Camp near Farnborough. Mobilization still progressing satisfactorily. Health of Troops Good.	J.N.W.

Army Form C. 2118.

WAR DIARY
or
INTELLIGENCE SUMMARY.
(Erase heading not required.)

Instructions regarding War Diaries and Intelligence Summaries are contained in F.S. Regs., Part II. and the Staff Manual respectively. Title pages will be prepared in manuscript.

Hour, Date, Place	Summary of Events and Information	Remarks and references to Appendices
NURSERY CAMP Nr. FARNBOROUGH 8 p.m. 10 – 8 – 14	Unit arrived Nursery Camp, authority, receipt of yesterday. Personal wheel to almost complete. War was drilled at the morning in the various duties, progress satisfactory. Health of troops continues good.	J.N.M.W. ✓
NURSERY CAMP Nr. FARNBOROUGH 8 p.m. 11 – 8 – 14	Major Potter Rawes arrived to take over command of unit. Handed same over to him satisfactory.	J.N.M.W. ✓
NURSERY CAMP 8 p.m. 11 – 8 – 14	Took over command. Dismiss at 11·15 a.m. — all satisfactory. Unit paraded at artillery lines for inspection by H.M. the King. Mobilization progress satisfactory — 39 personnel received T.V. at the Cambridge Hospital.	J.P.R. Major P.R.
NURSERY CAMP 7 p.m. 12 – 8 – 14	Army Books 64 completed & signed. Unit visited by G.O.C. 4th Div. Mobilization proceeding satisfactory.	J.P.R.
NURSERY CAMP 8 p.m. 13 – 8 – 14	2nd party of unit inoculated at the Cambridge Hospital. Everything proceeding satisfactorily — nothing further to record.	J.P.R.
NURSERY CAMP 8 p.m. 14 – 8 – 14	3rd party inoculated. Held kits inspected — a whole of unit completed with first field dressing, treasure, blue boxes, identity discs & iron ration covers.	J.P.R.

Army Form C. 2118.

WAR DIARY
or
INTELLIGENCE SUMMARY.
(Erase heading not required.)

Instructions regarding War Diaries and Intelligence Summaries are contained in F.S. Regs., Part II. and the Staff Manual respectively. Title pages will be prepared in manuscript.

Hour, Date, Place	Summary of Events and Information	Remarks and references to Appendices
NURSERY CAMP. 8/am 15 — 8 — 14	Progress satisfactory, drills & parades proceeded with - nothing of special note to record	J.J.P.
NURSERY CAMP. 8 pm 16 — 8 — 14	Initial Checking of Personnel & Equipment completed — the whole unit is complete in detail & efficient in its functions.	J.J.P.
NURSERY CAMP. 8 pm 17 — 8 — 14	Drills and practice in various duties of unit carried out. Afternoon devoted for personal attention — nothing of note to record	J.J.P.
SOUTHAMPTON DOCKS 8 pm 18 — 8 — 14	Unit paraded 9. left Camp. at 7-40 am. for entrainment at Government Siding, Aldershot. Equipment put on train half. Unit entrained & moved off at 10-2 am arriving here at 11-45 am. Second half arrived one hour later — Re entrainment, Water carts were found very awkward to place on single trucks. The second train load left S.Hampton at 5 pm on S.S. ADA, for Rouen.	J.J.P.
MOUTH OF SEINE "S.S. HONORIUS". 9 pm 19 — 8 — 14	1st Trainload left S'Hampton at 9 am. & arrived at mouth of seine at 9-20 pm.	J.J.P.

Army Form C. 2118.

WAR DIARY
or
INTELLIGENCE SUMMARY.
(Erase heading not required.)

Instructions regarding War Diaries and Intelligence Summaries are contained in F. S. Regs, Part II. and the Staff Manual respectively. Title pages will be prepared in manuscript.

Hour, Date, Place	Summary of Events and Information	Remarks and references to Appendices
BRUYRES - CAMP. 10 p.m. 20 — 8 — 14	Proceeded up the river SEINE to ROUEN at 4-30 a.m. which was reached at 4-30 p.m. The main party moved off to camp and did not reach camp until 10 p.m. Horses at Wag, did not work well — 23 horses had to be left on Ship until morning.	J.J.J.
TRAIN TO AUL-NOYE 12 mid-night 21 — 8 — 14	Remainder of horses brought from boat to Camp, & the day spent in final preparation — distribution of "Iron rations" etc. The whole unit moved off at 6-46 p.m. and reached "GARD DE NORD" at 8-15 p.m. Entrainment began at 9-18 p.m. whole unit occupied eleven "Long trucks" — Five Cattle Trucks & five Carriages for personnel. Vehicles, baggage etc. were put on very rapidly, & without confusion as soon as work was completed all entrained & bedded down to rest during journey.	J.J.J.
AUL.NOYE. 12 mid-night 22 — 8 — 14.	AUL.NOYE reached at 11-45 a.m., horses eating. Awaiting orders to move, men are breakfasting outside of Railway Station. Everything in readiness for moving off.	J.J.J.
BONNET 12 mid-night 23 — 8 — 14.	Reveille at 4 a.m., breakfast for Personnel at 5 a.m. Horses watered out at 6 a.m. unsaddled, followed at 6-15 a.m. from RAILWAY STATION at AUL-NOYE — BONNET reached at 1-15 p.m. Several halts were made en-road until Ammunition Column cleared the way. on 3298 2-45 p.m. proceeded towards GIVRY message received from Hd Qr	J.J.J.

Army Form C. 2118.

WAR DIARY
or
INTELLIGENCE SUMMARY.
(Erase heading not required.)

Instructions regarding War Diaries and Intelligence Summaries are contained in F. S. Regs., Part II. and the Staff Manual respectively. Title pages will be prepared in manuscript.

Hour, Date, Place	Summary of Events and Information	Remarks and references to Appendices
PONT. SUR SAMBRE 9pm 24 — 8 — 14.	6" Infantry Brigade at 3-3 p.m. not to proceed past SUGAR FACTORY but to take cover, not to Bivouac. The ready to move at once. Selected field & reported to Ad. Gro — Staff Officer ordered the Ambulance "back to a field 400 yards S. W. of Kilo no 12 road. BONNET — GIVRY Shell fire two miles distant to N.E. No casualties so far. 7-30 p.m. Casualties reported at GIVRY, sent out Bearer Sub-Division of B&C Section Water cart & Forage Cart with waggons to each Section. Proceeded to GIVRY — Met O.C. No 4 H. Ambulance at GIVRY. 9 took over 15 cases from him as transfers to No 6 Field Ambulance. Repaired to Hd. Qrs. No 6 Bgd. 2nd Div. to remain at GIVRY till 3 a.m. all wounded to be then sent on to Dressing Station at BONNET. Ambulance waggons not to walk on road after dawn, and advanced Dressing Station to fall back to SUGAR FACTORY. All transfers from No 4 attended to by 1-30 a.m. Orders received not 4-15 a.m. to relieve D.A.D.M.S. arrived at 4-30 a.m. & confirmed orders, recalled Bearer Sub Division & ambulance waggons from SUGAR FACTORY and evacuated wounded by Supply Column Empty lorries. & rail kept enough two cases which were brought on in the waggons. Ordered to relieve on RIEZ-LE-ERELLE at Bonnet — Received further orders to proceed on to LONGUEVILLE (from Hd Qrs) at 8 am. Bearer Subdivision of B&C Sections formed up, bringing 17 wounded between GIVRY.	M.J.M. M.J.M.

3208

WAR DIARY
or
INTELLIGENCE SUMMARY.
(Erase heading not required.)

Army Form C. 2118.

Instructions regarding War Diaries and Intelligence Summaries are contained in F.S. Regs, Part II. and the Staff Manual respectively. Title pages will be prepared in manuscript.

Hour, Date, Place	Summary of Events and Information	Remarks and references to Appendices
	Here the men & horses were fed. 9 a shot rest followed. One of the wounded died & was buried in the village Cemetery & a cross erected over grave. (70 Batt. R.F.A. 20.51372 G. Walker?). Proceeded on to PONT SUR SAMBRE at 9.45 am. Orders received to evacuate sick at AULNOYE where a Hospital train was in waiting — Arrived PONT SUR SAMBRE at 3.45 p.m. arrived short returned to Hd. Qrs. A.D.M.S. but Cycle orderly returned with same as he could not find Hd. Qrs. — Wounded evacuated to AULNOYE by motor lorries which were requisitioned for. Bivouaced in field on right of road — Men & horses fed & retired to rest at 7.30 p.m. Order given for no lights or fires.	J.J.
MAROILLE midnight 12 Aug. 25 — 8 — 14.	Reveille at 4 a.m. breakfast 4.30 a.m. — no orders received from A.D.M.S. & unit moved off at 5.45 a.m. to pick up column. — Column organised after passing to the left of AULNOYE, wounded picked up, evacuated to AULNOYE by Ambulance wagons. — MAROILLE reached at 5 p.m. arrival report rendered. 5.30 p.m. Runner move out 2 field into town. orders received from Dispatch Rider who said that Enemy were close. — moved back into field again at 7.30 p.m. — Rain falling very heavily. 10 p.m. received orders to move into town where Field Dressing Station was opened. — 14 wounded were treated here.	J.J.

Army Form C. 2118.

WAR DIARY
or
INTELLIGENCE SUMMARY.
(Erase heading not required.)

Instructions regarding War Diaries and Intelligence Summaries are contained in F.S. Regs., Part II. and the Staff Manual respectively. Title pages will be prepared in manuscript.

Hour, Date, Place	Summary of Events and Information	Remarks and references to Appendices
LA CARTE. 9 p.m. 26—8—14	Left MAROILLE hurriedly at 12·30 a.m. — marched all night, arrived PRISCHES —X— arrived in village until 11·30 a.m., could not get in touch with Head Qrs. — moved on to LA GROISE with a Battery of Artillery — arrived LA GROISE 3·30 p.m. after several lengthy halts owing to movement of troops. Unit bivouacing side of road for night. No more wounded received, no news of whereabouts of Hd Qrs.	X A section Ambulance troops & forage cart sent to Maroille for wounded, with 2 Officers & 12 horsemen. N.Y.R.
LA GROISE 10 p.m. 27—8—14	Left LA CARTE at 6 a.m., no British troops in the neighbourhood, proceeded on road & picked up stragglers near GUISE where we evacuated the wounded by rail. — Arrived at LA GROISE 7·45 p.m., where a dressing station was erected at the RUE DU THIL No. 2, formerly a CONVENT but now a PARISH SCHOOL.	Y.Y.R. Guise
AMRIGNY 10 p.m. 28—8—14	Arrived AMRIGNY at 3·30 p.m. Personnel & horses in a state of exhaustion. — Left Convent this morning at 4·45 a.m. marching continued till 3·30 p.m. — only 3 halts on road — great trouble with men's feet, horses in a bad state. Ambulances which were returned for wounded at MAROILLE also Officers & men not returned, reported same no messings. Boromany on side of road to night — men are again in food Spirits having attended to their feet etc. also have received a first meal first for 4 days, 28nd notified of arrival of troops	Y.Y.R.

WAR DIARY

INTELLIGENCE SUMMARY.

(Erase heading not required.)

Instructions regarding War Diaries and Intelligence Summaries are contained in F.S. Regs., Part II. and the Staff Manual respectively. Title pages will be prepared in manuscript.

Hour, Date, Place	Summary of Events and Information	Remarks and references to Appendices
SERVAIS — ARMIGNY 29 — 8 — 14 . 9 p.m.	Unit moved to a more sheltered position at 12.45 p.m. to day by order received from Head Qrs — about ½ a mile from where the unit bivouaced yesterday. Here, the wagons are completely hidden from aircraft & personnel enjoying good rest. Horses generally improved in condition. — Weekly returns rendered to HA. Qrs. at 6 p.m. 9 p.m. All quiet, men sleeping — wounded wounded a 5.30 to LA FERE.	J.J.P.
Three Kilos from SOISSON. 30 — 8 — 14. 9 p.m.	Unit moved suddenly at 9-40 p.m. last night, marching all night & reached camp near SOISSONS at 9-40 a.m. Men and animals again quite exhausted — Veterinary Officer sent for to attend to horses — Orders received to move off early tomorrow morning. DIVINE SERVICE held at 6 p.m.	J.J.P.
ST. DANDRY. 1 Kilo off. 31 — 8 — 14. 10 p.m.	Resting on side of ROAD near the village ready to move off at any moment. — Left Soissons this morning at 11-30 a.m. following in our right place in column — nothing special to note — now awaiting orders to move.	J.J.P.

2nd Div / Medical

5th Field Ambulance
Vol 4

S 12/11/84
Sept 1914

Army Form (C.) 2118.

WAR DIARY
or
INTELLIGENCE SUMMARY.
(Erase heading not required.)

No. 6 Field Ambulance

Hour, Date, Place	Summary of Events and Information	Remarks and references to Appendices
1 am 1/9/14 JMELENEL	ROADSIDE. Troops left again after two much field rations. Have put my men at enhances, farmers were very much upset for the whole of four hours. 42 sick & wounded evacuated by Supply Column on the THURY ROAD at 1 a.m. Those left hand collected between 9-12 a.m. Unit arrived at BOURSON, some sick, four injuries, & lt ? The personnel in a tent at GS. Billeted in a field also of road, nothing of interest occurred during rest.	
1 am 2/9/14 BOURSONE	Reveille 130 am Kits no moved ft towards OISE.	
10 pm — OISE	UNIT arrived at 9.30 pm. & billeted near the river, nothing of note to record — men & horses suffering severely from sore feet, very little chance of proper attention & cannot expect to move if not at... tomorrow	M.Walter Major 1/6 Ambulance

J/M/W.

Major Walter O.C. 6 Field Ambulance |

Army Form C. 2118.

WAR DIARY
or
INTELLIGENCE SUMMARY.
(Erase heading not required.)

Instructions regarding War Diaries and Intelligence Summaries are contained in F. S. Regs., Part II. and the Staff Manual respectively. Title pages will be prepared in manuscript.

Hour, Date, Place	Summary of Events and Information	Remarks and references to Appendices
11pm 3-9-14 PIERRE-LEVEE	Unit arrived 10 p.m. were enjoined to hold 7 horses in a very bad state. 27 cases of wounded evacuated at 6 am from MEAUX RAILWAY STATION.	
9am 4-9-14 MORDUX	UNIT left PIERRE-LEVEE en jour passing through VOISINS where short halt was filled. The road was bad and very exhausted horses to MORDUX arriving at 2 p.m. in very bad condition. 2 L.H. in hard on road. Nothing otherwise to record. Veterinary Officer applied for to attend to horses. Went out late.	J.J. Major T Kane O.P. 6 Fd. Ambulance
10pm 5-9-14 CHAUMES	Unit arrived 1.50 p.m. called for by Brig. Gen. L. Veterinary officer again applied for. Horses exhausted. No cattle casualties to day.	J.J. Major Kane O.T.C. Fd. Ambulance

Army Form C. 2118.

WAR DIARY
or
INTELLIGENCE SUMMARY.
(Erase heading not required.)

Instructions regarding War Diaries and Intelligence Summaries are contained in F. S. Regs., Part II. and the Staff Manual respectively. Title pages will be prepared in manuscript.

Hour, Date, Place	Summary of Events and Information	Remarks and references to Appendices
17pm 8/9/14 Place ?	2/Lt CHAUNES 11 am to noon 6 CLARE FARM 4 miles received from Brigade major evening place at 12 mid- day remaining until 3 pm. Unit moved it with 2nd Field Ambulance up to Chez at 5.15 pm. F. thing 6 cecil	M.J.J. Major Rawe O.C. 6 Fd. Ambulance
10 am 9/9/14 CHAILLY	Unit left billets at 4 am & proceeded to CHAILLY via BETHELLY MARESCATHINS arriving at 9 am. A thing D note is use.	M.J.J. Major Rawe O.C. Fd. Ambulance

Army Form C. 2118.

WAR DIARY
or
INTELLIGENCE SUMMARY.
(Erase heading not required.)

Hour, Date, Place	Summary of Events and Information	Remarks and references to Appendices
11 pm 8-9-14. REBAIS	Unit left CHAILLY at 6 am passing through JOUARCOURT (where 25 battle casualties evacuated) and ST MAGDALEN arriving REBAIS at 8 pm. Relief detailed by Officers in a ditch? Nothing to report. 4 pm. Bearers & dressing station sent to LA-BELLE-EDDIE. Reasonable? tent procured. Stand down at 8 pm. Wounded picked up 4 hundred. 4 Officers & 32 men — Germans 3 Officers — ? —	J.M. Major Rance O.C. 6 Fd Ambulance
10 pm 9-9-14 CHARLY	Unit left REBAIS at 5 am via Rupt BOITRON, LANOUNE & PEVANT, arriving CHARLY 9 pm. Have assisted picked up during journey & combined with those of the 5th Fd Ly Supply to camp at BOITRON	J.M. Major Rance O.C. 6 Fd Ambulance

Army Form C. 2118.

WAR DIARY
or
INTELLIGENCE SUMMARY.
(Erase heading not required.)

Instructions regarding War Diaries and Intelligence Summaries are contained in F.S. Regs., Part II. and the Staff Manual respectively. Title pages will be prepared in manuscript.

Hour, Date, Place	Summary of Events and Information	Remarks and references to Appendices
10 am 10/9/14 CHATILLON	Unit left CHATILLON 5-30 am, passing through DOMPTIN arriving at HAUTEVESNES at 3-30 pm where 3 hours halt was made. Enemy was said to be on artillery had been engaged. 3 of 4 the casualties were received. Unit again moved on from CHATILLON at 3/9 am arriving 7 km. Noting one of not to wound.	Major Rowe O.C 6 fld Ambulance V.P.R
10 pm 11/9/14 OULCHY-CHATEAU	Unit left CHATILLON at 5-30 am. enemy ing reported with st. arrived at Te CHATEAU at 9.30 am they have been very lost 4 men but tents. of from men work in the supposed of digging graves, where some fell in some. the first very overhead since beginning of hostilities. Nothing further to report	V.P.R Major Rowe O.C 6 fld Ambulance

Army Form C. 2118.

WAR DIARY
or
INTELLIGENCE SUMMARY.
(Erase heading not required.)

Instructions regarding War Diaries and Intelligence Summaries are contained in F. S. Regs., Part II. and the Staff Manual respectively. Title pages will be prepared in manuscript.

Hour, Date, Place	Summary of Events and Information	Remarks and references to Appendices
10 p.m. BRAISNE	Unit arrived at BRAISNE after a long march in very heavy rain & difficult roads. Men & horses exhausted. Billets obtained 9 p.m. in hard st. and floors to sleep on. Nothing further except scarcity of drying cloth. Sick evacuated by supply column.	[signature] Major Kaure O.C. 6 Fd. Ambulance
10 p.m. 13/9/14 NORTH OF MERCY ARCY	Unit left at 9 a.m. road very difficult from previous nights. That parts & 3rd of road quite unsafe f. horse mules. 6 p.m. when it moved it became necessary & mules & pulled in at 9 o'clock. men billeted in the yard.	[signature] Major Kaure O.C. 6 Fd. Ambulance

Army Form C. 2118.

WAR DIARY
or
INTELLIGENCE SUMMARY.
(Erase heading not required.)

Instructions regarding War Diaries and Intelligence Summaries are contained in F.S. Regs., Part II. and the Staff Manual respectively. Title pages will be prepared in manuscript.

Hour, Date, Place	Summary of Events and Information	Remarks and references to Appendices
10 am 14/9/14 VERNEUIL (CHATEAU BOURG-ET-COMIN)	Unit left VIEL-ARCY at 9 am. New road with Cavy at 3 am coming to a bury zone. Had tea send at 5 am. Shelter bivouac at CHATEAU at 12 pm. mid-day, remainder of unit proceeded to 5.20 pm. CHATEAU reached at 6.30 pm where a great number of wounded were awaiting attention.	[signature] Major Rawe O/C 6 Fd Ambulance
10 pm 15/9/14 CHATEAU	Unit working with 5th Field Ambulance on one front. Wounded coming in large numbers. A/E of 24 very seriously employed in carrying with numbers returned. No time possible for details.	[signature] Major Rawe O/C 6 F.A. Ambulance

Army Form C. 2118.

WAR DIARY
or
INTELLIGENCE SUMMARY.
(Erase heading not required.)

Instructions regarding War Diaries and Intelligence Summaries are contained in F. S. Regs., Part II. and the Staff Manual respectively. Title pages will be prepared in manuscript.

Hour, Date, Place	Summary of Events and Information	Remarks and references to Appendices
10 p.m. 16-9-14. CHATEAU	Whole D.A.H. staff busy dealing with wounded which are continually coming in. Lt. Reynolds secured last two very valuable appointments of supply column & ambulance wagons. CHATEAU under heavy shell fire, none of unit injured up to the present.	J.P. Major Rawe O.T.C. 2d Ambulance
17-9-14. CHATEAU	Everything going on the same, nothing of special importance to record.	J.P. Major Rawe O.T.C. 2d Ambulance

Army Form C. 2118.

WAR DIARY
or
INTELLIGENCE SUMMARY.
(Erase heading not required.)

Instructions regarding War Diaries and Intelligence Summaries are contained in F.S. Regs., Part II. and the Staff Manual respectively. Title pages will be prepared in manuscript.

Hour, Date, Place	Summary of Events and Information	Remarks and references to Appendices
12 midnight 18-9-14 (L'HOPITAL) VISU-ARCY.	Unit moved from CHATEAU NERMEUIL to L'HOPITAL VISU ARCY — 2-30 p.m. arriving here at 12-20 a.m. A Section remained behind at CHATEAU to follow in the morning.	[signed] Major Raine O.C. 6 Fd Ambulance
10 a.m. 19-9-14 L'HOPITAL VISU ARCY	Our field workshop & Bearer ambulance, nothing heard. Report — wounded brought from CHATEAU by A Sec who had been source in by supply column which arrived here 3-30 p.m. Nothing further of importance to report	[signed] Major Raine O.C. 6 Fd Ambulance

10.

Army Form C. 2118.

WAR DIARY
or
INTELLIGENCE SUMMARY.
(Erase heading not required.)

Instructions regarding War Diaries and Intelligence Summaries are contained in F. S. Regs., Part II. and the Staff Manual respectively. Title pages will be prepared in manuscript.

Hour, Date, Place	Summary of Events and Information	Remarks and references to Appendices
10 pm 20 Fy (2 HOSPITAL) NEIL AREY	Unit moved to the Chateau the village & groups of houses in the Chateau where all the wounded not be brought. Infirm remained in the field. No 6 Field Ambulance at Colony Green Roy.	J H Major Rawe O.C. 6 Fd Ambulance
10 am 21 Fy NEIL AREY	Wounded being received up to this time the counter mining groups of Russ attacks of shock infantry & c.	J H Major Rawe O.C. 6 Fd Ambulance

Army Form C. 2118.

WAR DIARY
or
INTELLIGENCE SUMMARY.
(Erase heading not required.)

Instructions regarding War Diaries and Intelligence Summaries are contained in F. S. Regs., Part II. and the Staff Manual respectively. Title pages will be prepared in manuscript.

Hour, Date, Place	Summary of Events and Information	Remarks and references to Appendices
10/pm 22nd Feb 1917	Nothing of importance to report, men still being admitted & evacuated by motor ambulance.	[signature] Major Rawle O.T.C. 6 Fd. Ambulance
" 23.2.14	— " —	[signature] Major Rawle O.T.C. 6 Fd. Ambulance
10pm 24 Feb	Nothing special to report.	[signature] Major Rawle O.T.C. 6 Fd. Ambulance

Army Form C. 2118.

WAR DIARY
or
INTELLIGENCE SUMMARY.
(Erase heading not required.)

Instructions regarding War Diaries and Intelligence Summaries are contained in F.S. Regs., Part II. and the Staff Manual respectively. Title pages will be prepared in manuscript.

Hour, Date, Place	Summary of Events and Information	Remarks and references to Appendices
Jan 25 14 VIEIL FKTY	Everything proceeding satisfactorily, holding own and recovered still further lost battle casualties. Show a decrease on yesterday.	J.Y.P. Major Payne O.C. 6 Fd Ambulance
10 pm 26 9/14 " "	Nothing of a special nature to report, average nightly sick & wounded being up anywhere 40 in number.	J.Y.P. Major Payne O.C. 6 Fd Ambulance
10 pm 27 9/14 " "	Progress as usual & took over duty temporarily The man of the time wounded at the outposts who were wounded by Japanese shrapnel were severely wounded & the Stretcher bearers had not the skill & energy. He was evacuated to base. Injury was received when supporting firing press.	J.Y.P. Major Payne O.C. 6 Fd Ambulance

Army Form C. 2118.

WAR DIARY
or
INTELLIGENCE SUMMARY.
(Erase heading not required.)

Instructions regarding War Diaries and Intelligence Summaries are contained in F. S. Regs., Part II. and the Staff Manual respectively. Title pages will be prepared in manuscript.

Hour, Date, Place	Summary of Events and Information	Remarks and references to Appendices
6 to 1 pm NEW ARCH	Place under very heavy shell fire and considerable damage to buildings & billets by H.E. & noxious & the usual amount of gas. Injured persons few, gassed [illegible]	[signature] Major Reeve O.C. 6 Fd. Ambulance
29 at 10 pm	Place still under fire of enemy shells. Everything else satisfactory	[signature] Major Reeve O.C. 6 Fd. Ambulance
30 at 10 pm	Place again [illegible] shells, the enemy [illegible] early afternoon. Several [illegible] amongst the civilian population & have had some to treat, were left in our care. The men received injuries & the case named [illegible] [illegible] the woman received a [illegible] wound featuring 9 rights side with shock & [illegible] [illegible]	[signature] Major Reeve O.C. 6 Fd. Ambulance

Army Form C. 2118.

WAR DIARY
or
INTELLIGENCE SUMMARY.
(Erase heading not required.)

Instructions regarding War Diaries and Intelligence
Summaries are contained in F. S. Regs., Part II.
and the Staff Manual respectively. Title pages
will be prepared in manuscript.

Hour, Date, Place	Summary of Events and Information	Remarks and references to Appendices
20th continued.	Great danger accompanies the movement of men & the sent & all have been carried to Rly & made comfortable as possible	[signature] Major Reeve O.C. 6 Fd Ambulance

(9 26 6) W 257—976 100,000 4/12 H W V 79/3298

8th Field Ambulance.

Vol III

12/11/965
Oct. 1914

Army Form C. 2118.

WAR DIARY
or
INTELLIGENCE SUMMARY.
(Erase heading not required.)

Hour, Date, Place	Summary of Events and Information	Remarks and references to Appendices
8 P.M. 1-10-14 VIEIL ARCY	One unfit attack case of interior — 2 cases Christmas. The Ellis advocator took my lt — inoculated 2 and 8 —— brought by M. Ambulance. Instructions re letter cards received from A.D.M.S. 2nd Div. — Clothing issued to Unit. Shopped in Fère all day. She is always more useful in Coffee & c. — the road — Ambulances drew fur, jam. Consulted S.M.O. — that of Oxford R.A.M.C. re owning this place in last resort. Went to the Mill — but dis recommends. One Ordering A.P.D. work in Fère. Noiselle threw once bullets were found in his upper ingested in No 3. Fur find — officer account when away @ HQ.D. VERNEUIL with head Unit.	[signature] R.A.M.C.

Army Form C. 2118.

WAR DIARY
or
INTELLIGENCE SUMMARY.

(Erase heading not required.)

Instructions regarding War Diaries and Intelligence Summaries are contained in F. S. Regs., Part II. and the Staff Manual respectively. Title pages will be prepared in manuscript.

Hour, Date, Place	Summary of Events and Information	Remarks and references to Appendices
8 P.M. 2/10/14 VIEIL ARCY.	Very little sleep for Divisions 29 of whom 12 were medical cases. Two clashes during night — suspicion of we. moves by Intelly Officer but no return to see Intelligence — Scare of spies reported to one case of impostor found — Impostors to D.A.D of M.P. Evidence — suspects — also villagers — Most of the latter left today on interference of Maire fear. Health of Troops good.	N.P.A
8 P.M. 3/10/14 VIEIL ARCY.	Admirarous.11 — Battle Aircrafts — 8 shrapnel his to noon and at 6 — Lieut High Explosive Shells occasionally — McCoy's can no longer being made, for with a rate can not be feel.	J.M

(9 26 6) W 257-976 100,000 4/12 HWV 79/5298

Army Form C. 2118.

WAR DIARY
or
INTELLIGENCE SUMMARY.
(Erase heading not required.)

Instructions regarding War Diaries and Intelligence Summaries are contained in F. S. Regs., Part II. and the Staff Manual respectively. Title pages will be prepared in manuscript.

Hour, Date, Place	Summary of Events and Information	Remarks and references to Appendices
6 P.M. 4/10/14 VIEIL ARCY	Pte Terry wounded after sentry — on returning from BOURG — Divisional Reserve Field.	V.J.M.
8 P.M. 5/10/14 VIEIL ARCY	Blankets & Mackintosh sheets arrived. Horse lines moved ½ Coy. 1st Advance Party 34 — Sub. Kaffo C? 14 including 4 duplicated 6x. Movement of ambulance taken in an open 2 farmer to A.D.M.S. Lord Murray. Twenty of Ambulance carried more out. One from fire, officer that he should not proceed to the lines of A.L.1.	V.J.M.
8 P.M. 6/10/14 VIEIL ARCY	Inspection of Units — Kit etc. reported. 17 — changes from Supplies. 19 — Medical — 3 Soft. hypodermic. Said Units Except delays recovered. Prepared lens.	V.J.M.

Army Form C. 2118.

WAR DIARY
or
INTELLIGENCE SUMMARY.
(Erase heading not required.)

Instructions regarding War Diaries and Intelligence Summaries are contained in F. S. Regs., Part II. and the Staff Manual respectively. Title pages will be prepared in manuscript.

Hour, Date, Place	Summary of Events and Information	Remarks and references to Appendices
8 P.M. 7-10-14 VIEIL ARCY	A.D.M.S. N.Midt. at 10-30 A.M. Attest by Returns & took arrangements were completion of Equipment – however as Cigarettes received from D.M. Stores. Ambulance – ordered to Infantry Brigade 6th Bgde. – Class of Enteric Suspects are becoming more frequent – took over School for these cases, in addition to farm in use up to date	N.Y.D.
8 P.M. 8-10-14 VIEIL ARCY	Visited by Colonel Lee (P.O.) Inspector Enteric fevers with Lieut. Jefferies R.E. – lecture – dose so Millians – satisfactory in all cases as to close with data given to same with patient. He came to see us in all cases of Enteric to ensure where Anti-Tetanus serum used	N.Y.D.

79

Army Form C. 2118.

WAR DIARY
or
INTELLIGENCE SUMMARY.
(Erase heading not required.)

Instructions regarding War Diaries and Intelligence Summaries are contained in F.S. Regs., Part II. and the Staff Manual respectively. Title pages will be prepared in manuscript.

Hour, Date, Place	Summary of Events and Information	Remarks and references to Appendices
8 P.M. 9/10/14 VIEIL ARCY	Four suspected cases of Enteric – from Soupir – Cigarettes & magazines received from Lord McCarthy. Cigarette sent up by bike ambulance forwarded from Jeffery's point for 9 men of white.	W.S.S.
8 P.M. 10/10/14 VIEIL ARCY	No stores for us immediate neighbourhood. No direct galvanised. Uneven to tent-men unav. Dysentery – one man isolated on Private Avenue – five days Z.J. col. to Private Avenue of men who ate on crop lettuce in vicinity. Asked for by Major J. Moore R.A.M.C Brigade with	J.M.
8 P.M. 11/10/14 VIEIL ARCY	One case suspected Enteric from PONT ARCY – 11 Coy Mr Saviter by P.S. M.O. at 6.45 P.M.	J.P.

(9 26 6) W 257—976 100,000 4/12 HWV 79/3298

Army Form C. 2118.

WAR DIARY
or
INTELLIGENCE SUMMARY.
(Erase heading not required.)

Instructions regarding War Diaries and Intelligence Summaries are contained in F. S. Regs., Part II. and the Staff Manual respectively. Title pages will be prepared in manuscript.

Hour, Date, Place	Summary of Events and Information	Remarks and references to Appendices
8 P.M. 12/10/14 VIEIL ARCY	Following on instructions from HQrs all equipment was unloaded and prepared. We anticipate ... ?	J.V.
8 P.M. 13/10/14 VIEIL ARCY	Visited by H.D.M.S. at about 11 A.M. — Received orders that N° 6 Fld Amb. Temporary attached to 1st Division. Reported frequency to H.Q of H.S.I.R. Div after having reported in writing.	H.J.
8 P.M. 14/10/14 VIEIL ARCY	Visited by A.D.M.S. 1st Div. 9 A.M. — Received instructions re disposal of sick from him — Matters just before the afternoon when horse lines were heavily attacked and one Farrier, 12 servants, which were attended, passed on bound — A.D.M.S. & A.D.V.S. notified. — One of horses slightly wounded — Order received at 9 P.M. to write to move to BAZOCHES at 4 A.M. (1) agons packed Patients evacuated by motor amb	V.V.

WAR DIARY
or
INTELLIGENCE SUMMARY.
(Erase heading not required.)

Army Form C. 2118.

Hour, Date, Place	Summary of Events and Information	Remarks and references to Appendices
VIEIL ARCY Conf^d	and unit: ready to move by 11 P.M.	
8 P.M. 15/9/14 BAZOCHES	# Regiment at 2 A.M. and unit prepared 3.30 A.M. Moved off at 4 A.M. — Weather very bad — been gave — road difficulty with transport over hill at LONGUEVAL — stopped at 5 A.M. Horses had to be taken out & used as leaders — also the wagons had to be near handy — Progress very slow & difficult — VAUXCERE reached at 6.50 P.M. 7 P.M. met Supply Train & got sure food. Had to wait for the Infantry Cover some — they opened road very far. — Arrived at BAZOCHES at 8 A.M. & moved with Butt^y at 8.30 A.M. owing to much use of roads for the wagons & interference in road with fires & baggage &c & yet troops booked. — Uncle came from aeroplane infantry orders received from his H^d Qrs 6 Bde — & acknowledged.	

WAR DIARY or INTELLIGENCE SUMMARY

Hour, Date, Place	Summary of Events and Information	Remarks and references to Appendices
8 P.M. 16/10/14 On Train	Reveille Midnight — Unit arrived at 1 A.M. for France — arrived at 2.50 A.M. Entrained took 45 minutes — train then not occupying Train — Train left 6.45 A.M. Arrived Paris 1.25 P.M. left at 1.55 P.M. Weather dull - cool - occnl showers. 10 sick accompany unit who were not fit for travel attached place along Our stores were taken over from R.A.R. at FISMES — Nothing further to note. Details yet to follow:— Pierce officers 2 — Oult num 13 R.H.H. ord Drvrs 9, 17 sc. Coft. O.L. 15 H.S. — Vehicles — wagons in charge of [illegible] G.S. 2 — Ambulance Wagons 9, Water Cart 1	M.A.R.

WAR DIARY
or
INTELLIGENCE SUMMARY.
(Erase heading not required.)

Army Form C. 2118.

Hour, Date, Place	Summary of Events and Information	Remarks and references to Appendices
8 P.M., 17/10/14 HAZEBROUCK	BOULOGNE oL 4 P.M. Left at 8-15 P.M. — went to Calais and arrived at 10-45 P.M. Left at 11-10 P.M. Arrived at St OMER at 1.35 P.M. and left STRAZEELE at 3 P.M. and left to detrain at 3 P.M. and left to Billet at HAZEBROUCK at 4-25 P.M. Arrived at Headquarters LE MERTER-RUE CASSEL at 7.30 P.M. — Arrival reported. Staff Officer forward absent on detach — Dan then found absent to H.Q. On Duty. Hence journies to Proved M. Dur	N.R.

Army Form C. 2118.

WAR DIARY
or
INTELLIGENCE SUMMARY.
(Erase heading not required.)

Instructions regarding War Diaries and Intelligence Summaries are contained in F.S. Regs., Part II. and the Staff Manual respectively. Title pages will be prepared in manuscript.

Hour, Date, Place	Summary of Events and Information	Remarks and references to Appendices
8.P.M. 18/10/14 HAZEBROUCK	Received on Recruits as our Armorer's Artificer. Evacuated sick to Clearing Hospital. N.F.R. for troops.	N.F.R.
8.30 P.M. 19/10/14	Marched at 4.15 P.M. from billets at HAZEBROOK and arrived GODEWAERSVELD at 8.30 P.M. Rain very heavy — Troops in billets (part) & the others under cover there was.	N.F.R
8 P.M. 20/10/14	Marched out at 7.30 a.m. in rear of Bn. Rr. Gd. Jewish Rev. Ld & J the Canal at HERZEN — received order to halt at St JEAN — afterwards VLAMERTINGHE — sent on Officer CAPT JONES to meet Bullion & give his Bn. gone forward orders from the Bn. Div. 2 to bivouac VLAMERTINGHE — returned & informed I Transport Left — remained — transport found — went on & left Wildbush & went to Coy? arrived & had Bivouac in rear of Bn.	N.F.R.

WAR DIARY
or
INTELLIGENCE SUMMARY.
(Erase heading not required.)

Army Form C. 2118.

Hour, Date, Place	Summary of Events and Information	Remarks and references to Appendices
8 P.M. 21/10/14	Marched out of Billets at 9.15 a.m. reached YPRES at 11 A.M. — Journey happens in transit — & — appeared all day for orders. received at 7.45 P.M. to proceed along YPRES — POPERINGHE road for purpose of taking over Belgian Hospital at E. CHATEAU — Cut away to Madame Lallemand wounded Battalion unit, trek to point on a side road — arrived into Ops at or near front.	Shrapnel intensified Ding that bit the fare extensive damage caused You Press Nie
22/10/14	9 a.m. CHA — preformed interview a Lt. Col. Dewitt — Divisional Cavalry. Moved over to M.D.M.S. — Received info after Acting Appointment for purposes & RO. at 2 P.M. Informed at 4 Rue St. JEAN Liège Group at 11 a.m. at the Rue St. JEAN would proceed to HQ 3. which had moved to HP. Pu accompanied with instructions and ambulances into Ypres and to the Rue Subdin Rue d'Ipré latet reported at first the Cavalry Keep. Motor ambulances ordered	V.P.J.

WAR DIARY
or
INTELLIGENCE SUMMARY.
(Erase heading not required.)

Army Form C. 2118.

Hour, Date, Place	Summary of Events and Information	Remarks and references to Appendices
8 P.M. 23rd/10/16	Awaiting orders	
8 P.M. 24th/10/16	3.30 P.M. Left [illegible] [illegible] [illegible]. [illegible] — Reply by [illegible] [illegible] [illegible]. [illegible] at [illegible] [illegible] [illegible] [illegible] [illegible] — [illegible] [illegible]. [illegible] [illegible] much [illegible] [illegible] [illegible] [illegible] [illegible] [illegible] [illegible] [illegible] — [illegible] [illegible] [illegible] [illegible] [illegible] [illegible] [illegible] [illegible] [illegible] [illegible] [illegible] to [illegible]	J.M.
8 P.M. 25. 10.16	Preparing [illegible] — [illegible] up the 6.30 P.M. 208 Arrg [illegible] [illegible] [illegible] [illegible] [illegible] [illegible] — [illegible] yet [illegible] [illegible] [illegible] [illegible] — [illegible] [illegible] [illegible] — [illegible] [illegible] [illegible] [illegible] [illegible] — and an officer [illegible]	J.M.

Army Form C. 2118.

WAR DIARY
or
INTELLIGENCE SUMMARY.
(Erase heading not required.)

Instructions regarding War Diaries and Intelligence Summaries are contained in F. S. Regs., Part II. and the Staff Manual respectively. Title pages will be prepared in manuscript.

Hour, Date, Place	Summary of Events and Information	Remarks and references to Appendices
	Self accommodation for 90 Infy Offrs Cas. — Total accommodation in R & no. — but capacity approxim about 80% of true admittance on stretcher cases, no Chairette or Units up to date.	
8 P.M. 26/10/16	Admissions 92 — Evacuations 28 — Progress satisfactory — All patients enjoy...	L.W.
8 P.M. 27/10/16	Admissions 240 — Evacuated 44 — High Inspection of Winchester Case...	L.W.

Army Form C. 2118.

WAR DIARY
or
INTELLIGENCE SUMMARY.
(Erase heading not required.)

Instructions regarding War Diaries and Intelligence Summaries are contained in F.S. Regs., Part II. and the Staff Manual respectively. Title pages will be prepared in manuscript.

Hour, Date, Place	Summary of Events and Information	Remarks and references to Appendices
8 P.M. 27/10/14	Strength 166 – Reinforcements 125 – Reinforcements 24 – Nothing to report.	N.V.
8 P.M. 28/10/14	Strength 57 – Evacuated 119 – Received 133 – Sick from France – Division H.Q. – 1 officer for Duty.	N.V.
8 P.M. 30/10/14	Strength 68 – Evacuated 21 – Geo. H. Card Private C. dislocation – Return to Unit 25-1 –	N.V.
8 P.M. 31/10/14	Cases in R.R.H. – Evacuated at 7 P.M. – 124 – All Cases with Unit. All Forms Completed to date together.	N.V.

6th Field Ambulance.

Vol IV

S 12/250 6
Nov. 1914

WAR DIARY
or
INTELLIGENCE SUMMARY.
(Erase heading not required.)

Army Form C. 2118.

Instructions regarding War Diaries and Intelligence Summaries are contained in F.S. Regs., Part II. and the Staff Manual respectively. Title pages will be prepared in manuscript.

Hour, Date, Place	Summary of Events and Information	Remarks and references to Appendices
5 P.M. 1-11-14 YPRES	Patrols in occupation 184 — evacuated.— Battery opposite to support quarter Recon.	
8. P.M. 2-11-14 YPRES	142 in occupation — Captain Houston. Critical state.	
8.10 P.M. 3-11-14 YPRES	L. Battery in occupation — Your Regt. relieved Ml. — Honor on trench — gas mask also to enlarge — cooling. Officer on duty. Issuing dispatch 6p.m. Dublin Fus. relieved shelling.	XXX suffering
9 P.M. Wed. 11-11-14 YPRES	All Coys. ordered Place to Rem dugout quarters — trail 8 corps to be 4 full Regt. — half Corps to 2 forward Recon mile way of YPRES. Second Battery Y-POPERINGHE RD. L. Dillon forward trench	

Army Form C. 2118.

WAR DIARY
or
INTELLIGENCE SUMMARY.
(Erase heading not required.)

Instructions regarding War Diaries and Intelligence Summaries are contained in F. S. Regs, Part II. and the Staff Manual respectively. Title pages will be prepared in manuscript.

Hour, Date, Place	Summary of Events and Information	Remarks and references to Appendices
8 P.M. 5-11-14 Kittets	Went to Billets at front village —	MPS
	On 6-11-14. Reinforcements to Regt. Prepared for next journey — 2 Guns to H.Q. Ambulance for duty — Rest rest to Bren —	
8 P.M. 6-11-14 Bircts	Went on rome Billets — gone out Officers — look over other Companys Headquarters. Troops came regular, men started for duty one per and one Sub officer. Infantry section before advance to —	MPS
8 P.M. 7-11-14 Kittets	Nothing to note	MPS
8 P.M. 8-11-14	Entery Ypres to tents	MPS

Army Form C. 2118.

WAR DIARY
or
INTELLIGENCE SUMMARY.
(Erase heading not required.)

Instructions regarding War Diaries and Intelligence Summaries are contained in F. S. Regs., Part II. and the Staff Manual respectively. Title pages will be prepared in manuscript.

Hour, Date, Place	Summary of Events and Information	Remarks and references to Appendices
8 A.M. 9-11-14 Same Bivouac	Nothing special to note — Officers arranging transport to move in at short notice.	
1 P.M. 10-11-14 Same Bivouac	Two officers went for stay H. Mercer + H. McClintock left to Havre	H.M.
8 P.M. 12-11-14 Same Bivouac	Lands of pork for Mens' Beans — personal fit ever varying. Beans sent to Havre. Commence ammu. storm.	S.P.S
8 P.M. 13-11-14 Same Bivouac	Continued in same & reverse-ranking funeral to fronts	S.P.
11 P.M. 18-11-14 Same Bivouac	Received orders to that one Coy command to Major J.H.R. WINDER R.A.M.C. Hospital over and over 6 No 6 detachments from Bergen 2 Woodie R.G.M.C. Received and counts 30 6 detachments from Bergen 2/8.	J.R. McK Major J.R.A.M.C. J.H.R. Winder Major R.A.M.C.

Army Form C. 2118.

WAR DIARY
or
INTELLIGENCE SUMMARY.
(Erase heading not required.)

Instructions regarding War Diaries and Intelligence Summaries are contained in F.S. Regs., Part II. and the Staff Manual respectively. Title pages will be prepared in manuscript.

Hour, Date, Place	Summary of Events and Information	Remarks and references to Appendices
8 P.M. 15. Nov. 1914.	Unit still Billeting in same area. Troops exercised in the morning. Transport inspected. Officers re-appointed to declined evening to Exchange of C.O.s. Visiting horses improved. Snow in the morning, cold, wet at day. Health of troops good. Five (5) Officers on leave, and one hundred + three (103) men evacuated to No. 4 F.A.	J/H H Wrigdet. Major Junior.
8 P.M. 16. Nov. 1914.	Unit still in Billeting in same area. Troops exercised in the morning. Transport inspected. Horses however visited by vet, every thing found satisfactory. Weather colder and ground wet mostly stated. Sanitation in camp attended to as much as possible. One Officer + 72 men evacuated to No. 4 F.A.	J H W
8 P.M. 17. Nov. 1914.	Unit still Billeting in same area. Troops exercised with the morning. Transport inspected. Orders received from A.D.M.S. 2 Divn. M 122. for the Bearer Divisions of No. 6 F.A. to report tomorrow at Unit Lislay. Two 3 Ambulance Wagons which were to remove with R. Bearer Division of No. 5. F.A. this was attended to. The Bearer returned, less 3 wagons mentioned + 4 Officers. The Health of the men was good. Weather cold + wet: ground very wet and hilly. Sanitation attended to. 5 N.C.O.s + men evacuated to No. 4 F.A.	J H W

WAR DIARY
or
INTELLIGENCE SUMMARY.
(Erase heading not required.)

Army Form C. 2118.

Instructions regarding War Diaries and Intelligence Summaries are contained in F.S. Regs., Part II. and the Staff Manual respectively. Title pages will be prepared in manuscript.

Hour, Date, Place	Summary of Events and Information	Remarks and references to Appendices
8 P.M. 18th Nov. 1914	Unit still billeting in same area. Weather still very unfavorable. One horse died during night from Pneumonia. Transport inspected. Health of troops good. Orders received from A.D.M.S. that until two 3 Ambulance wagons already with 70 S. 7 C. to proceed to CAESTRE at 7 a.m. morning of 19-11-14. Nothing further of note to record.	J.H.N.W
8 P.M. 19th Nov. 1914.	Reveille at 5:30 a.m. Breakfast at 6 a.m. Unit paraded at 6:45. moved off at 7.20 a.m. & they decide to difficulty of transport. Arrived at Billets at CAESTRE at 3.45 p.m. after a very trying march. Owing to weather conditions. Usual halls were given, and one horse at mid-day for watering & feeding horses & dinner to men. Snow was falling freely towards end of march. On arrival in Billets. The billets were placed in their various batteries. Lot of and billeted and a proper inspection given. Horse arrival superintended. One Row-bolt. 3 men went about. Nothing further to record.	J.H.N.W
8 P.M. 20th Nov. 1914	Reveille at 6 a.m. Breakfast 7 a.m. Paraded at 8.15 a.m. and detained. Weather still very cold. Frozen hard. Hot baths were arranged for, and as many men as possible were sent down. Symbd. Cavs. charged with two to completing. At a Small hospital was fitted up 6. Ry. Bn. officers with Downs. 20 beds accommodation.	J.H.N.W

WAR DIARY
or
INTELLIGENCE SUMMARY.
(Erase heading not required.)

Army Form C. 2118.

Hour, Date, Place	Summary of Events and Information	Remarks and references to Appendices
20. Nov. 1914.	2 M.O. & 3 N.C.Os. with a small escort & general duty Mess with an Sanit's orderly put into a c. 16 were admitted during day. no serious cases. Healthy troops good. Nothing further to note.	J.H.H.W
21. Nov. 1914.	Same routine adopted as yesterday. Hospital visited frequently. & progress satisfactory. Admissions during day 12. Discharges to duty 3. Convoys to 90 s Clearing Hosp. 17. Remain 8. Transport inspected on horse lines & pneumonia. Healthy troops good. breaks very cold. Nothing further to note. Guns has been parts to men to leave Billets & proceed to town before Dinner. & 12 & 5.30 p.m. all necessary arrangements	J.H.H.W
22. Nov. 1914.	Same routine adopted as yesterday. Hospital visited frequently. Shelters were started to be horsed. Admission during day 5. Discharge to duty 6. Transported to 90 s Clearing Hosp 4. Remaining 5. Health of troops good. Weather still very cold.	J.H.H.W
23. Nov. 1914.	Same routine adopted as yesterday. Hospital visited frequently. Shelters inspected. Transport inspected. Admissions to Hosp during day 14. Discharges to duty 1. Transport 12. Remaining 9. Health of troops good. Weather still cold. Condition continues good & improving. Warm clothing for troops arrived Q.M.S. Stell Hume. proceeded on leave to ENGLAND.	J.H.H.W

Army Form C. 2118.

WAR DIARY
or
INTELLIGENCE SUMMARY.
(Erase heading not required.)

Instructions regarding War Diaries and Intelligence Summaries are contained in F.S. Regs., Part II. and the Staff Manual respectively. Title pages will be prepared in manuscript.

Hour, Date, Place	Summary of Events and Information	Remarks and references to Appendices
24th Nov. 1914	Same routine adopted as yesterday. Had all wagon wheels & plates in line Hospital visited frequently. Admissions during day, 19. Discharges to duty. 7. Transferred 15. Missionary 2. Camp — Hospital visited by O.C. No S. Sgt OTHEN. OSC proceeded to France L ENGLAND. 10.30 am. Hot baths arranged for Troops. Health of troops good. Weather still cold but not freezing	J.H.T.W
25th Nov 1914	Same routine adopted as yesterday. Transport inspected and men began work to each device O.S.C. gave per hour. Hospital visited frequently. Admissions 9. Discharges to duty, 1. Transferred to War 5. Remaining 5. Health of troops good. Weather rather cold. Nothing special to report.	J.H.T.W
26th Nov. 1914	Same routine adopted as yesterday. Transport inspected. Health of troops good. Weather still bad. Prospects not satisfactory arrangements of all the work of M.T. by Mechanical subspecialty. Hospital visited frequently. Admissions 5. Sickness to hospital 1. Transferred 4. Remaining 5. O detachment of 1.N.C. + 2 men sent to FLETRIE to turn a transport driver shelter at HEADQuarters. Nothing further to note.	J.H.T.W

WAR DIARY
or
INTELLIGENCE SUMMARY.

Army Form C. 2118.

Hour, Date, Place	Summary of Events and Information	Remarks and references to Appendices
8 p.m. 27 Nov 1914 St Eloi S	Same routine adopted as yesterday — from nature of ground and reports that our correct — Position of vicinities changed — New shelter works for horses. Health of Troops good — Major Linden, Captn Walsh sick again proceed to England a short leave. Nothing further to record.	O Jones Capt & Adj
8 p.m. 28 Nov 1914 St Eloi S	Troops employed during the morning in cleaning roads, billets etc — Interviewed D. Knip left for road at St Eloi — P? Parkin — New man was sent back from the trenches on N.W. 10 to N° S. 7. A by L? Armstrong Maine. Inspected "D" Coy Knip left & 157 men 107 had vaccinated 26 were sore today & 24 infused — have of letter reported to O.C. Knip left — Inoculated 14 admitted Convalescent with Tropical Fever 13, Dysentery 9	O.J.

Army Form C. 2118.

WAR DIARY
or
INTELLIGENCE SUMMARY.
(Erase heading not required.)

Instructions regarding War Diaries and Intelligence Summaries are contained in F. S. Regs., Part II. and the Staff Manual respectively. Title pages will be prepared in manuscript.

Hour, Date, Place	Summary of Events and Information	Remarks and references to Appendices
8 am Nov. 29. 1914 In billets.	Sunday – Church parade C of E 12 noon – R.C. 8 a.m. Hospital 9 admissions, 8 transferred. Lt. Holroyd + Lt. Lanigan left 10 remaining – for leave to England to 5-12-14.	J
8 am Nov. 30 1914. In billets.	Fatigue parties employed in cleaning billets and surroundings – Smarden Squad proceeded on route march from 10.30 a.m. to 12.30 p.m. A supply of hot water for baths for the men is now available daily – Hospital 11 admissions, 4 discharges, 5 transferred to base, 12 remaining – weather stormy but milder – shortage of troop food –	D. Scutro Capt + R.A.M.C

30/11/14

8th Field Ambulance.

Vol V

12/5907
Dec. 1914

Army Form C. 2118.

WAR DIARY
or
INTELLIGENCE SUMMARY.
(Erase heading not required.)

Hour, Date, Place	Summary of Events and Information	Remarks and references to Appendices
8 pm Dec 1st 1914 In Hutts at CAESTRE	Reveille 6.30 am. Reconnaissance? on truck galore. Parade 8.45 am. Work of brickmaking red - erection of autonome wagons completed — Inspected hunt of tools [?] — KRR & Berkshires touch line [?] satisfactory — Capt Hoffmann (wounded) Major Corrie 2nd Div Sign Co — admitted to hospital — Lieut Hughes discharged to duty this morning; reported to A.A.A.S. Hospital 7 admitted, 5 discharged. Duty, 3 transferred, 11 remaining. 16 Officers admitted — 1 discharged —	Steven Capt RAMC to OC no 6 Field Amb. on leave.

WAR DIARY
or
INTELLIGENCE SUMMARY.
(Erase heading not required.)

Army Form C. 2118.

Instructions regarding War Diaries and Intelligence Summaries are contained in F.S. Regs., Part II. and the Staff Manual respectively. Title pages will be prepared in manuscript.

Hour, Date, Place	Summary of Events and Information	Remarks and references to Appendices
8 a.m. Dec. 2. 1914. In billets.	Routine duties as yesterday. Hospital 7 omitted, 3 discharged to unit, 8 transferred to base. 6 remaining. Game of football. Letting fixture to reserve.	D.T.
8 p.m. Dec. 3rd 1914. In billets.	Lieut. Ambrose proceeded on leave to parents at 9 a.m. and marched under my command to METEREN for inspection by His Majesty the King. On returning to billets at 1.15 p.m. Hospital 7 omitted, 1 discharged to duty, 7 temporary sick remaining. Weather wet and stormy. L/Cpl. Giles and Pte. Hardcastle were presented with the Distinguished Conduct Medal by His Majesty the King.	D.T.

WAR DIARY or INTELLIGENCE SUMMARY

Army Form C. 2118.

Hour, Date, Place	Summary of Events and Information	Remarks and references to Appendices
8 p.m. Dec 4. 1914. Lille.	Routine duties as yesterday — Route march 10.30 a.m. to 12 noon — Hospital 9 admitted, 1 to duty, 3 transferred to train, 10 remaining. Weather very wet.	D.J.
8 p.m. Dec 5. 1914. Lille.	Routine duties as yesterday. Enquiries for information of D.S. + L. + Major Capt. + arrangements had been made to return in reporting of 6th Bele. Scottish reply from O.C. 9 South Battalion. Hospital, 1 man admitted + transferred & tr, 10 admitted, 1 discharged to duty, 9 to base 10 remain. Weather very wet. Lieut Booth Kaine (S.R.) arrived for duty last night.	O.J.

Army Form C. 2118.

WAR DIARY
or
INTELLIGENCE SUMMARY.
(Erase heading not required.)

Hour, Date, Place	Summary of Events and Information	Remarks and references to Appendices
8 b.y. Dec. 6. 15/14. Billets	Routine duties as yesterday. Troops exercised in Billets. Hospital - 7 admitted, 2 discharged to duty, 9 transferred to Base. 6 remain. 2 returned to duty. Lieut A. Came [?] leave & returned command, also returned. Capt Waller, Lt. Carrere, Lt. Camper + Lt. G.C. Welch. Capt Snow & Capt Thorold in command of rear & right. Healthy troops condition good. Weather mild but exceedingly wet.	[signature]
8 b.y. Dec 7. 15/14. Billets.	Routine duties as yesterday. Troops taken out for a route march in the morning. Hospital 9 admitted, 1 discharged to duty, 4 transferred to Base. 10 remain. Nothing further to report. New Herold A.S. Left with Base to duty.	[signature]
8 b.y. Dec. 8th 15/14. Billets.	Routine duties as yesterday. Troops exercised in Billets & cleaning up. Hospital. 8 admitted. 4 discharged to duty, 7 transferred to Base. 7 remaining. The Brig. of the 6 Bg. Maj. visited Billets.	[signature]

Army Form C. 2118.

WAR DIARY
or
INTELLIGENCE SUMMARY.
(Erase heading not required.)

Instructions regarding War Diaries and Intelligence Summaries are contained in F. S. Regs., Part II. and the Staff Manual respectively. Title pages will be prepared in manuscript.

Hour, Date, Place	Summary of Events and Information	Remarks and references to Appendices
8 p.m. Dec 9th 1914. Billets.	Routine duties as yesterday. Troops exercised in Billets being wet day raining all day. Transport washed & Vet. Off. One horse (Bay) was shot by his order and was suffering w/ colic. Hospital 12 admitted. 2 Discharged totals, 11 Transferred B'Base, 6 Names. DGDMS. visited Billets. Capt. Jones & Thornton Manor arrived & have this morn. Pt. Dent procured 5 days on leave till 12th inclusive.	J. H. P. W.
8 p.m. Dec 10th 1914. Billets.	Routine duties as yesterday. Troops taken out for a route march. Very wet afternoon. Hospital. 13. admitted. 2 discharged totals, 11 Transferred CWT B'Base 6 Names. Capt. Seaton Manor reported to duty with 30 & 2 C. V.W. & Lt. Armstrong Manor (Sids). Lt. Cesari reported to D/5 6 & 1' Kings (Liverpools) Rgt. 25 prs of hosts arrived & B'apr. Motorpul [...] tspt.	J. H. P. W.
8 p.m. Dec. 11th 1914. Billets.	Routine duties as yesterday. Troops exercised in Billets. Fatigue party employed cleaning up. Hospital 6. admitted. 4 discharged 2 Duty. 1 Transferred B'Base. 2 Remaining. The Rev. E. P. Burnt, C.D. reported his arrival + duty. The 2/Lt. Ind E Cesari to th. MARIE Est. enemy.	J. H. P. W.

Army Form C. 2118.

WAR DIARY
or
INTELLIGENCE SUMMARY.
(Erase heading not required.)

Instructions regarding War Diaries and Intelligence Summaries are contained in F.S. Regs., Part II. and the Staff Manual respectively. Title pages will be prepared in manuscript.

Hour, Date, Place	Summary of Events and Information	Remarks and references to Appendices
8 p.m. Dec. 12th 1914. Billets.	Same routine as yesterday. Troops exercised & Billets. Clothing & necessaries J.H. Dr. inspected. Hospital: 1 Officer admitted & transferred T.Base. other Mentors. 4 admitted. 3 discharged to Duty. 4 transferred to Base. 4 hernia. A.D.M.S. inspects Billets & transport. Made its Hazebrouck with Lieut. to see a dispepter under intestine Couq. foul record. breaks kidney, rupture of big gut. (and. One horse died of colic — (recent of P.M. made))	J. H. R. W.
8 p.m. Dec 13th 1914. Billets	Sunday. There was church parade of R.C.s & C.of.E. Billets cleaned up as much as possible. Very wet day. Hospital = 11. Admitted. 1. discharge to duty. 6 horses from T.Base. 8 remaining. Nothing particular to report. 2nd Lieut. Hame (S/y R) should have returned from leave last night but has not done so. there is none reported as absent.	T. H. R. W.
8 p.m. Dec 14th 1914. Billets	By air way. Same weekly routine carried out. Mess and Horses inspected in Billets. An order received from C. in of army to be ready to move in two hours from 9.15 9 am. This was carried out. The party from FLETRE was ordered to rejoin unit and reported possible up as two as possible ready to move if necessary, but still kept open inspection. Hospital = 12. Admitted. and 1 Officer. 6 discharge to S/Duty. 14 Transferred to Base. None admitted. 1 Officer. 1 slight Enteric. 1 Nasopharyngitis. 2nd Lieut. Hame (S/y R) reported this arrived from leave to station he was late to arrive but nothing before will be done. nothing further to report. Weather still bad. W. CROOKS A.S.C. attached 70 6 2 A was brought in by the Military police to Camp, having fined by Mr. French order of d/r VLAMERTINGHE. he has been missing Since 15 11 14. He was bring it back his lined.	J. H. R. W.

Army Form C. 2118.

WAR DIARY
or
INTELLIGENCE SUMMARY.
(Erase heading not required.)

Instructions regarding War Diaries and Intelligence Summaries are contained in F. S. Regs, Part II. and the Staff Manual respectively. Title pages will be prepared in manuscript.

Hour, Date, Place	Summary of Events and Information	Remarks and references to Appendices
8 p.m. Dec. 15th. 1914. Billets.	Same routine as yesterday. Troops & Horses exercised in Billets, orders still to move in 2 hours time if necessary. Hospital 8. Admitted 0. Discharged 6. Sick 8. Transferred 1. Remaining. Remounted Pt Evants for Court Martial Evidence & statements taken by Capt Sime were forwarded. Weather still cold & very wet.	J.H.T.W.
8 p.m. Dec. 16th 1914. Billets.	Troops taken out for a route march. Horses also taken out on exercise. Order issued that we were to be ready to move in 2 hours time if force. Hospital 1 Officers admitted 13. other Wounded. Total 14. admitted. Transferred 1 officer, 12 other wounded, Remaining one. E Coy Hqs visited by 7. 9. A.M. R. Fort A.V.S. was inoculated & clear. Horse Park wall tested carries. Horses inoculated Vet. Off. one horse (Nr. Nouster) killed, arm this wound but is in danger with ? manages. Weather still cold & wet. Hostility Hospital pres. 3 N.C.O. were inoculated before going up. Future terms.	J.H.T.W.
8 p.m. Dec. 17th 1914. Billets.	Same routine as usual in Billets. men & horses exercised. Transport inspected by Senior A.S.C. Officer and Horses inspected by O.D.V.S. Doc Sims sent to rest town with suspected mange (Pt Evants) Hospital. Admission 10. Transferred Heart of Remounts. 2. R' Crosho punished. No 1. It was sent into HAZEBROUCK to O. Coy 2.7. Sergeants for punishment. 2 N.C.O.'s of No 6 Coy & S A.S.C. were issued Field Urgent in Paris.	J.H.T.W.

79/3298

Army Form C. 2118.

WAR DIARY
or
INTELLIGENCE SUMMARY.
(Erase heading not required.)

Instructions regarding War Diaries and Intelligence Summaries are contained in F.S. Regs., Part II. and the Staff Manual respectively. Title pages will be prepared in manuscript.

Hour, Date, Place	Summary of Events and Information	Remarks and references to Appendices
8 p.m. Dec. 18th 1914. Billets.	Same routine as usual. Troops Thomas exercised in fields. Still under orders to move at 2 hours. Hospital. 5. Admitted 2. Remaining Total 7. Transferred to Base. 6. Remaining 1. Pte Reynolds was transferred to nurse sick will Cadets. Pte Taylor A.S.C. was granted 5 days leave to try and see his wife who was stated to be dying. But was faced out. Weather still very bad, but health of troops good.	J.H.R.W.
8 p.m. Dec. 19th 1914. Billets.	Same routine as usual. Troops therin exercised in fields. Still under orders to move at 2 hours. Hospital 4 admitted. 1 remain. 4 Transferred to Base. Remains. 6. Inspected our large bucket of H2O. Issues rising. Inhalers of zinc. Worked shirts was but health of troops good.	J.H.R.W.
8 p.m. Dec. 20th 1914. Billets.	Sunday. Same routine as usual. Troops there exercised. Church parade. 1 moved at 12.30 p.m. Hospital. 6. Remained. 6. Admitted. 1. Discharged to Duty. 8. Transferred to Clearing Hosp. Remaining. 3.	J.H.R.W.
8 p.m. Dec. 21st 1914. Billets.	Same routine as usual. Troops there exercised. Hospital. 3. Remained 4 admitted. 4 Transferred to Base. 3. Remaining. Inspected water carts. Weather still very bad. but health of troops good. Received the orders to move at 7.30 A.M. by G. BETHUNE at 7 am tomorrow.	J.H.R.W.

Army Form C. 2118.

WAR DIARY
or
INTELLIGENCE SUMMARY.
(Erase heading not required.)

Instructions regarding War Diaries and Intelligence Summaries are contained in F.S. Regs., Part II. and the Staff Manual respectively. Title pages will be prepared in manuscript.

Hour, Date, Place	Summary of Events and Information	Remarks and references to Appendices
8 p.m. Dec. 22nd 1914. on line of march.	Left CAESTRE Billet about 7 a.m. for BETHUNE. Wagons arrived until march, and there were a lot of halts due to delays in such a long column. We were billeted after much delay as there was no place for us with Horsn in the Indian Field Ambulance at SEMINAIRE ST VAAST. The 7.C. arrived all correct. Hospital 2. Reinforcing.	J.H.T.W.
8 p.m. Dec 23rd 1914. Billet at BETHUNE COLLEGE des JEUNES FILLES. RUE MARCELLIN BERTHELOT BOULEVARD VICTOR HUGO.	at 10.30 a.m. sent out an advance dressing party to BEUVRY of the Bearer Sub. Division of A Sec under Capt. SEXTON assisted + Lt. SMITH with instructions to get in touch with the O. by the 1st and Lt. SMITH, as Liaison Officer to Bng H.Q. 4 wounded wounded to No.1 F.A. SCHOOL JULES FERRY, one nunbury, crossing in BOULEVARD d'ARTOIS BETHUNE. The rest had orders to proceed to rue Ribote's Town, on his wagon, arriving about 11.30 p.m. Town Hospiece in a very dirty state. The men employed in cleaning up the place. Hospital 2. Reinforcing. Dispatches 2.	J.H.T.W.
8 p.m. Dec. 24th 1914. Same billets.	Employed in cleaning up building which was left in a dirty state. No 1 Clearing Hosp. moved into same building. They accepts two wings and we occupy one wing. We asked them to clean up their place with our men. I went up and visited the dressing station relieved by Capt SEXTON. a Vet. Officer visited + inspected our horses. Heallh of host good.	J.H.T.W.
8 p.m. Dec 25th 1914. Xmas Day. Same billets.	Holiday for F.A. as much as possible. Proceeded to LOCON by making A.D.M.S. and inspected billets for a Dtty. troops in case we had orders to move. Capt. CATTERY, Capt. LLOYD JONES were also there. Well A.D.M.S. We 2.0. spend a happy day with 9. in ____ mess	J.H.T.W.

Army Form C. 2118.

WAR DIARY
or
INTELLIGENCE SUMMARY.
(Erase heading not required.)

Instructions regarding War Diaries and Intelligence Summaries are contained in F.S. Regs., Part II. and the Staff Manual respectively. Title pages will be prepared in manuscript.

Hour, Date, Place	Summary of Events and Information	Remarks and references to Appendices
8 p.m. Dec 26th 1914. Same billets	Same routine as usual. Troops + Horses exercised, + Billets cleaned up as much as possible. A fatigue party sent to 30 1 Clearing Hosp. to help them clean up their place. Horses inspected by Vet Officer. Visited the Beaver Sub. Division & present everything correct. Weather still cold & wet but healthy bracing frost.	J.H.R.W.
8 p.m. Dec 27th 1914. Same Billets.	Same routine as usual. Troops & Horses exercised. Usual fatigue employed. Horses inspected by Vet Officer. Brewer Sub. Division returned to H.C.V. by order of A.D.M.S. A great many of promotions to act. Mounts went made in the Div. by order. Visited CHOCQUES. with a view to moving No. 6. F. a. to that bul-found no 4. Clearing Hosp. taking over the buildings. Pte BICKERS never reported sick will absents. Horses were being freed & 2 of 5 Clear Hosp	J.H.R.W.
8. p.m. Dec 28th 1914. Same Billets.	Same routine as usual. Troops & Horses exercised. Usual fatigue employed. Horses inspected by Vet Officer. Nothing further to report. Healthy frost from Pts F.S. WILKS, C.S. refected for exempt for duty from No. 6. F. a. + Pts W.H. SATCHET. With Chaps reported sin arrived for duty. Qs SHEEHAN + Pt WHITE transferred to 301 Clearing Hosp sick. Pt. CLARKS have made life on parade.	J.H.R.W
6 p.m. Dec. 29th 1914. ECOLE PAUL BERT. RUE DU MARAIS. BETHUNE	Under orders of S.O.C. 1st Divn. No. 6. F.a. moved to Billets mentioned in margin. 4 Officers billeted in house used Inspected by A.D.M.S. + went with A.D.M.S. to inspect CHOCQUES – houses suggested for use as we F.a.D & new F.a.D Billets were in a very dirty state & men employed in cleaning up. 6 pa. bly 1 N.C.o. + 10 men will be back war. + personnel. Sent to LOCON. + horses drinking station.	J.H.R.W.
8 p.m. Dec 30th 1914. Same Billets	Usual routine carried out. Troops taken out riding & horse exercise + Inspected by 5 A.D.V.S. & 10 a.m. + Pt W. attended to bty. org. 2 Horses sent to sick lines. A fatigue party were sent to first Billets to help No. 4 Clear. Hosp. to a consult with their re defacts & extra & Weather. Nothing further to report.	J.H.R.W.

Army Form C. 2118.

WAR DIARY
or
INTELLIGENCE SUMMARY.
(Erase heading not required.)

Instructions regarding War Diaries and Intelligence Summaries are contained in F. S. Regs., Part II. and the Staff Manual respectively. Title pages will be prepared in manuscript.

Hour, Date, Place	Summary of Events and Information	Remarks and references to Appendices
8 p.m. Dec 31st 1914. Same Billets.	Usual routine carried out. Troops & Horses Bivouaced. Violent storm raging. Station at LOCON. Sag A.D.M.S. Lt. Col. E. BIRCH. having reported for duty, is taking for this Brigade Health of Troops Good	J.H.R.W.

2ND DIVISION
MEDICAL

NO. 6 FIELD AMBULANCE

JAN - DEC 1915

No. 6. Field Ambulance.

Vol VI.

121/4259
Jan 1915

Army Form C. 2118.

WAR DIARY
or
INTELLIGENCE SUMMARY.
(Erase heading not required.)

Instructions regarding War Diaries and Intelligence Summaries are contained in F. S. Regs., Part II. and the Staff Manual respectively. Title pages will be prepared in manuscript.

Hour, Date, Place	Summary of Events and Information	Remarks and references to Appendices
8 P.M. 1st January 1915. ECOLE PAUL BERT. RUE DU MARAIS. BETHUNE.	Same routine carried out. Troops and Horses examined. Horses inspected by ADVS all satisfactory. Billets inspected by ADMS. Two NCO's & 18 men were sent by order of ADMS & VIEILLE CHAPPELLE to look after the bathing arrangements of the 2nd Division for the troops under Capt THURSTON. Nothing further to report. Health of troops good.	J.H.T. WIMBER. MAJOR R.A.M.C. O.C. No 6 FIELD AMBULANCE
8 p.m 2nd January 1915. Same Billets	Same routine carried out in Billets. Horses exercised and inspected by Vet Officer. Bearer training with war chest from ⅔ 4, 7 and bearer Capt Nicholls. Routine work day. Nothing further to report.	J H T W
8 p.m 3rd January 1915. Same Billets.	Same routine carried out in Billets. Getting all the Billet rooms washed out while bearers are away. Visited bearers at bearer dressing stations with ADM. No divine service held & MASS. but men sent out to Church Parade.	J H T W
8 p.m 4th January 1915. Same billets.	Same routine carried out in Billets. Report from O.C. Bearers during last 24 hours 12 NCO's & men evacuated sick & wounded. 11 from LE TOURET, 1 one from HALTE. Nothing further to report. Health of troops good.	J H T W
8 p.m 5th January 1915. Same Billets.	Same routine carried out in Billets. Visited Bearers. Report from O.C Bearers during last 24 hours. One Officer & 42 NCO's & men sick & wounded. Remained in routine. The JOY's, not sick. Horses inspected by Vet. Off. Health of troops good.	J H T W
8 p.m 6th January 1915. Same Billets.	Same routine carried out in Billets. Examined numerous buildings The town for a suitable place for a convalescent Camp and found billets round the Tk but have prepared men for 100 beds. Report from O.C Bearers during last 24 hours 2 Officers & 37 men sick & wounded. Rev Fry Mason sent back to early again.	J H T W

Army Form C. 2118.

WAR DIARY
or
INTELLIGENCE SUMMARY.
(Erase heading not required.)

Instructions regarding War Diaries and Intelligence Summaries are contained in F. S. Regs., Part II. and the Staff Manual respectively. Title pages will be prepared in manuscript.

Hour, Date, Place	Summary of Events and Information	Remarks and references to Appendices
8 p.m. 7th January. 1915. Same billets.	Same routine as usual. Have opened three billets for 100 patients. 30 were transferred from O.C. Beavers about 6 p.m. today mostly cases of some feet, colds, rheumatism. Report from O.C. Beavers, LE TOURET during last 24 hours. Officers 1 + 46 other ranks sick + wounded. Four O.C. dressing station at HALTE 4 sick. Very hot day. Health of troops good. All the troops in these billets have had a hot bath. Clean clothes.	J.H.R.W.
8 p.m. 8th January 1915. Same Billets.	Same routine as usual. Visited HALTE and LOCON dressing stations. Division Cav. heavy draft horse sent sick to Hospital with an unusual rash of hands and heart. A.D.M.S. visited billets + Hospital. Report from O.C. Beavers LE TOURET during last 24 hours. 1 Officer wounded (slight) 29 other ranks sick wounded from HALTE 3 sick, 25 N.C.O. + men sent sick from advanced dressing stations with frostbitten persons and so on. Weather still very bad but health of troops good.	J.H.R.W.
8 p.m. 9th January. 1915. Same Billets.	Same routine as usual. 8 (eight) patients were transferred to No. 4 Fld. Amb. Report from O.C. Beavers LE TOURET during last 24 hours. 5 Officers wounded. Officers sick 2 Officers wounded 1 Officer, sick other ranks, 10 wounded + 37 sick. From O.C. dressing station HALTE other ranks 2 sick. Four wounded H. horses – have them treated U.	J.H.R.W.
8 p.m. 10th January. 1915. Same Billets.	Same routine as usual. Report from O.C. Beavers LE TOURET during last 24 hours. Wounded. Officer Nil. Other Ranks 25. Sick. Officer Nil. Other Ranks 38. 2 fld. S.B. from HALTE M. Ranks wounded 1. Sick 9. Visited Beavers at LE TOURET Patients + Amb. doing well. Health of troops good.	J.H.R.W.
8 p.m. 11th January. 1915. Same Billets.	Same routine as usual. Report from O.C. Beavers LE TOURET during last 24 hours. Wounded. Officer 1. Other Ranks 12. Sick. Officer Nil. Other Ranks 25. From HALTE 2 sick. Two checking. Sergeant Wooding nothing particular to report.	J.H.R.W.

Army Form C. 2118.

WAR DIARY
or
INTELLIGENCE SUMMARY.
(Erase heading not required.)

Instructions regarding War Diaries and Intelligence Summaries are contained in F.S. Regs., Part II. and the Staff Manual respectively. Title pages will be prepared in manuscript.

Hour, Date, Place	Summary of Events and Information	Remarks and references to Appendices
8 p.m. 12th January 1915. Same Billets.	Same routine as usual. Report from O.C. Bearers LE TOURET during last 24 hours. Wounded officers nil. other ranks 6. Sick. Officers nil. other ranks 43. from HALTE sick 3. Checking equipment as before. Nothing further to report.	J.H.T.W
8 p.m. 13th January 1915. Same Billets.	Same routine as usual. Report from O.C. Bearers LE TOURET during last 24 hours. Officers nil. Other ranks. Wounded 5. Sick 11. from HALTE. 6 sick. Nothing further to report. Inspected various Cacolony Horses & mules.	J.H.T.W
8 p.m. 14th January 1915. Same Billets.	Same routine as usual. I visited dressing stations at HALTE & LOCON. Seen A.D.M.S. received an order 6.1570/4910 now position HALTE, LE TOURET. Bearers have moved to ESSARS & have moved our cart and dressing station East of GORRE. Nothing further to report.	J.H.T.W
8 p.m. 15th January 1915. Same Billets.	Same routine as usual. The G.O.C. 2nd Division & the A.D.M.S. inspected the Hospital this afternoon. Have instituted baths for the patients and supplied them with clean underclothes. Report from O.C. Bearers for last 24 hours. 1 Officer Sick 4 n.c.o. Other ranks. Nothing further to report.	J.H.T.W
8 p.m. 16 January 1915. Same Billets.	Same routine as usual. Report from O.C. Bearers during last 24 hours. 6 N.C.O.s & men (4 sick & 2 wounded) were evacuated. The dressing stations at HALTE two cleared up and regiment. means dressing station at ESSARS. Further report from O.C. Bearers 13. N.C.O.s & men sick. Reinforcement of bearers & stations is no fullness. A small dressing station has been formed at ESSARS under C.E.M.C. MACINTOSH. Advance dressing station has been formed in small workhouse in BETH UNE MOR F.S.A.	J.H.T.W

Army Form C. 2118.

WAR DIARY
or
INTELLIGENCE SUMMARY.
(Erase heading not required.)

Instructions regarding War Diaries and Intelligence Summaries are contained in F.S. Regs., Part II. and the Staff Manual respectively. Title pages will be prepared in manuscript.

Hour, Date, Place	Summary of Events and Information	Remarks and references to Appendices
8 p.m. 17th January 1915. Same Billets.	Same routine as usual. Sunday church parade paraded from VIEILLE CHAPELLE. Came in to H.A. bathing establishment too slack. Nothing further to report.	J.H.R.W.
8 p.m. 18th January 1915. Same Billets.	Same routine as usual. Report from O.C. Bearers during last 24 hours evacuated sick + 2 wounded officers. Nothing further to report.	J.H.R.W.
8 p.m. 19th January 1915. Same Billets.	Same routine as usual. Report from O.C. Bearers during last 24 hours. 9 sick + 5 wounded, all other hands. Inspected various buildings with Barrow for a suitable building to form a Divisional Rest in.	J.H.R.W.
8 p.m. 20th January 1915. Same Billets.	Same routine as usual. Visited Bearers yesterday, found everything satisfactory. Report from O.C. Bearers during last 24 hours. (20 N.C.O's + men) 17 sick + 3 wounded were evacuated. Inspected more buildings with A.D.M.S. for a toll hand.	J.H.R.W.
8 p.m. 21st January 1915. Same Billets.	Same routine as usual. Report from O.C. Bearers for last 24 hours. Evacuated 12 W.O.S + men sick. No wounded. Still looking for a building establishment. Nothing further to report.	J.H.R.W.
8 p.m. 22nd January 1915. Same Billets.	Same routine as usual. Report from O.C. Bearers for last 24 hours Evacuated 8 N.C.O's + men = 7 sick + 1 wounded. Visited Bearers all satisfactory.	J.H.R.W.
8 p.m. 23rd January 1915. Same Billets.	Same routine as usual in Billets. Visited new Building with A.D.M.S. + S.O. a Brewery + Margarine Factory, as to forming a bathing establishment there. There seems to much to do as to heat + lighting in brewery many fittings thereby. Report from O.C. Bearers for last 24 hours, 12 N.C.O's + men 11 sick + 1 wounded.	J.H.R.W.

WAR DIARY
or
INTELLIGENCE SUMMARY.
(Erase heading not required.)

Army Form C. 2118.

Instructions regarding War Diaries and Intelligence Summaries are contained in F.S. Regs., Part II. and the Staff Manual respectively. Title pages will be prepared in manuscript.

Hour, Date, Place	Summary of Events and Information	Remarks and references to Appendices
8 p.m. 24th January 1915. Same Billets.	Same routine as usual. Church Parade. Visited Cases - all satisfactory. Report from O.C. Bearers Evacuated Ret. 24 hours - 9 N.C.O.s & men. (7 sick 2 wounded.) Nothing further to report.	J.H.T.W.
8 p.m. 25th January. 1915. Farm belonging to M. CANTRAINNE. ROBECQ.	Received an order from A.D.M.S at 10 a.m. to evacuate present Billets & proceed to Village of ROBECQ. The first division of Field Ambulance moved to new Billets, arriving 4.30 p.m. This move was due to BETHUNE being shelled in the morning.	J.H.T.W.
8 p.m. 26th January 1915. Same Billets.	Same routine as in the Billets, all men employed cleaning up. Report from O.C. Bearers. 1 East 24 hours evacuated 1 Officer sick & 15 N.C.O.s & men = 10 men wounded & 5 men sick. One Thos. R. Kings. R.w. Mgt. sent to O.C. Bearers. Steam coffee at his dressing Station. No change since its inception.	J.H.T.W.
8 p.m. 27th January 1915. Same Billets.	Same routine as usual in Billets. Sent by order of A.D.M.S. Capt. IEVERS + 32 N.C.O's + men. + 3 Ambulance wagons to BETHUNE to form a Rest House full. 2nd Division. Hay and litter. ECOLE PROFESSIONELLE now but late - Capt. SEXTON + 21 N.C.O.s + men were sent to LES LOBES, to form a dressing station there. Our Ambulance Wagons were on car wagons. Capt. THURSTON reported his departure as M.D.N. 36 Bde. R.F.A. letters by motor G.A.D.M.S. We dispatched 100 Blankets + half of K Box Annex Cpt Station here. Report from the Bearers during past 24 hours evacuated 11 N.C.O.s & men 21 wounded. + 10 Sick. - Permanent Convalescent The BRIDGE Room Deck.	J.H.T.W.
8 p.m. 28th January 1915. Same Billets.	Same routine as usual in Billets. Re-fitted 200 Blankets yesterday & same Clothing. Transport inspected by Senior Transport Officer. Capt. IEVERS + party returned to H.Qu. 2nd McINTOSH + men (Sp.Vs) sent to help Capt. SEXTON at LES LOBES. + 7 men. one Sunbeam motor far. Sent to Capt. SEXTON's dressing station. Report from O.C. Bearers Evacuated last 24 hours. 6 N.C.O.'s & men. sick. wounded. Nil. Report from Capt. SEATON dressing station. Nil. Capt. SAMPSON T. 330 N.A.M.C. reported his arrival to this Field Amb. for Duty from 36 Bde. R.F.A. in place of Capt. THURSTON. returned who is to his Bde. Station.	J.H.T.W.

Army Form C. 2118.

WAR DIARY
or
INTELLIGENCE SUMMARY.
(Erase heading not required.)

Instructions regarding War Diaries and Intelligence Summaries are contained in F.S. Regs., Part II. and the Staff Manual respectively. Title pages will be prepared in manuscript.

Hour, Date, Place	Summary of Events and Information	Remarks and references to Appendices
8 p.m. 29th January 1915. Same Billets.	Same routine as usual in Billets. The A.D.M.S. visited the Billets. Reinspected another 200 Blankets. Report from O.C. Bearers – unsuccessful chimney test. 24 horses. 1 S.I.W.O.S. + more = 1 wounded = 14 sick. – wounded man sent to MERVILLE. Report from O.C. Infirmary Station at CHATEAU LOISE evacuated 4 sick cases (one case of Diphtheria). The men were taken too a Hospital Branch. Weather very cold. Health of Troops Good.	J.H.R.W.
8 p.m. 30th January 1915. Same Billets.	Same routine as usual in Billets. Re-inspected morning messing. Report from Advanced Party at CHATEAU LOISE evacuated out 24 hours. 2 sick cases + other matters.	J.H.R.W.
8 p.m. 31st January 1915. Same Billets.	Same routine as usual in Billets. Church Parade. Re-inspected writing of my Satisfactory. Report from CHATEAU LOISE, during 24 hrs. evacuated. Other matter 4 sick. Report from O.C. Bearers. 1 Officer + 9 men sick. 9/o wounded. Nothing further: Report Health of men Good.	J.H.R.W.
Entry – 1		J.H.R.Walker Major [illegible] O.C. 3rd. &.2. amb.

79
3298

121/4643

Ans

No. 6. Field Ambulance.

Vol VII

121/4643
Feb. 1915

WAR DIARY No. 6 Field Ambulance

INTELLIGENCE SUMMARY

Army Form C. 2118.

Instructions regarding War Diaries and Intelligence Summaries are contained in F.S. Regs., Part II. and the Staff Manual respectively. Title pages will be prepared in manuscript.

(Erase heading not required.)

Hour, Date, Place	Summary of Events and Information	Remarks and references to Appendices
8 p.m. 1st February. 1915. ECOLE de GARCONS. VENDIN-LEZ-BETHUNE.	Under orders received from A.D.M.S. last night at 10 P.M. We moved 6.2 amb. from our Billets at ROBECQ to new Billets as per allotted program, arriving at ECOLE de GARCONS. at VENDIN-LEZ-BETHUNE d' 11.30 a.m. Present orders during the day is have to BETHUNE during the day. Report from O.C. CHATEAU LOBE. evacuating station - evacuated officers wounded 5 - sick and 1 officer. Capt. DRAKE - BROCKMAN - W. + N.9. of R.F.A. Lt. Comm. Gden. (Confusion Kme). 6. 90. 3. ? amb. BETHUNE - 15. sick. Nothing further to report. Report from O.C. Bearers evacuated during last 24 hours. other Ranks. 2. wounded -	J.H.T. Wilmer Major R.A.M.C. OC. 6. Field Ambulance 2nd Division
8 p.m. 2nd February. 1915. COLLEGE. St. VAAST. BETHUNE.	Under orders. We moved from our night R Billets to Billets as per margin, arriving at 10.A.M. and took over billeting from 30.2 Field Ambulance. A.D.M.S. visited R.R.O.P. this afternoon and gave instructions to continue a bathe house, washing, arrangements in within buildings for the 2nd Division. Same as 30.2.? amb. etc. our 1st Division. The LOCOM. detachment rejoined H.Q.S. live at 6.45.1.2. Report from O.C. evacuating station at CHATEAU LOBE. evacuated during last 24 hours. 1. officer sick. + 2. other Ranks. Report from O.C. Bearer Division at LE HAMEL evacuated during last 24 hours 2 wounded + 8 sick cases. The Sanitary Section attached to 2 Division M.D. and billets in same billet as ourselves. Also No. Section of 30.2. ? amb. sept billet	J.H.T.W.
8 p.m. 3rd February. 1915. Same Billet.	Unit has been working all day getting the building for Baths ready, + Guniumus things have been put with Tomas on purchased by Supreme Secretary personum purchase. A.D.M.S. a Senior Staff Officer visited the building. Report from O.C. Bearers to R.O. 24 hours - evacuated other Ranks. - Sick = 9, wounded 2. Returned to Battalion 2 Officers.	J.H.T.W.

WAR DIARY N° 6 Field Ambulance

INTELLIGENCE SUMMARY.

(Erase heading not required.)

Army Form C. 2118.

Instructions regarding War Diaries and Intelligence Summaries are contained in F.S. Regs., Part II. and the Staff Manual respectively. Title pages will be prepared in manuscript.

Hour, Date, Place	Summary of Events and Information	Remarks and references to Appendices
8 p.m. 4th February 1915. Same Billet	Bathing arrangements started today. 224. Bathed today. A.D. of S. + two Staff Officers visited the arrangements. Report from O.C. Bearers evacuated had 24 hours. Wounded 2 Officers, + Other Ranks. Sick. 6. " Lieut Smith A.N. Moved (S/n) sent 7th Fd a 2 Bomb for temporary duty. " Lieut R.S. McINTOSH F.W. Massie (S/n). sent 7th 1st Herts Inf) no M.O. at the temporary duty.	J.H.R.W.
8 p.m. 5th February 1915. Same Billet	2 SD. Bathed today. Report from O.C. Bearers evacuated during last 24 hours. Officers 1. Sick. Other Ranks. 11 Sick. Two cases of Scabies admitted to this F.A. today.	J.H.R.W.
8 p.m. 6th February 1915. Same Billet.	170. Bathed today. Report from O.C. Bearers evacuated during last 24 hours. Officers - Nil. Other Ranks - Wounded = 1. Sick = 14.	J.H.R.W.
8 p.m. 7th February 1915. Same Billet	Sunday - Bathing establishment closed, but the women were working as usual. 137 orders of A.D. of S. S7. contacts of a Diphtheria case were Bathed and their clothes chlorotoluated with aspirates? report from O.C. Bearers evacuated during last 24 hours. Officers - Nil - Other Ranks = Wounded 1. Sick 12.	J.H.R.W.
8 p.m. 8th February 1915. Same Billet	Monday. 390 Bathed today. Everything very satisfactory. Two cases of Scabies admitted to Hosp. A.A. & Q.M.G. visited the Bathing Establishment. Report from O.C. Bearers evacuated during last 24 hours. Officers - Sick = 2. Other Ranks - Sick = 8. Wounded = 4.	J.H.R.W.
8 p.m. 9th February 1915. Same Billet.	Tuesday. 541 Bathed today. A.A. & Q.M.G. visited the building. Capt. SEXTON sent on duty with Armoured Cars. 2nd WILLIS W. 704.3 and 2nd SMITH from 9th & 2 Bomb & 1st Herts Inf) no M.O. Report from O.C. Bearers evacuated during last 24 hours. Officers - Nil - Other Ranks - Sick = 5. Wounded = 1.	J.H.R.W.

Army Form C. 2118.

WAR DIARY No 6 Field Ambulance

INTELLIGENCE SUMMARY.

(Erase heading not required.)

Instructions regarding War Diaries and Intelligence Summaries are contained in F.S. Regs., Part II. and the Staff Manual respectively. Title pages will be prepared in manuscript.

Hour, Date, Place	Summary of Events and Information	Remarks and references to Appendices
8 p.m. 10th February 1915. Same Billet.	Wednesday. 561. Batted Listing. The S.O.C. 2nd Division visited the arrangements. Report from O.C. Bearers evacuated during last 24 hours. Officers = Nil. Other Ranks - Sick = 6. Wounded = 1.	J.H.T.W.
8 p.m. 11th February 1915. Same Billet.	Thursday. 484. Batted Listing. Report from O.C. Bearers evacuated during last 24 hours. Officers Nil. Other Ranks - Sick = 7.	J.H.T.W.
8 p.m. 12th February 1915. Same Billet.	Friday. 365. Batted Listing. Report from O.C. Bearers evacuated during last 24 hours. Officers Nil. Other Ranks = Sick = 15. Wounded = 2. Heavy draught horse Lilly I accepted. Destroyed.	J.H.T.W.
8 p.m. 13th February 1915. Same Billet.	Saturday 165. Batted Listing. Report from O.C. Bearers evacuated during last 24 hours. Officers Sick = 1. Other Ranks: Wounded = 5. Personnel Casualties. Sgt SMITH and Stoke.	J.H.T.W.
8 p.m. 14th February 1915. Same Billet.	Sunday 90 Batting Listing. Ruthless closed. Report from O.C. Bearers evacuated during last 24 hours. Officers = Sick = 2. O.R. Trades = Sick = 12 + Wounded = 3.	J.H.T.W.
8 p.m. 15th February 1915. Same Billet.	Monday 565. Batted Listing. Report from O.C. Bearers evacuated during last 24 hours Officers Nil. Other Ranks = Sick = 17. Wounded = 2.	J.H.T.W.
8 p.m. 16th February 1915. Same Billet.	Tuesday 560. Batted Listing. All the Bearers returned to H.Qrs by order of A.D.M.S. + The Division. G.S. 2 carts lost their horses. Fresh re-inforcements joined this unit today from the Base.	J.H.T.W.
8 p.m. 17th February 1915. Same Billet.	Wednesday. 510. Batted Listing. Everything going on satisfactory.	J.H.T.W.
8 p.m. 18th February 1915. Same Billet.	Thursday. 465. Batted Listing. 2nd Lt ARMSTRONG and Lts 2 H.L.I. + party of R. SCOTS who has joined this unit for duty	J.H.T.W.

WAR DIARY No 6 Field Ambulance Army Form C. 2118.

INTELLIGENCE SUMMARY.

(Erase heading not required.)

Instructions regarding War Diaries and Intelligence Summaries are contained in F.S. Regs., Part II. and the Staff Manual respectively. Title pages will be prepared in manuscript.

Hour, Date, Place	Summary of Events and Information	Remarks and references to Appendices
8 p.m. 19th February 1915. Same Billet.	Rating. S.10. Rested today. Surg Gen. McPherson. A.M.S. inspected the Bathing arrangements today.	J.H.T.W
8 p.m. 20th February 1915. Same Billet.	Saturday. S.70. Rested today. Six disinfected 1028. Blankets today.	J.H.T.W
8 p.m. 21st February 1915. Same Billet.	Sunday. No Bathing done today, but the men were employed as usual washing & ironing. A party of men attended church Parade.	J.H.T.W
8 p.m. 22nd February 1915. Same Billet.	Monday. 666. Rested today. Divisional Visitors ship stand in new Billet another Sgt. JENKINS meanr 6.2 amb. There are 12 Métres in all. 4 from each Brigade.	J.H.T.W
8 p.m. 23rd February 1915. Same Billet.	Tuesday. 410. Rested today. RE J.M. WILSON. name (T.C) joined this afternoon from 70 M. Gun. Shops at the Base.	J.H.T.W
8 p.m. 24th February 1915. Same Billet.	Wednesday. 949. Rested today. Capt. 2.W.O SEXTON. Capt. for SHIRLEY. Reported to A.D.M.S. 2nd Div. two med with 70 22. 7 amb, Lieut J#T. CHARLES. name (T.C) reported for duty from 30.2. 7 amb. 7th 9.O.C. 2nd Div. ordered Medals yesterday. Gun today. place was opened for the management Forking off town. at which places 289 other Ranks. Were are expecting returns.	J.H.T.W
8 p.m. 25th February 1915. Same Billet.	Thursday. 156. Rested today. I did not knew why to pass Part Hands that was an attack being made. Temp. Lieut J.M. WILSON (T.C.) sent the Corps Hdty on 27.0.V.2.1 to a Betting Installer. Temp. Lieut. T.E.S. WILLIS. name (T.C.) proceeded on leave letting to Billings.	J.H.T.W
8 p.m. 26th February 1915. Same Billet.	Friday. 976 followed today in 696 at Sam N'Doul on 276 at Say anne bathing Installers. In Ambulance BIRCH (wounded in leave to George) also died SCOTT ( ) however on leave for N84.7 where his Temporary attache	① Owen Capt. Adam

79
3298

(9 26 6) W 267—976 100,000 4/12 H W V

WAR DIARY N° 6 Field Ambulance, Army Form C. 2118.

or

INTELLIGENCE SUMMARY.

(Erase heading not required.)

Instructions regarding War Diaries and Intelligence Summaries are contained in F.S. Regs., Part II. and the Staff Manual respectively. Title pages will be prepared in manuscript.

Hour, Date, Place	Summary of Events and Information	Remarks and references to Appendices
8/m. Feb 27. 1915 Same kent.	Major NINDER left for AIRE for temporary duty with HQ 1st Army. I assumed command during his absence. 5 A99 balls to Coy B.18 at Sam H. Vaast (2nd Glastman) and 181 at temporary hut Detachment at Ecole PAULBERT moved to Ecole LIBRE	D. Lewis Capt RAMC i/c.
8/m. Feb 28. 1915 Same kent	Sunday. No parades. 700 blankets 2nd WORCESTER Regt disinfected All inspection of their ambulance laundry at work as usual	D. Lewis Capt RAMC i/c

121/4896
March 1915

No. 6. Field Ambulance

Vol VIII

Army Form C. 2118.

No. 6 Field Ambulance

WAR DIARY
or
INTELLIGENCE SUMMARY.
(Erase heading not required.)

Instructions regarding War Diaries and Intelligence Summaries are contained in F. S. Regs., Part II. and the Staff Manual respectively. Title pages will be prepared in manuscript.

Hour, Date, Place	Summary of Events and Information	Remarks and references to Appendices
8 pm March 1st 1915. SEMINAIRE ST VAAST. BETHUNE	Baths - 569 at Seminaire and 232 at Margarine Factory. Total 801 (3" Chatham Gunrs). 912 Blankets of same unit disinfected.	O. Ivens Capt RAMC
8 pm March 2nd 1915. Same place.	Baths 610 at Seminaire and 258 at Margarine Factory. Total 868 (Oxf & Bucks L.I.). 950 Blankets disinfected.	O. Ivens Capt RAMC
8 pm March 3rd 1915. Same place.	Baths 544 at Seminaire + 251 at Margarine Factory. Total 795. Blankets disinfected 950.	O. Ivens Capt RAMC
8 pm March 4th 1915. Same place.	Baths 588 at Seminaire + 270 at Margarine Factory. Total 858. Blankets disinfected 560. D/Cols – G.O.C. 1st Army Corps Inspected the Baths, Laundry, tailors shops etc. at S.S.O. Lieut F.E.S. Willis (T.C.) returned from leave and res N° 5. F.A. to temporary duty by orders of A.D.M.S. 2nd Divn.	O. Ivens Capt RAMC
8 pm March 5th 1915.	Baths 665 at Seminaire + 346 at Margarine Factory. Total 1031. Blankets disinfected 1008.	O. Ivens Capt RAMC

# WAR DIARY or INTELLIGENCE SUMMARY

1/6 Field Ambulance

Army Form C. 2118.

Hour, Date, Place	Summary of Events and Information	Remarks and references to Appendices
8pm March 6. 1915 Same place	Batts. 721 at Clery St Vaast 245 at Margonne Factory Total 966. Sanitary Division – Blanket disinfector 950.– Lieut Colonel BIRCH. E. returned from leave – notification that No 11939 STEVENS. O. who was sent here yesterday WR5 TR has been dangerous centre – general meningitis. The man to the last 7 days had occupied a room with 8 others at the entrance gate. These contacts were sent to RD STA (isolation) The room was fumigated with sulphur and subsequently scrubbed out with Cresol – same of system unknown. The room was not overcrowded. H.R.H. the Prince of WALES inspected the "Baths", laundry, tailors shop etc at 11am.	O. Stevens. Capt Raine
8am March 7, 1915 Same place	Sunday. Baths used by parties of Clergy. Blankets disinfected 1250 (1st Royal Fusiliers) French uniforms disinfected in steam disinfector, & cape in sulphur Room.	O. Stevens Capt Raine
March 8. 1915.	Received orders to report to D.M.S. to take over command of No 8 Motor Ambulance Convoy; handed over to Captain SIMPSON. C. B.S.O. Raine – taken over 21. F.E.S. WILLIS	O Stevens Capt Raine J Lampson Capt Raine A.M.C reported his departure for duty with 2nd South Staffords

N° 6 Field Ambulance.

Army Form C. 2118.

WAR DIARY
or
INTELLIGENCE SUMMARY.
(Erase heading not required.)

Instructions regarding War Diaries and Intelligence Summaries are contained in F.S. Regs., Part II. and the Staff Manual respectively. Title pages will be prepared in manuscript.

Hour, Date, Place	Summary of Events and Information	Remarks and references to Appendices
8 p.m. 9th March 1915. Sailly Labourse	Taken over command again of No 6 F. Amb. on return from Renescure. Rec'd an O.O. from General Staff 1st Army. No washing to troops being done today, but the washing + disinfecting of clothes + blankets being continued. Have partitioned the building to facilitate accommodation about 200 men. Capt. J.A. RENSHAW from No 8 M.A.C. reports for duty, also the following officers. Lieut. J.P. CHARLES. name C (T.C.) from 2nd Cav Div. — Lieut. A.W. SMITH. name (S.p.R) from 1st Hus'. Hspt. + Lieut. E.A.C. MITCHELL. name. (T.C.) + R.S.C. + Lieut. J.R. SCOTT. name (Sp.R) from No 4. Fd Amb. Sick and wounded sick, wounded both Btals. 6 No 4. F. Amb. suffering from Influenza — Diarrhoea. Also. Lieut.Colonel CORNU. J.C. has taken over the duties of Interpreter in place of Sub-Lieut SAUVAGE S.M.	J.H.N.W. Major
8 p.m. 10th March 1915. Sailly Labourse.	The Bearer Division under Capt WALSHE + Lt SMITH + Lt CHARLES. left H.Q.s at 4.30.am. + proceeded on advanced training station at A.B.C. MAP BETHUNE. Washing, drying + airing of clothes, being continued + disinfecting of blankets continued, nothing further to report	J.H.N.W.
8 p.m. 11th March 1915. Sailly Labourse.	Report from O.C. Bearers evacuated during last 24 hours 5 Officers + 222 N.C.O.s + men, all more or less severely wounded. I visited the advanced dressing station opened every thing satisfactory. Washing of clothes disinfection being continued as usual at 7.30. pm proceeded in order to A.D.M.S. record of Beuvre to HQ's. Bethune to report. Nothing further to report.	J.H.N.W.

Army Form C. 2118.

WAR DIARY
INTELLIGENCE SUMMARY.
(Erase heading not required.)

Instructions regarding War Diaries and Intelligence Summaries are contained in F.S. Regs., Part II. and the Staff Manual respectively. Title pages will be prepared in manuscript.

Hour, Date, Place	Summary of Events and Information	Remarks and references to Appendices
8 p.m. 12th March. 1915. Same Billet.	651. Battle Listing. The Reserve Bargmen returned at 10 am this morning. Roll resumed listing. Nothing unusual tonight.	J.H.R.W.
8 p.m. 13th March. 1915. Same Billet.	Total 30 of Battle for listing 920. at H.Qr. 695 – at Army Packing 225. Received orders to be ready to move at 2 hours notice. Lieut J.B. SCOTT Manne (S.R.) reported for duty from 90 4. R. Lieut J.M. WILSON Manne (T.C.) reports proceeding from 2/ INNIS. Fuss on completion of temporary duty. The A.H. Q.M.G. inspected the Battery's armoury &c.	J.H.R.W.
8 p.m. 14th March. 1915. Same Billet.	Sunday. No Battle. Divine service of protestants & worshipers of other combined and usual Church parade held at 10.30 am. nothing further to report.	J.H.R.W.
8 p.m. 15th March. 1915. Same Billet.	Monday. 961 Battle Listing. (711 at H.Qr. & 250 at Army Packing.) all of H. 1st K.R.R.S. Blankets dis-infected. 231. (Units Res. 3rd AmP). + 832. (1st K.R.R.S.). Nothing further to report.	J.H.R.W.
8 p.m. 16th March. 1915. Same Billet.	Tuesday. 984 Battle Listing (721 at H.Qr. & 263 at Army Packing.) the 1st Hamp Rainforts + 1114. Blankets dis-infected. The A.D.M.S. inspected the Bath House.	J.H.R.W.
8 P.M. 17th March. 1915. Same Billet.	Wednesday. "St. Patrick's Day." 1027. Battle Listing (750 at H.Qr. & 277 at Army Packing.) The Shirts. 641. Blankets dis-infected. The G.O.C. 2nd Division inspected the Bath House.	J.H.R.W.
8 P.M. 18th March. 1915. Same Billet.	Thursday. 729. Battle Listing. (546 at H.Qr. & 183 at Army Packing.) Div R.E. & Div R.F.A. Rainforts, consist of Blankets. Service Dress – Underclothes. D.A.D.M.S. inspected the Bath House.	J.H.R.W.
8 P.M. 19th March. 1915. Same Billet.	Friday. 1010. Battle Listing. (721 at H.Qr. & 289 at Army Packing.) Wrought Up. Disinfection of Blankets. 750.+ Service Dress & Winter clothing. A.H. Q.M.G inspected the Bath House & Motor Shop.	J.H.R.W.

Army Form C. 2118.

WAR DIARY
INTELLIGENCE SUMMARY.
(Erase heading not required.)

Instructions regarding War Diaries and Intelligence Summaries are contained in F.S. Regs., Part II. and the Staff Manual respectively. Title pages will be prepared in manuscript.

Hour, Date, Place	Summary of Events and Information	Remarks and references to Appendices
8 P.M. 20th March 1915. Same Billet.	Saturday. 990 Bathed today. (663 at H.Qrs, 307 at Mary Factory). Brit Col + R.E + Supply Coy + Train. Disinfected Blankets 249. + Some Service dress + underclothing. The Director General of the French Medical Service & his Staff were shown over the Bath House by the D.M.S. 1st Army & his Staff + Col. Sir W. LEISHMAN. D.G.A.T. our A.D.M.S. & his other Staff Officers.	J.H.T.W.
8 P.M. 21st March 1915. Same Billet.	Sunday. Baths closed today. The D.G. of H.O.M.S. (Sir G. Sloggett) accompanied by Surg. General MacPherson, + the A.D.M.S. 2nd Division visited the Bath House.	J.H.T.W.
8 P.M. 22nd March 1915. Same Billet.	Monday. 682 Bathed today. (507 at H.Q. + 175 at Mary Factory). 110 of No. 3 Field Ambl. + the H.L.I. Disinfection of Blankets + service dress + under clothing.	J.H.T.W.
8 P.M. 23rd March 1915. Same Billet.	Tuesday. 1014 Bathed today. (765 at H.Qrs + 249 at Mary Factory). Brig Mr Joseph 1st Guards. Disinfection of clothing as usual. Sir Arthur Sloggett + Apl. + this Ext. = 1008 + 3-2 each. Disinfection of clothing as usual. Sir Arthur Sloggett + Br Herrington visited the Bath House accompanied by A.D.M.S.	J.H.T.W.
8 P.M. 24th March 1915. Same Billet.	Wednesday. 1020 Bathed today. (711 at H.Q. + 309 at Mary Factory). The Division Zoo. We disinfected the Blankets, 885. + some clothing service dress + underclothing.	J.H.T.W.
8 P.M. 25th March 1915. Same Billet.	Thursday. 770 Baths today. (555 at H.Q. + 215 at Mary Factory). The Blankets disinf. + 27 full disinfection of Blankets + clothing as usual.	J.H.T.W.
8 P.M. 26th March 1915. Same Billet.	Friday. 963 Bathed today. (686 at H.Q. + 277 at Mary Factory). The Colds Guards. Coy. disinf. + some clothing service dress underclothing. The A.D.M.S. of the 7th + Br Division visited the Bathing Installation."	J.H.T.W.

Army Form C. 2118.

WAR DIARY
INTELLIGENCE SUMMARY.
(Erase heading not required.)

Instructions regarding War Diaries and Intelligence Summaries are contained in F.S. Regs., Part II. and the Staff Manual respectively. Title pages will be prepared in manuscript.

Hour, Date, Place	Summary of Events and Information	Remarks and references to Appendices
8 PM. 27th March Same Billet	Taken over from Major J.H.R. Brooks, RAMC who proceeds on leave. 1087 baths today, blankets 1150	Stampson Cpl R.AMC
8 PM 28th March Same billet	Lt. Wilson A Charles returned of leave. Godsmith Wilson Charles Mitchell and Scott have proceeded to take over temporary duty with Regimental Units. The horses were inspected by the A.D.V.S. II Division	RJ
8 PM 29th March Same billet.	The linen called 517 BEHAPS. Blankets disinfected 1000 2 WLC guards inspected at the afternoon by I D.A.A & D.M.S. London Division II Surgn General O'Donnell D.S.O. A.M.S and A.D.M.S II Div III Major Gen Munro. Staff. It had been officially reported that Lt A.N. Smith RAMC has been seriously wounded	RJ

No. 6 Field Ambulance

WAR DIARY
-or-
INTELLIGENCE SUMMARY.
(Erase heading not required.)

Army Form C. 2118.

Instructions regarding War Diaries and Intelligence Summaries are contained in F. S. Regs., Part II. and the Staff Manual respectively. Title pages will be prepared in manuscript.

Hour, Date, Place	Summary of Events and Information	Remarks and references to Appendices
8 PM 30th March Same billet	Total baths 1036 - 698 at Hd Qrs 338 at Hayrinis factory. Total blankets 1083. Baths visited by Major Gen Parsons + Staff and by Major Ready Staff Officer 2nd Division	P. Sampson Capt RAMC
8 AM 31st March Same billet	Total number Baths 836 Hd Qrs 588 Hayrinck factory 248 Blankets disinfected 1000 belonging to Ox + Bucks Shoe Regt. Paid The brokers + Ironers.	P.S

121/5195

121/5195
April 1915

Co. C. Field Ambulance

Vol IX

WAR DIARY
INTELLIGENCE SUMMARY.
(Erase heading not required.)

Army Form C. 2118.

Hour, Date, Place	Summary of Events and Information	Remarks and references to Appendices
8 PM 1st April Same Billet	Total no. of Baths 659 - 470 at Hd Qrs and 189 at Margarine Factory 866 Blankets were disinfected Six Sunbeam Motor ambulances, one Ford Motor Ambulance and one Motor Bicycle (Douglas) have arrived. One Sgt & 12 Drivers A.S.C. M.T. have arrived and have been taken on the Strength	Stanfoau Capt. RAMC

WAR DIARY

INTELLIGENCE SUMMARY.

(Erase heading not required.)

Army Form C. 2118.

Hour, Date, Place	Summary of Events and Information	Remarks and references to Appendices
8 P.m. 2nd April Same billet	Total no of baths 692. Hts 8546 8 pyjama suits 224 one Sunbeam and three Ford motor ambulance cars sent to 9th Division and were directed to report to A.D.M.S. That Division four Drivers A.S.C. M.T. have been struck off the strength	B Sampson Capt R.A.M.C
8 P.m. 3rd April Same billet	Total no of baths 884. 613 a/ Hd Qrs 271 at pyjama factory 0 1000 Blankets disinfected two-horse ambulances as complete equipments were sent via Fullers and to Fouquières to be handed over to No I Reserve Park	[signature]
8 P.m. 4th April Same billet	No baths available. Return Capt S.G.A.H. Walsh D.S.O. assumed temporary medical charge 2nd Division R.E. Five horse drawn ambulances completely equipped with Drivers A.S.C. proceeded to Chocques and those were entrained for ROUEN. Five drivers A.S.C. proceeded with these ambulances and were struck off the strength.	[signature]

Army Form C. 2118.

WAR DIARY
INTELLIGENCE SUMMARY.
(Erase heading not required.)

Instructions regarding War Diaries and Intelligence Summaries are contained in F.S. Regs., Part II. and the Staff Manual respectively. Title pages will be prepared in manuscript.

Hour, Date, Place	Summary of Events and Information	Remarks and references to Appendices
8 P.M. 5th April Same Billet.	36 Monday. 874. Bathel Estay (593 at H.Q. + 278 at Mawy Factory). The H.R.T.L Blankets disinfected 1019. and other articles of service dress & underclothing. The A.D.M.S. 1st London Div. This inspected the Bathing arrangements. I returned from Leave at 7 any. this morning, & took over from Capt. SAMPSON.	J.H.R. Wickett Major R.A.M.C.
8 P.M. 6th April Same Billet	Tuesday. 1030. Bedford Estay. (720 at H.Q. + 310 at Mawy Factory.) & 778 Guests Blankets disinfected = 1030. & other clothing, Lt. McNeill & L/Cpl Williams sent returns from Temp duty with Maj. Woods.	J.H.R.W
8 P.M. 7th April Same Billet	Wednesday. 912. Bathel Estay. (616 at H.Q. + 236 at Mawy Factory). Blankets disinfected = 404 + other clothing. PICHOT. S.S. returned from Leave & will act here as S.C.M. Sent to 2/-James R.A.D. per duty as M.O. & ordering of RESERVES Field.	J.H.R.W.
8 P.M. 8th April Same Billet	Thursday. 951 Bathel Estay (684 at H.Q. + 267 at Mawy Factory) 15 Kings Tea rec.d. Blankets disinfected = 1040. & other clothing. 2/ Lt Williams sent to 2/- James here in relief of Sgt. Scott who returned to H.Q.	J.H.R.W.
8 P.M. 9th April Same Billet	Friday. 858. Bathel Estay (629 at H.Q. + 229 at Mawy Factory). Rec.d and recopied Blankets disinfected 469. & other clothing. Pte MITCHELL proceeded on Leave, Tuesday. + Pte CHARLES went on leave 9/OR.9. 2/L.T. Sinclair & Sgt. MARTIN who are transferred Sect. l. 7.O. & 7 and 6.	J.H.R.W.
8 P.M. 10th April Same Billet	Saturday. 1152. (Bathel Estay. (807 at H.Q. + 345 at Mawy Factory) 2 French Travellers Blankets disinfected 1152. = 1016 other clothing.	J.H.R.W.
8 P.M. 11th April Same Billet	Sunday. No Bathing Estay. Sunday, articles 42 received. Blankets disinfected 821 + other clothing.	J.H.R.W.

Army Form C. 2118.

WAR DIARY
INTELLIGENCE SUMMARY.
(Erase heading not required.)

Instructions regarding War Diaries and Intelligence Summaries are contained in F. S. Regs., Part II. and the Staff Manual respectively. Title pages will be prepared in manuscript.

Hour, Date, Place	Summary of Events and Information	Remarks and references to Appendices
8 P.M. 12th April Same Billet.	Monday. 1006. Battle Valley. (672 at H.Q. + 334 at Army Post). Men Surpees - Blankets disinfected 50 + other clothing.	J.H.R.W.
8 P.M. 13th April Same Billet.	Tuesday. 946. Battle Valley. (645 at H.Q. + 301 at Army Post), 2nd H.L.I. Blankets disinfected 20. other clothing.	J.H.R.W.
8 P.M. 14th April Same Billet.	Wednesday 1138. Battle Valley (850 at H.Q. + 288 at Army Post) Baths by. Portable disinfector - 1070. other clothing.	J.H.R.W.
8 P.M. 15th April Same Billet.	Thursday. 723. Battle Valley. (569 at H.Q. + 154 at Army Post) Men Troops Blankets disinfected 127. other clothing. 2nd T. BOURNE B.R.C. No 4 (T.F.) appears went to Brit: troops. Dis: to L Band.	J.H.R.W.
8 P.M. 16th April Same Billet.	Friday 997. Battle Valley (670 at H.Q. + 327 at Army Post) & C.A. Ranges. Blankets disinfected. 1039. other clothing.	J.H.R.W.
8 P.M. 17th April Same Billet.	Saturday, 958. Battle Valley (686 at H.Q. + 272 at Army Post). Own M.O. Blankets disinjected. 859. other clothing. 1st S.C.O. inspection plant.	J.H.R.W.
8 P.M. 18th April Same Billet.	Sunday. NO bathing today. Laundry work continued as usual. Blankets disinfected. 560. other clothing. 1st sergeant arranged. S. Supt Arthur W/S Cpl WALSH repaired in ceremony.	J.H.R.W.
8 P.M. 19th April Same Billet.	Monday 806 Battle Valley (578 at H.Q. + 228 at Army Post). Herts Rct Patt. Blankets disinfected 1278. other clothing	J.H.R.W.
8 P.M. 20th April Same Billet.	Tuesday 791 Battle Valley (501 at H.Q. + 290 at Army Post). Aus Troops. Blankets disinfected 244. other clothing. Regt. T.F.R.S. Ft. Joseph. Commanded Gore	J.H.R.W.

Army Form C. 2118.

WAR DIARY
INTELLIGENCE SUMMARY
(Erase heading not required.)

Instructions regarding War Diaries and Intelligence Summaries are contained in F.S. Regs., Part II. and the Staff Manual respectively. Title pages will be prepared in manuscript.

Hour, Date, Place	Summary of Events and Information	Remarks and references to Appendices
8 P.M. 21st April Same Billet	Wednesday. 965 Bathed today (699 at H.Qrs. + 266 at Many Post) 1st, 12th, 72nd, 73rd Blankets disinfected = 1064. nothing clothing	J.H.T.W.
8 P.M. 22nd April Same Billet	Thursday. 1020 Bathed today (707 at H.Qrs. + 313 Many Post). Blankets Dis- infected 1028 rather clothing. Lieut A.C. TURNER R.A.M.C. (T.C.) attached here proceeded to Rly Stn Souchel, A.D.M.S. inspected in line Barracks. got hour	J.H.T.W.
8 P.M. 23rd April Same Billet	Friday. 990. Bathed today (699 at H.Qrs. + 291 at Many Post) 3rd Bns 2n Blankets disinfected. 1021, rather clothing. Lieut T. BOOZIE - Price M.O.M.E (T.C) reported this unit to duty on completion of Reinf. Duty with 3rd Cav R.E.A.	J.H.T.W.
8 P.M. 24/5 April Same Billet	Saturday. 1193. Bathed today (830 at H.Qrs. + 363 at Army Post) Bonn. + 3rd Bns. The R.a.# Blankets disinfected = 1143. rather clothing	J.H.T.W.
8 P.M. 25th April Same Billet	Sunday. No bathing today. Laundry work continued as usual + Transportation	J.H.T.W.
8 P.M. 26th April Same Billet	Monday. 969. Bathed today (659 at H.Qrs + 310 at Magazine Bathing). Bnd Guards Blankets disinfected = 1050 + rather clothing. Lieut. J.O. SCOTT R.a.m.c (Pte Bn.) returned from leave about 16 hrs.	J.H.T.W.
8 P.M. 27th April Same Billet	Tuesday. 991 Bathed today (696 at H.Qrs + 295 at Army Post). S. Bonn Bn. Blankets disinfected = 1300. rather clothing. + French Gunst = 300.	J.H.T.W.
8 P.M. 28th April Same Billet	Wednesday. 881. Bathed today. (567 at H.Qrs + 314 at Army Post). 9th H.L.I. Blankets disinfected. 926. rather clothing. Capt WALSHE D.S.O.+ Capt RENSHAW R.M.P.D.ed N.E. Kelly returned from lunch. The DDoS. 15th Army inspected 16 Bathing before dinner.	J.H.T.W.

Army Form C. 2118.

WAR DIARY
or
INTELLIGENCE SUMMARY

(Erase heading not required.)

Instructions regarding War Diaries and Intelligence Summaries are contained in F. S. Regs., Part II. and the Staff Manual respectively. Title pages will be prepared in manuscript.

Hour, Date, Place	Summary of Events and Information	Remarks and references to Appendices
8 P.M. 29th April Same Billet.	Thursday. 993 booked today (681 N.H. Cros. + 312 at Army Rest). Sonorial troops. Blankets turned in total = 153. + other clothing. 2/Lt CHARLES reported to duty. from leaving Winter ready with 9th R.E.	J.H.R.W.
8 P.M. 30th April Same Billet.	Friday. 1085 booked today (783 at H.Cas. + 352 at Num. Rest), 2 Cold Feucks. Blankets disinfected = 100, + other clothing.	J.H.R.W. Maj. R.a.m.c. O.C. No 6 Field Ambulance.

121/5574

May 1915.

2nd Division

Co. 6. Field Ambulance

Vide

Summarized

13/5574

Army Form C. 2118.

WAR DIARY
or
INTELLIGENCE SUMMARY.
(*Erase heading not required.*)

Instructions regarding War Diaries and Intelligence Summaries are contained in F. S. Regs., Part II. and the Staff Manual respectively. Title pages will be prepared in manuscript.

Hour, Date, Place	Summary of Events and Information	Remarks and references to Appendices
8 P.M. 1st May. 1915. COLLEGE ST. VAAST. BETHUNE.	Saturday. 100 S. batted today. (643 ct H.ᵈ Qrs + 352 at Mary Dressing.) 2 ᵈ H.L.I. Blankets disinfected = 30 rollers clothing + a lot of summer drawers. The A.D.M.S. inspected to bathing establishment at 6 p.m.	J.H.R.W. Major R.A.M.C. O.C. No 6 Field Amb.
8 P.M. 2ⁿᵈ May. 1915. Same Billet.	Sunday. No bathing today. Laundry work continued as usual.	J.H.R.W.
8 P.M. 3ʳᵈ May. 1915. Same Billet.	Monday. 1099 bathed today. (754 at H.ᵈ Qrs. = 345 at Dressing Factory). S. Staffords. Blankets disinfected = 987 rollers clothing.	J.H.R.W.
8 P.M. 4ᵗʰ May. 1915. Same Billet.	Tuesday. 947 Bathed Today (662 at H.ᵈ Q. + 265 at Mary Dress) 1 Divisional Troops. Rattenkoli disinfected = 171 rollers clothing. Sap. T.ᵉ Claus 11 Coy R.E. fell into the baths today & disturbed the night Identity which was reclosed under Sheaf. Patient was taken in & 90 S.S. and Lieut. T.A. D'Oyly Dawes (T.C.) proved too shaky from Paris.	J.H.R.W.
8 P.M. 5ᵗʰ May. 1915. Same Billet.	Wednesday. 900 Bathed today (335 at H.Q. 4200m + 265 at Mary Dress.) Dr Mercher E.R. Blankets disinfected = 618 rollers clothing.	J.H.R.W.
8 P.M. 6ᵗʰ May 1915. Same Billet.	Thursday. 1062 bathed today (721 at H.Q.Qrs + 341 at Mary Dress.) 1st Roy. Hosps. Blankets disinfected = 938 rollers clothing. Pt. 9 R.D. M.S 9 F.A.S.H. Reeves (T.F.) updated for duty, from ROUEN.	J.H.R.W.
8 P.M. 7ᵗʰ May. 1915. Same Billet.	Friday. 1051. Bathed today. (621 at H.Q.Qrs + 430 at Mary Dress.) Royal Scots. Blankets disinfected = 1050 rollers clothing. 15 Cas. J.A. Ruston. R.A.M.C and Robert L. Hope. Quartered by Army of Ireland. Ships went 8/4 yr.	J.H.R.W.

Army Form C. 2118.

WAR DIARY
or
INTELLIGENCE SUMMARY.
(Erase heading not required.)

Instructions regarding War Diaries and Intelligence Summaries are contained in F.S. Regs., Part II. and the Staff Manual respectively. Title pages will be prepared in manuscript.

Hour, Date, Place	Summary of Events and Information	Remarks and references to Appendices
8 P.M. 8th May 1915. Same billet.	Saturday. No tactical today. Lieut BLACK & C. Ramsay (?C) [on?] went this round for duty from Las Bains.	J.H.R. W.
8 P.M. 9th May 1915. Same billet.	Sunday. Battery stopped to the front. Not to be relay but is undertaking to wound tell out the Sarha à pernacht. We have opened our hospital accommodated from the Dressed Railway & received about 10 cases. Took on him a off till return of May. The B[?] RI. 18 Butt of Prints 2 — Day. Wounded to Hospital. [illegible several lines] ...remained 17. ...remained 135.	J.H.R. W.
6 P.M. 10th May 1915. Same billet.	Monday. Return for last 24 hours. Remaining sick 24. ... sick 1 — wounded 7. evacuated sick [?] ... other ranks. Evacuated other ranks sick 2 — ...wounded ... Dutch [?] 2 — 4.R.R.B. (1) 2nd Essex Fus. (1). The Bearers have done ... work so far. They have been on [illegible].	J.H.R. W.
8 P.M. 11th May 1915. Same billet.	Tuesday. Return for last 24 hours. admitted 54 sick, other ranks. Evacuated other ranks. 8 sick. 5 wounded. Retained. 56 sick, 15 wounded. Retained 15 sick, other ranks. 17. To light duty 3. Report from O.C. Bearers at X.12.a. Returning NAP sick — ... Evacuated other ranks. 1 wounded, 2 sick.	J.H.R. W.

Army Form C. 2118.

WAR DIARY
INTELLIGENCE SUMMARY.
(Erase heading not required.)

Instructions regarding War Diaries and Intelligence Summaries are contained in F. S. Regs., Part II. and the Staff Manual respectively. Title pages will be prepared in manuscript.

Hour, Date, Place	Summary of Events and Information	Remarks and references to Appendices
8. P.M. 12th May 1915. Same billet.	Wednesday. Return for last 24 hours. Admitted other ranks. 2.5. Sick. 4 Wounded. Evacuated other ranks 8. Sick 5. Wounded. Remaining this date 32. Sick. 9 Wounded. Retained to duty 19. Convalescent Coy 28. Report from O.C. Bearers of X 12.a. Evacuated. Sick 2. by any S.B. Batty. Ruins.	J H R W
8. P.M. 13th May 1915. Same billet.	Thursday. Return for last 24 hours. Admitted other ranks 23 sick 34 wounded. Evacuated other ranks 7. sick 2. wounded. Remaining other ranks 40. sick. 83 wounded. Retained to duty 6. Convalescent Coy. 15. (but cases of poisoning of unknown nature, 1 included in above sick evacuated) Report from O.C. Bearers X12.a. Evacuated. 1 officer wounded. 4 13. N.C.O.s & men. Stretcher bearers employed carrying wounded from the Ridges, being shelled in open country.	J H R W
8 P.M. 14th May 1915. Same billet.	Friday. Return for last 24 hours. Admitted other ranks. 14. sick 34 wounded. Evacuated other ranks 10 sick. 34 wounded. Remaining other ranks 34 sick. 18 wounded. Retained to duty. 3. Convalescent Coy 10. Daily wounded 2. (1. man of 8 Suffolk Regt. R.A.M.C. Company of sick 2. 59. Report from O.C. Bearers X12a. Evacuated 2 men sick, v 1. wounded.	J H R W
8. P.M. 15th May 1915. Same billet.	Saturday. Return for last 24 hours. Admitted other ranks. 16 sick 129 wounded. Evacuated other ranks 10 sick. 88. wounded. Remaining other ranks 45. Sick. 111 wounded. Retained to duty 3. Convalescent Coy. 15 Transferred 510.4 wgh 1 coy of sick & wounded from Armentieres. F.W. Bucks. Died in Motor Service & Hainault arms I 31 1. D.F.A.9. B.2.4 40 DRs. Report from O.C. Bearers. S. 9.a. Evacuated 27 Officers wounded other ranks 5.35. wounded.	J H R W
8. P.M. 16th May 1915. Same billet.	Sunday. Return for last 24 hours. Admitted other ranks. 9 02 wounded. Evacuated other ranks 1036. Remaining other ranks. 30 sick. Report from O.C. Bearers. C Sec at S 8 a. Evacuated 36 Officers +1063. other ranks wounded. "A" Sec. bearers in support at X 12.a. No.11160 Pte. E.O. SASSE of this unit who has been slightly recommended for intelligent work.	J H R W

Army Form C. 2118.

WAR DIARY
INTELLIGENCE SUMMARY
(Erase heading not required.)

Instructions regarding War Diaries and Intelligence Summaries are contained in F.S. Regs., Part II. and the Staff Manual respectively. Title pages will be prepared in manuscript.

Hour, Date, Place	Summary of Events and Information	Remarks and references to Appendices
8 P.M. 17th May 1915 Same billet	Monday. Return for last 24 hours. Admitted other ranks 32, sick 413 wounded. Evacuated other ranks 18, sick 286 wounded. Remaining other ranks 32 sick, 121 wounded. Returned to duty 1 Capt. Bay 15. Died of wounds 1 Maj. Clarke & other Ranks. Received (29th sqn L)(27 sqn L) 2 NCOs wounded, 7 NMB Report from O.O. Pearson. Evacuated wounded 3 officers & 394 other ranks. Remount Canadian. DAT.ESS? & hrs & over Steenvoorde. Emergency material.	J.N.R.W.
8 P.M. 18th May 1915 Same billet	Tuesday. Return for last 24 hours. Admitted other ranks 15, sick 271 wounded. Evacuated other ranks 12 sick 264 wounded. Remaining other ranks 16 sick, 125 wounded. Returned to duty Oy 19. DIED 1st Kent. R.Sch. 15.4 H.Simpson D.2" S.Staff (?) Total 3. German wounded admitted 4. Report from O.C. Pearson 3 officers 244 other ranks wounded.	J.N.R.W.
8 P.M. 19th May 1915 Same billet	Wednesday. Return for last 24 hours. Admitted other ranks 24, sick 134. Evacuated 21 other ranks 5 sick & 134 wounded. Remaining other ranks 24 sick. 95 wounded. Returned to duty Oy 18. German wounded admitted 1. 3. DIED (2) 2nd Welsh Pvt L. 2nd Devon. 1. Report from O.C. Pearson. Evacuated 1 other ranks 48 wounded.	J.N.R.W.
8 P.M. 20th May 1915 Same billet	Thursday. Return for last 24 hours. Admitted other ranks 14 sick 21 wounded. Evacuated 121 other ranks 4 sick 58 wounded. Remaining other ranks 29 sick 21 wounded. Two clean cases sent by M.O. & Capt. & Hotella to Convalescent Cap 16 Romano admitted 1. DIED (4) 1" Congo R. 1, 2" S.Staff R. 2, 1" Quex Peach 1. Report from O.C. Pearson 380. Evacuated 1 officer 205. 16 other ranks wounded. Sgt Clarke & men. Tournamant general.	J.N.R.W.

Army Form C. 2118.

WAR DIARY
INTELLIGENCE SUMMARY.
(Erase heading not required.)

Instructions regarding War Diaries and Intelligence Summaries are contained in F.S. Regs., Part II. and the Staff Manual respectively. Title pages will be prepared in manuscript.

Hour, Date, Place	Summary of Events and Information	Remarks and references to Appendices
8 P.M. 21st May. 1915. Same billet.	Friday. Return for last 24 hours. Admitted when results 26 sick, 2 wounded. Evacuated other ranks. 97 sick, 28 wounded. Remaining other ranks 121. Returns to duty 3. Evacuated by 2 Coy 3 Field Amb. ranks nos. 3. DIED (1) 12 Gurk. Guards. The persons 13 swing horses, stabled here just now are in orders to be evacuated all sick & wounded to CHOCQUES. Report from O.C. Bearers. Evacuated other ranks. 14 sick, 1 wounded.	J.H.R.W.
8 P.M. 22nd May. 1915. BURBURE Boys School.	Saturday. Got sick & wounded were increased by 12 midnight. Half of "B" Bearer Div. has moved H.Q. at Wing. Received the following orders at 1.30 p.m. "A+C Sect. will move to RAIMBERT & open there also B Sec. will move to ECQUEDECQUES. We arrive on this schd. 5 P.M. BURBURE & open two patients or boys school. The Bearer Division will move to ECQUEDECQUES.	J.H.R.W.
8 P.M. 23rd May. 1915. Same Billet.	Sunday-Whit. Have opened for 100 patients. (Infants + O.R. Bearers. Evacuated 1 Officer sick, + 32 other ranks sick, wounded.) Admitted sick 4, 2 Prisoners Ps: 2, 8.2.4. 24 pc:	J.H.R.W.
8 P.M. 24th May. 1915. Same Billet.	Monday. Capt. WALSHE + the Bearers opened N. Qr. Group. Return for last 24 hours N.I. the 24 hours.	J.H.R.W.
8 P.M. 25th May 1915. Same billet.	Tuesday. Return for last 24 hours. Admitted. 8 sick. Evacuated. 2 Wounded 9 from M.E. MORGAN from out officers. 6 th. 1st time	J.H.R.W.
8 P.M. 26th May 1915. Same Billet	Wednesday. Return for last 24 hours. Admitted 8 sick. Evacuated 1 Returns 4, 11 Capt. 46 2.0 ? Dis-- admitted on Hostel pt. A.C. D.E. 3 + 9	J.H.R.W.
8 P.M. 27th May 1915. Same Billet.	Thursday. Return for last 24 hours. Admitted I.N. (1 Officer sick (9 + 41 Jenvillen) 11 Officer sick: Evacuated (officers 12 other ranks sick. Remaining 4 + other ranks. Returned to duty. 3.	J.H.R.W.

Army Form C. 2118.

WAR DIARY
—or—
INTELLIGENCE SUMMARY.
(Erase heading not required.)

Instructions regarding War Diaries and Intelligence Summaries are contained in F. S. Regs., Part II. and the Staff Manual respectively. Title pages will be prepared in manuscript.

Hour, Date, Place	Summary of Events and Information	Remarks and references to Appendices
8 P.M. 28th May 1915. Sans Pareil	Friday. Return of sick 24 hours. Admitted, other ranks 4 sick. Nominating other ranks 8 sick.	9 N.T.W. O.
8 P.M. 29th May 1915. Sans Pareil	Saturday. Return of sick 24 hours. Admitted other ranks 13 sick. Evacuated O.R. Nominating 15. Returned to duty 3. (For-casting orders were transmitted 7p.m. 9 a.m.)	9 N.T.W.
8 P.M. 30th May 1915. Sans Pareil	Sunday. Return of sick 24 hours. Admitted other ranks 1 sick. Evacuated 4 sick. Nominating 7. 11 sick. Returned to duty 1.	9 N.T.W.
8 P.M. 31st May 1915. CHATEAU. @ MONT EVENIS D.19.b. France Sheet 36c. 1/40000.	Monday. Return of sick 24 hours. Admitted other ranks N/c Nominating 9 sick. Returned to duty 5. 2. Removed from Q. 15.000 & carried over about 12 noon. Today with A.D.S. - to Sec' as mountings at RAMBERT	9 N.T.W. in day. Major memor. O.C. No. 6 (?) Amb.

121/5885

Summarised

121/5885

2nd Division

No. 6. Field Ambulance

Vol XL

June 1915

Army Form C. 2118.

WAR DIARY
INTELLIGENCE SUMMARY
(Erase heading not required.)

No. 6 FIELD AMBULANCE

Instructions regarding War Diaries and Intelligence
Summaries are contained in F. S. Regs., Part II.
and the Staff Manual respectively. Title pages
will be prepared in manuscript.

Hour, Date, Place	Summary of Events and Information	Remarks and references to Appendices
1st June 1915. 8 P.M. CHATEAU LE MONT EVENIC D. 19.b.	Tuesday. Return for last 24 hours. 6 New Pat, other ranks. 1 sick. Evacuated 1 sick. Remaining 3 sick. Returned to duty 6.	J.H.N. Wincer Major. O.C. No. 6 Field Amb.
2nd June 1915. 8. P.M. Same Billet.	Wednesday. Return for last 24 hours. Admitted other ranks. 2 sick. Evacuated 1/1 sick. Remaining 3 sick. Returned to duty 1. The D.M.S. visited this building & got some "C" Sect. Fwd Cars drivers under Cpl. H55203 Pte W. Turner was ordered to report for To duty in the school at GOSNAY. Egt. Pte H55175 Pte. Ryl. at S.A.J.	J.H.N.W.
3rd June 1915. 8. P.M. Same Billet.	Thursday Return for last 24 hours. Admitted other ranks 10 sick. Remaining 12 sick. Returned to duty 1. Sent an Orderline Sjt. by No. 5. 2 bus to the Station there.	J.H.N.W.
4th June 1915. 8. P.M. Same Billet.	Friday. Return for last 24 hours. Admitted other ranks 6 sick. Remaining 7 sick.	J.H.N.W.
5th June 1915. 8. P.M. Same Billet.	Saturday. Return for last 24 hours. Admitted other ranks 6 sick. Evacuated 5 sick. Remaining 15. Returned to duty 3.	J.H.N.W.
6th June 1915. 8. P.M. Same Billet.	Sunday. Return for last 24 hours. Admitted other ranks. 8 sick. Evacuated 7 sick. Remaining 16 sick. 13 Sick. bus moved to LE CHATEAU. F.F.R. F.A.Y. B.18.6.	J.H.N.W.
7th June 1915. 8. P.M. Same Billet.	Monday. Return for last 24 hours. Admitted other ranks 8 sick. Evacuated 4 sick. Remaining 15 sick. Returned to duty 4. 2I.C. J.W. CLAYTON name (T.C.) Enofficer Psd Unit. visited T. C. Sect.	J.H.N.W.

Army Form C. 2118.

WAR DIARY
INTELLIGENCE SUMMARY
(Erase heading not required.)

Hour, Date, Place	Summary of Events and Information	Remarks and references to Appendices
8th June. 1915. 8 P.M. Same Billet.	Tuesday. Return for past 24 hours. Admitted other ranks. 12. sick. Evacuated 4 sick. Remaining 22 sick. Return to duty. 2. Pte. A.C. TURNER. manor (T.C.) kept dept this unit & proceeded to MALASSISE Hosp. ST. OMER. for study.	J. H. N. W.
9th June. 1915. 8 P.M. Same Billet.	Wednesday. Return for past 24 hours. Admitted other ranks 15 sick. Evacuated 16 sick. Remaining. 16. sick. Return to duty. 5. "O" Sect returned to H.Qrs. from LE CHATEAU FERFAY. B.18.B.	J. H. N. W.
10th June. 1915. 8 P.M. Same Billet.	Thursday. Return for past 24 hours. Admitted other ranks. 8. sick. Evacuated 7. sick on account of moving – from No.1 Amb. 4 sick on account of moving. from H.Qrs. one sections. Remaining. 9. sick. Pte. MITCHELL went to hosp to-day. C.1. St. Hubts.	J. H. N. W.
11th June. 1915. 8 P.M. ECOLE. VERQUIN. E.29.C.	Friday. Under orders from A.D.M.S. 21'S" Sect. moved to this village here then morning and found a small Hosp. for sick & section at the School. S4 accommodate. Return for past 24 hours Admitted 14 sick. Evacuated 11 sick. Remaining 11 sick. Return to duty. 1.	J. H. N. W.
12th June. 1915. 8 P.M. Same Billet.	Saturday. Return for past 24 hours. Admitted 9 sick Transferred to 30 & 7 & 4 sections. Evacuated. 3. To duty. 1. Remaining. 20.	J. H. R. W.
13th June. 1915. 8 P.M. Same Billet.	Sunday. Return for past 24 hours Admitted 11 sick Transferred to 30, 4 & 2 & 2 sections. Evacuated 6. Remaining. 27. Health of troops good.	J. H. N. W.

Army Form C. 2118.

WAR DIARY
INTELLIGENCE SUMMARY.
(Erase heading not required.)

Hour, Date, Place	Summary of Events and Information	Remarks and references to Appendices
14th June 1915. 8 P.M. Same Billet.	Monday. Return for last 24 hours. Admitted other ranks 5, sick transferred from No. 4, 3 A.I. section. Evacuated 5 sick. Remaining 26. Sick relieved to duty 4. 20 convalescent coy 1. Men had a bath & enjoyed same.	J.H.T.W.
15th June 1915. 8 P.M. Same Billet.	Tuesday. Return for last 24 hours. Admitted other ranks 16 sick. Transferred to 3°4, 7.0. 6, 4 + 70.5.3 a. 1. Evacuated 16 sick (including 1 ? Enteric + 1 measles.) Remaining 29 sick relieved to duty 4.	J.H.T.W.
16th June 1915. 8 P.M. Same Billet.	Wednesday. Return for last 24 hours. Admitted other ranks 12 sick. Transferred from No 4, 7 & 5. Evacuated 13. 2° Enty 4. Remaining 29. Sick of the admitted 6 cases were ? Pyraemia. N.Y.D. Received a verbal order from A.D.M.S. to pack up & ready to move in 2 hours notice. 25 MCGEAGH 9 L.D. name (T.C.) Sent 7 Ent. 44 Munz N.E.A.	J.H.T.W.
17th June 1915. 8 P.M. Same Billet.	Thursday. Return for last 24 hours. Admitted other ranks 26 sick + 1 wounded. Evacuated 19 sick + 1 wounded. Remaining 29. 2° Enty 7. Verbal orders cancelled. Ration Rev. H.L. HORNBY C.F. eye attached to this unit from 3d Army 13 FA 4 servant.	J.H.T.W.
18th June 1915. 8 P.M. Same Billet.	Friday. Return for last 24 hours. Admitted other ranks 13 sick. Evacuated. 6. 2° Enty 4. Remaining 82. (3 ? Pyraemia).	J.H.T.W.
19th June 1915. 8 P.M. Same Billet.	Saturday. Return for last 24 hours. Admitted other ranks 26 sick. Evacuated 23 2° Enty 9. Remaining 26 (1 ? Pyraemia). Rev HORNBY left for brigade duty, 1.6" Brig.	J.H.W.W.
20th June 1915. 8 P.M. Same Billet.	Sunday. Return for last 24 hours. Admitted other ranks 6 sick. Evacuated 9. 2° Enty 3. Rem. Coy. 2. Remain. 18. (3. ? Pyraemia). a. v. 13. Sgt left found Billet for BETHUNE to open 70 3298 College St. VAAST when there we received an order postponing move. We returned to present Billet.	J.H.W.W.

Army Form C. 2118.

WAR DIARY
INTELLIGENCE SUMMARY.
(Erase heading not required.)

Hour, Date, Place	Summary of Events and Information	Remarks and references to Appendices
21st June 1915. 8 P.M. Same Billet.	Monday. Return for tent 24 hours. Admitted other ranks 14, sick evacuated 8, Zebulj 4. Remaining 20. (5 Pyrexia). Pte. TALBOT name (Sp.Re) from 25 2 Camb 8th Div. admitted for study. Pte. MORGAN returned from leave. Pte. SARGENT western leave. Our move of yesterday is cancelled for the present. I visited C Sect - the O.C. wished an accident by yesterdays fulling go horse.	J.H.R.W.
22nd June 1915. 8 P.M. Same Billet.	Tuesday. Return for tent 24 hours. Admitted other ranks 12, Sick, Transport 10, 7.C. 4. 2.&.C.1. (5 Pyrexia), Evacuated 8. To duty 2. Remaining 28.	J.H.R.W.
23rd June 1915. 8 P.M. Same Billet.	Wednesday. Return for tent 24 hours. Admitted other ranks. 15 Sick. (3 Pyrexia) Evacuated 15. To duty 5. Remaining 18.	J.H.R.W.
24th June 1915. 8 P.M. COLLEGE ST. VAAST. BETHUNE.	Thursday. Return for tent 24 hours. Admitted other ranks. 10. sick (5 Pyrexia) Transport. No. 2. 3. amb. 15 Division 71 Evacuated 86. 2 Sdrofs, 2. Remaining 35. No. 6. 2 Camb. A Sect moved to new Billet in marquise 15 rest 2 Sect. Hears moved to ANNE 2 I N. & opened I School Rue.	J.H.R.W.
25th June 1915. 8 P.M. Same Billet.	Friday. Return for tent 24 hours. Admitted other ranks. 3 Sect Transport from No. 4. 7 amb. 3. Evacuated. 13. Zebulj 8. Im by 15 Div 1. Remaining 35. C Sect. Sect took over opened head Quarters from GOSNEY.	J.H.R.W.
26th June 1915. 8 P.M. Same Billet.	Saturday. Return for tent 24 hours. Admitted other ranks, 9 sick, Transport from 9e St. 2.&.C.1. (2 Pyrexia). Evacuated 15. Zebulj 8. Remaining 22. Sergt MEALE reserve was evacuated with NYD Pyrexia.	J.H.R.W.

Army Form C. 2118.

WAR DIARY
—or—
INTELLIGENCE SUMMARY.
(Erase heading not required.)

Instructions regarding War Diaries and Intelligence Summaries are contained in F. S. Regs., Part II. and the Staff Manual respectively. Title pages will be prepared in manuscript.

Hour, Date, Place	Summary of Events and Information	Remarks and references to Appendices
27th June. 1915. 8. P.M. Same Billet.	Sunday. Return for last 24 hours. Admitted other ranks 5. Sick. Evacuated 2. 2.Body; 5. Remaining. 20.	J H R W
28th June. 1915. 8. P.M. Same Billet.	Monday. Return for last 24 hours. Admitted other ranks. 8 sick. Transferred from 30. 4,7 and 1. – from 5. 3 and 1. Evacuated 11. 2.Body; 3. to Ambulance by 1. Remaining 15.	J H R W
29th June. 1915. 8. P.M. Same Billet.	Tuesday. Return for last 24 hours. Admitted other ranks. 15. sick. Evacuated 2. 2.Body; 2. Am. Coy. 2. Remaining 24. Detachment was paid yesterday. A D M S. inspected the Evening Station J R's det at ANNEZIN.	J H R W
30th June. 1915. 8. P.M. Same Billet.	Wednesday. Return for last 24 hours. Admitted other ranks 17. sick. Evacuated 12. 2.Body; 1. Remaining 22. (3 Byronic). Went with A.D.M.S. in the morning and selected an Advd. Dressing Station near the Canal junction on the north side of the railway at F.I.D. at 6.8. Capt. WALSHE & Lt. CLAYTON. with A Sect. Bearers proceeded with Officers and took over dressing station and the evacuating the GIVENCHY section from No. 23 7.9.7th Division	J H R Windles Major Commdg. No. 6 F. Amb.

121/6243

2nd 2-5 Division
—
121/6243.

No. 6. Field Ambulance
—
Vol XII.

July 115.

Army Form C. 2118.

WAR DIARY
INTELLIGENCE SUMMARY.
(Erase heading not required.)

Instructions regarding War Diaries and Intelligence Summaries are contained in F.S. Regs., Part II. and the Staff Manual respectively. Title pages will be prepared in manuscript.

Hour, Date, Place	Summary of Events and Information	Remarks and references to Appendices
1st July. 1915. 8. P.M. Same Billet.	Thursday. Return for last 24 hours. Admitted other ranks. 23 sick transport from No 3. F. amb. 1. & Wounded admitted 12. Evacuated 12. sick 3 wounded. Infantry 3, 2 Am. Cy, 1. Remaining 25 sick. 10 wounded. The Bathing Establishment started opening yesterday 276 R.O.R. was given. C.R. General reports Sun. all their Imperial Bearers & instructors(?) were again posted. This is a new idea, the East-harm was and looks the Serbest there was not administered. Therefore went baths couts to prison. We also have one administrator Ear. Report from O.C. Reserves at F.10.A. Evacuated 14. other ranks. wounded & 9. sick during last 24 hours.	J.H.T. Winchar Major name as No 6. 2 amd.
2nd July. 1915. 8. P.M. Same Billet.	Friday. Return for last 24 hours. Admitted other ranks. 17. sick transfer from No 2. F. amb. 1 (scabies). & from No.3. 3 (scabies). Evacuated 8 sick & 8 wounded. Totally. 6. 2c Am. Cy. 3. (2 wounded). Remaining. 35. sick. Baths given = 340. Capt. SAMPSON R.O. proceeded on leave. Capt. HESLOP proceeded to A.N.W.E.2.IN to take over charge of it sick in relay. Report from O.C. Reserves at F.10.A. for last 24 hours. Evacuated 14, other ranks sick. [A premature explosion in the muzzle of an anti-aircraft gun. 21 section N.O. occurred at 8.30 a.m. this morning (3-7-15) at F.17.b.2.4, one man killed one died of wounds admission. 2 wounded severely.]	J.H.T.W.
3rd July. 1915. 8. P.M. Same Billet.	Saturday. Return for last 24 hours. Admitted other ranks. 21. sick transport from No S.A.A. 3. (scabies) 4 wounded. (Pyrexia 8) Evacuated. 16 sick 2. wounded. Totally. 2. 2c Cav Cy. 2 Cav. Cy. = 337. Repart from O.C. Reserves at F.10.A. Remaining 36. sick 1 wounded. Baths given N.C.O.'s + men wounded + 10 sick. = 5. DIED of wounds = 1. gun accident. Remaining 36. sick 1 wounded. Baths given 6	J.H.T.W.

Army Form C. 2118.

WAR DIARY
INTELLIGENCE SUMMARY.
(Erase heading not required.)

Instructions regarding War Diaries and Intelligence Summaries are contained in F.S. Regs., Part II. and the Staff Manual respectively. Title pages will be prepared in manuscript.

No 6 FIELD AMBULANCE

Hour, Date, Place	Summary of Events and Information	Remarks and references to Appendices
4th July, 1915. 8. P.M. Same Billet.	Sunday Return for last 24 hours. Admitted other ranks. 18 sick. 3 wounded. Evacuated 4 sick. 1 wounded. To-day 3. 2 Cav Cy. 4. Remaining 43 sick + 3 wounded. No Baths given today being Sunday. I visited the Bearers at Cav Tre SE of F.10.d. 4 found everything satisfactory. Report from O.C. Bearers for last 24 hours. Evacuated. 9 other ranks, sick. 3. wounded.	J.H.R.W.
5th July, 1915. 8. P.M. Same Billet.	Monday. Return for last 24 hours. Admitted other ranks. 26 sick. transfer from No 5. F.A. 1. (J. Cyrcoux). Evacuated. 25 sick. 3 wounded. To-day 1. 2 Cav Cy. B. Remaining. 41. Baths given = 362. Report from O.C. Bearers at F.10.d. Evacuated during last 24 hours. Wounded. 1. man. Sick. 2 Officers + 14. NCOs + men. PEOPLE has been posted to Home Rly by order War Office being sent.	J.H.R.W.
6th July, 1915. 8. P.M. Same Billet.	Tuesday. Return for last 24 hours. Admitted other ranks. 18 sick. (4 Cyrcoux). 2 wounded. Evacuated. 6 sick + 1. wounded. To-day 3. 2 Cav Cy. 2 Remaining. 48. sick. 1 wounded. Baths given = 286. (5th Hants Lrs). Report from O.C. Bearers at F.10.d. Evacuated. Sick. 6. NCOs + men. Wounded. 1. Officer. 13. NCOs + men. Geared. 2. men.	J.H.R.W.
7th July, 1915. 8. P.M. Same Billet.	Wednesday. Return for last 24 hours. Admitted other ranks. 20 sick (5 Cyrcoux) + 14 Wounded. Evacuated. 8 sick. 4 wounded. To-day 1. Cav Cy. 3. DIED = 1. Remaining. 56 sick. 10 wounded. Baths given = 202. Report from O.C. Bearers at F.10.d. Evacuated other ranks. 11 sick = 3 wounded.	J.H.R.W.

Army Form C. 2118.

WAR DIARY
or
INTELLIGENCE SUMMARY.
(Erase heading not required.)

Hour, Date, Place	Summary of Events and Information	Remarks and references to Appendices
8th July, 1915. 8 P.M. Same Billet.	Thursday. Return for last 24 hours. Admitted other ranks. 22 sick 5 wounded. Evacuated. 9 sick 2 wounded. Totals 2. 2 Gen Hos. 9. Remaining 5.8 sick. 13 wounded. Baths given = 289. Report from OC Bearers evacuated other ranks. sick 4 wounded 4.	J H R W
9th July, 1915. 8 P.M. Same Billet.	Friday. Return for last 24 hours. Admitted Officer 1 sick & transport & No. 5 ? Amb other ranks. 24 sick & 17 wounded. (? Pyrexia.) Evacuated. 7 sick 8 wounded. Totals. 7. 2 Gen Hos. 14. Remaining 5.9 sick 14 wounded. Baths given = 74. Report from OC Bearers. F 104. Evacuated Officers 2 wounded other ranks. 7 sick & 18 wounded. Lieut. CHARLES Moore (T.C.) reported for duty for 2. H.L.I.	J H R W
10th July, 1915. 8 P.M. Same Billet.	Saturday. Return for last 24 hours. Admitted other ranks. 19 sick & 5 wounded. Evacuated. 11 sick & 9 wounded. Totals 1. 2 Gen Hos, 3 sick & 4 wounded Remaining 61 sick & 6 wounded. Baths given = 290. Report from OC. Received at F 10 a. Officers 1 wounded other ranks. 7 sick 3 wounded. O D & 3. inspected our Horses & transport.	J H R W
11th July, 1915. 8 P.M. Same Billet.	Sunday. Return for last 24 hours. Admitted other ranks. 10 sick 15 wounded. Evacuated. 2 sick 2 wounded. Totals 2. 2 Gen Hos, 3 sick 4 wounded known. 64 sick 8 wounded. No bathing today being Sunday. Report from OC Bearers. Evacuated = 1. Officer wounded. 7 other ranks sick & 3 wounded. am Bearing Company marching too fast. 1/1st Bonny H Div. Unfortunary claiming M930 Pte am Attornet on leave am Humston & 5 Cpl Sampson.	J H R W

WAR DIARY
INTELLIGENCE SUMMARY
(Erase heading not required.)

Army Form C. 2118.

Hour, Date, Place	Summary of Events and Information	Remarks and references to Appendices
12 July 1915 6 P.m. Same Billet	Took over charge Field Ambulance from Major Louden Rauric who proceeded 1st Corps H.Q. for temporary duty. B Section moved from Annezin to Mondack Farm Bethune. Centered map 1. 4.9.0.0. @ 21. D. 8.2. by orders of A.D.M.S. II Division. Patients were moved to Hd Qrs of unit. Return for last 24 hours admitted other ranks 10 sick five wounded evacuated 2 sick 2 wounded to duty 2 Conval Co 3 sick + one wounded Remaining 64 sick and 8 wounded. No 3 Baths pm 351.	G Simpson Capt RAMC
13 July 6 P.m. Same Billet	Admissions for last 24 hrs 20 sick five wounded evacuated 14 sick two wounded to duty 14 + Conv Co 9 sick two wounded. Remaining. Held a P.m. on No 12756 Pr W Harlor II Div Am Col R.F.A who died suddenly in his unit. Cause of death Rupture of aneurism of Coeliac Arci B. No 3 Baths pm 206.	BL

WAR DIARY
INTELLIGENCE SUMMARY
(Erase heading not required.)

Army Form C. 2118.

Hour, Date, Place	Summary of Events and Information	Remarks and references to Appendices
14 July 1915. 8 PM Same Billet	Admissions for last 24 hrs 24 sick 8 wounded. On duty 9 to Conv. Co. Eight. Evacuated 7 sick eight wounded. Remaining 33 sick 7 wounded. OC Bearers wounded. Bulking for 14th = 349. 12 sick 5 wounded. Spendt Lieut Subdivision J B. section at Mordone Farm and transferred all cases of Skin diseases	[signature]
15 July 1915 8 PM Same billet.	Admissions for last 24 hrs. 8 sick 8 wounded. Returned to duty one Conv Co 2. Remaining 27 sick six wounded. 1 a.f 7 wright RAMC 1c reported for actual from No 11 General Hospital was posted to C section. Lt O.M.S. reposted B section at Mordone Farm. Capt A H Heslop returned from temporary duty with 1st Corps total wo of Bullhy J 398	[signature]
16th July 1915 8PM Same Billet.	Admissions for last 24 hrs 14 sick 9 wounded evac 4 sick 8 wounded to duty one to Conv Co. Remaining 35 sick seven wounded Total Bulhs 393 Lt E C Black proceeded on leave	[signature]

WAR DIARY
INTELLIGENCE SUMMARY.
(Erase heading not required.)

Army Form C. 2118.

Hour, Date, Place	Summary of Events and Information	Remarks and references to Appendices
17 July 1915 8 PM Same billet	Total admissions for the last 24 hours 19 sick two wounded evac six sick two wounded to duty. No Conv Co. One Remaining 47 sick five wounded. Total no of baths 344. OB section inspected by ADMS	[signature]
18 July 1915 8 PM Same billet	Total no of admissions for last 24 hrs 9 sick 3 wounded evac 4 sick 4 wounded to duty 4 to Conv. Co. One Remaining 47 sick four wounded out of these remaining 14 at a Rest No. 1 at Gallone Farm with B section. No Ret ESD Health Report form	[signature]
19 July 1915 8 PM Same billet	Total no of admissions for last 24 hrs 13 sick 4 wounded evac 3 sick to duty B Conv Co one Remaining 52 sick 4 wounded (50 at B section) Total Baths 386	[signature]
20 July 1915 8 PM Same billet	Total no of admissions for last 24 hrs 8 sick two wounded evac 4 sick three wounded to duty nil No Conv Co 2 Total remaining 57 sick six wounded total no of baths 333. Lt Burch returned from leave. Lts Clayton & Talbot proceeded on eight days leave	[signature]

WAR DIARY
INTELLIGENCE SUMMARY

Army Form C. 2118

Hour, Date, Place	Summary of Events and Information	Remarks and references to Appendices
21 July 1915 8 P.m. Same billet	Total no. of admissions for last 24 hrs 3 wounded 10 sick 3 wounded evac 2 sick 2 wounded to duty 4 sick. Remaining 61 sick seven wounded. Total no. of Baths 164. Lt A.T. Wright R.A.M.C. T.C. joined the advanced dressing Station.	[signature]
22 July 1915 8 P.m. Same billet	Total no. of admissions for last 24 hrs 19 sick 31 wounded evacuated 3 sick 28 wounded to duty 12 sick to conv.B & sick 3 wounded died (1) wounds three one died out B Hospital Transferred to No 5 field amb (1) 2 sick five wounded. Remaining 63 sick 8 wounded owing to this billet being shelled all wounded and sick were sent to B Section. Lt R Skerman R.A.M.C. (2C) reported but arrival from no 6 Stationary Hspl and was later ordered to report to No 4 field amb for duty. Baths 262	[signature]

Army Form C. 2118.

WAR DIARY
or
INTELLIGENCE SUMMARY.
(Erase heading not required.)

Hour, Date, Place	Summary of Events and Information	Remarks and references to Appendices
23rd July, 1915. 8 P.M. Same Billet.	Friday. Returned from Temp. Duty at 13th Coy., H Co. and others over the Command of the Unit from Capt. SAMPSON D.S.O. Major, who acted as C.O. starting away advance. Q.T.M. was held on NO. 3046. Pte SELBY. 901 Coy. 12th Hld., by order of O.D.M.S. This man was treated Dead. His Character returned was Good. G.O. % No.6 Returning LILLIERS. Result – 7 short terms yet. Return from O.C. Brewery Incorrigible appeared outside & other wounds. 10 sick & 4 wounded. Return Fd. Post 2a, Horses. Admitted other wounds. 13 sick & 4 wounded. Evacuation 8 sick & 3 wounded. Unnecessary 43 sick & 5 wounded. To Duty 4. 2 Can Coy. 12. (37 sick & 4 wounded Cases at "B" Sect). Lieut. N.L. JOYNT Name C. (No. 12) reported for duty from 70. 10. Station Hosp STOMER	J.H.R. Winshot Major N.O.N.C.
24th July, 1915. 8 P.M. Same Billet.	Saturday. Return Fd. Post 24. Horses. Admitted other wounds 12. Evacuated 17 Sick – 1 wounded. To Duty 5. 2 Can Coy. 5. Unnecessary. 29 sick + 3 wounded. 3 Officers admitted. No. of Beds – 359. 2nd N.L. JOYNT Zan Sept. Pte. [illegible] wounded order to report to O.C. No.4. F. Amb. Report from O.C. Brewers. – Evacuated other wounded 5 sick. Health of Unit good.	J.H.R.W.
25th July, 1915. 8 P.M. Same Billet.	Sunday. Return Fd. Post 24. Horses. Admitted other wounds. 13 sick & 4 wounded 5 wounded. (14 sick + 3 wounded at "B" sect.). No further pain. History being Knocking – Cpl. BLACK 12 reported sick from Cant. Report from O.C. Brewers, Evacuated Officers wounded. = 1. other wounds sick = 10. wounded 4.	J.H.R.W.

Army Form C. 2118.

WAR DIARY
— of —
INTELLIGENCE SUMMARY.
(Erase heading not required.)

Instructions regarding War Diaries and Intelligence Summaries are contained in F. S. Regs., Part II. and the Staff Manual respectively. Title pages will be prepared in manuscript.

Hour, Date, Place	Summary of Events and Information	Remarks and references to Appendices
26th July, 1915. 8 P.M. Same Billet.	Monday. Return for last 24 hours. Admitted, other ranks. 23 sick & 8 wounded. Evacuated. 14 sick & 2 wounded. To July, 6. 2/o Can Cav. 2. Remaining 36. sick & 10 wounded. ((27 sick & 3 wounded are at "B" sect.) 5 cases were admitted with Pyrexia. No. y Battn. from = 390. Report from O.C Bearers. Evacuated during last 24 hours. Officers, wounded 1, other ranks. sick 15. wounded 10.	J. H. R. W.
27th July, 1915. 8 P.M. Same Billet.	Tuesday. Return for last 24 hours. Admitted other ranks. 16 sick & 3 wounded. Evacuated. 10 sick & 10 wounded. To July, 7. Cm Cry. 2. Remaining. 33 sick & 3 wounded. ((23 sick 13 wounded are at "B" sect.) 4 Cases were admitted with Pyrexia. No y Battn from = 322. Report from O.C. Bearers. Evacuated during last 24 hours. Officers sick = 1. Other ranks. sick = 18. wounded = 3.	J H. R. W.
28th July, 1915. 8 P.M. Same Billet.	Wednesday. Return for last 24 hours. Admitted other ranks. 14 sick & 5 wounded. Evacuated. 8. sick & 1. wounded. To July, 7. Cm Cry. 5. Remaining. 27. sick & 7 wounded. ((18 sick & 3 wounded are at "B" sect). 2. Cases were admitted with Pyrexia. No y Battn from = 334. Report of O.C Bearers. Evacuated during last 24 hours. Officers wounded. 2. Other ranks. sick 3 & wounded 3. 2 visited Bearer posts today.	J H. R. W.
29th July, 1915. 8 P.M. Same Billet.	Thursday. Return for last 24 hours. Admitted other ranks. 28 sick & 12 wounded. Evacuated. 15 sick & 13 wounded. To July, 8. 2 Cm Cry. 2. Remaining 36 sick & 6 wounded ((22 sick & 3 wounded are at "B" sec.) 7 cases were admitted with Pyrexia. No y Battn from = 346. Report from O.C Bearers. Evacuated during last 24 hours. Other ranks. sick 18. & wounded. 11. Capt Talbot & Lt Clayton relieved Lt Beavor & Lt Clayton. Lt Beavor went to join them.	J H. R. W.

Army Form C. 2118.

WAR DIARY
—or—
INTELLIGENCE SUMMARY.
(Erase heading not required.)

Instructions regarding War Diaries and Intelligence Summaries are contained in F. S. Regs., Part II. and the Staff Manual respectively. Title pages will be prepared in manuscript.

Hour, Date, Place	Summary of Events and Information	Remarks and references to Appendices
30th July, 1915. 8 P.M. Same Billet.	Friday. Return for last 24 hours. Admitted other ranks, 27 sick & 6 wounded of Evacuated, 16 sick & 6 wounded. Details, 2 W. Cy Cy. 2. Remaining, 43 sick & 6 wounded (29 sick & 3 wounded at "B" Sect.) 7 cases were admitted with B' remain. No. of Meetings given = 282. Report from O.C Bearers. Evacuated. Other ranks. Died = Sick wounded = 1. Capt. T. C. Clout went for Temp. Duty. R. Montes Rgt.	J H P. W.
31st July, 1915. 8 P.M. Same Billet.	Saturday. Return for last 24 hours. Admitted other ranks. 13 sick & 4 wounded Evacuated. 9 sick. Details, 2 sick & 1 wounded. 2 Con Coy 3 sick. Remaining, 42 sick & 9 wounded (32 sick & 3 wounded at "B" Sect.) 1 case of Pyrexia was admitted. No. of Beds = 348. Report from O.C Bearers. Other ranks. Admitted = Sick = 6. Wounded = 4. Pte WRIGHT. Went for Temp Duty. L.H. Cos. R.E. The O.C. 2 — Fd. G.S.C. Train. Inspected our transport yesterday am in the morning.	J H P. Windel Major Marrow O.C. No. 6. F. Amb.

2nd Division

No. 6. 7.0.

Aug 1915

Army Form C. 2118.

WAR DIARY
—of—
INTELLIGENCE SUMMARY.
(Erase heading not required.)

Instructions regarding War Diaries and Intelligence Summaries are contained in F.S. Regs, Part II. and the Staff Manual respectively. Title pages will be prepared in manuscript.

Hour, Date, Place		Summary of Events and Information	Remarks and references to Appendices
1st August 1915. 8 P.M. SÉMINAIRE. ST VAAST. BÉTHUNE.		Sunday. Return for last 24 hours. Admitted other ranks. 27 sick & 4 wounded. Evacuated. 19 sick & 8 wounded. Totals; 7 sick. 2 Can. Cav. 3 sick. Mons Cav. Corp. 4 D sick & 5 wounded. (23 sick & 4 wounded at "B Sect). 7 cases were suffering from Pyrexia N.Y.D. No Baths given today. Being travelling. Return from O.C. Bearers evacuated. Officers sick. 2. other ranks. sick 18 wounded. 2.	J H R WINDER MAJOR R.A.M.C. O.C. No 6. F. Amb.
2nd August 1915. 8 P.M. Same billet.		Monday. Return for last 24 hours. Admitted. other ranks. 30 sick & 2 wounded (Bomb accident). Evacuated. 17 sick & 1 wounded 2 Buffs. 2 sick. 2 Can Cav. 14 sick. Remaining 37 sick & 5 wounded. (25 sick & 4 wounded at "B Sect"). 7 cases were suffering from Pyrexia. N.Y.D. No of Baths given. 384. Report from O.C. Bearers evacuated. Officer sick 1. other ranks sick. 18. wounded 2. [illegible]	J H R Winder
3rd August 1915. 8 P.M. Same billet.		Tuesday. Return for last 24 hours. Admitted other ranks. 32 sick & 3 wounded. Evacuated. 10 sick. Totals; 3 sick. 2 Can Cav. 3 sick & 1 wounded. Remaining 53 sick & 4 wounded. (28 sick & 3 wounded at "B Sect"). 2 cases were suffering from Pyrexia. N.Y.D. No of Baths given. 390. Report from O.C. Bearers evacuated. other ranks. sick = 12. wounded = 1. 2nd Lt TALBOT refunded having for duty this evening from 2 Bearer dept.	J H R Winder

Army Form C. 2118

WAR DIARY
INTELLIGENCE SUMMARY.
(Erase heading not required.)

No 9 FIELD AMBULANCE

Instructions regarding War Diaries and Intelligence Summaries are contained in F.S. Regs., Part II. and the Staff Manual respectively. Title pages will be prepared in manuscript.

Hour, Date, Place	Summary of Events and Information	Remarks and references to Appendices
4th August 1915. 8 P.M. Same Billet.	Wednesday. Return for past 24 hours. Admitted other ranks 35 sick & 5 wounded. Evacuated 20 sick & 2 wounded. Totals: 4 sick 2s Can Coy, 5 sick Remaining. 59 sick & 6 wounded. (27 sick & 3 wounded at is' beer.) 6 cases of Pyrexia N.Y.D. were admitted. No of Isolns. = 106. Report from O.C. Bearers, evacuated other ranks: 19 sick & 10 wounded. Lt. CHARLES proceeded on leave.	J.H.R. Winslow
5th August 1915. 8 P.M. Same Billet.	Thursday. Return for past 24 hours. Admitted other ranks 30 sick & 8 wounded. Evacuated. 13 sick & 10 wounded. Totals: 1 sick 2s Can Coy 2 sick Remaining 73 sick & 4 wounded. (52 sick & wounded at is' beer). 3 cases of Pyrexia N.Y.D. were admitted. No of Isolns. = 52. Report from O.C. Bearers other ranks: 12 sick & 12 wounded. evacuated.	J.H.R. Winslow.
6th August 1915. 8 P.M. Same Billet.	Friday. Return for past 24 hours. Admitted other ranks. 42 sick & 9 wounded. Evacuated. 22 sick & 3 wounded. Totals: 11 sick & 1 wounded. 2s Can Coy, 15 sick Remaining. 66 sick & 9 wounded (36 sick & 3 wounded at is' beer) 10 cases of Pyrexia N.Y.D. were admitted. No of Isolns. = 181. Report from O.C. Bearers, evacuated Bat Officer wounded = 1. Other Ranks: Sick = 12. wounded 13. Capt. JOHNT. proceeded on leave.	J.H.R. Winslow
7th August 1915. 8 P.M. Same Billet.	Saturday. Return for past 24 hours. Admitted other ranks 38 sick & 9 wounded. Evacuated 18 sick & 9 wounded. Totals: 10 sick 2s Can Coy 3 sick Remaining. 69 sick & 9 wounded (37 sick & 4 wounded at is' bed) 9 cases of Pyrexia N.Y.D. were admitted. No of Isolns. = 49. Report from O.C. Bearers. evacuated other ranks sick = 16 wounded = 4.	J.H.R. Winslow.

Army Form C. 2118.

WAR DIARY
or
INTELLIGENCE SUMMARY.
(Erase heading not required.)

Hour, Date, Place	Summary of Events and Information	Remarks and references to Appendices
8th August. 1915. 8 P.M. Same Billet	Sunday. Return for last 24 hours. Admitted other ranks. 19 sick + 3 wounded. Evacuated 25 sick + 2 wounded. To Duty 9 sick. To Con: Dep: 7 sick + 1 wounded. Remaining. 47 sick + 9 wounded. (26 sick + 6 wounded at 13 sect.) 1 case of Pyrexia & 7 O.R. were admitted. No. of Deaths = Nil. bearer panelling. Report from O.C. Bearers. evacuated other ranks. sick = 14. wounded. 4.	J.H.R. Winter
9th August 1915 6PM Same billet	Monday. Return for last 24 hrs. Admitted 37 sick 11 wounded evacuated 12 sick 4 wounded to duty 4 to Conv B 6 Remaining 64 sick 11 wounded (31 sick 6 wounded at 13 section) No of deaths 369 8 cases of Pyrexia. B.O bearers evacuated other ranks Sick 16. wounded 14	C Simpson Capt
10th August 1915 8PM Same billet	Took over command of unit from Major Wurtele Rowe who proceeded on eight days leave. Return for last 24 hrs. Admitted 19 sick + 3 wounded evacuated 16 sick + 5 wounded today. Sick to Conv Co. 4. Cases of Pyrexia Three (Remaining 57 Sick 9 wounded 39 sick + 9 wounded at B section. Total Deaths 357	C Simpson

WAR DIARY
INTELLIGENCE SUMMARY
(Erase heading not required.)

Army Form C. 2118.

Hour, Date, Place	Summary of Events and Information	Remarks and references to Appendices
11th August 1915 8PM Same billet	Returns for last 24 hrs Admitted other ranks 20 sick two wounded evacuated 16 sick 4 wounded to duty eight to C. Co 5. Remaining 48 sick 15 wounded 5 pyrexia 2 sick 10 wounded at B section total no of baths 381	E Simpson
12th August 1915 8PM Same billet	Returns for last 24 hrs Admitted other ranks 39 sick two wounded evacuated 23 sick 4 wounded to duty 6 to Cav Co 9. Remaining 53 sick seven wounded 4 pyrexia 39 sick five wounded in B Section total no of baths 111 L/Cpl E.C Black R.A.M.C (T.C) reported from Neuroparry on duty with II Divisional Train	
13th August 1915 8PM Same billet	Returns for last 24 hrs Admitted other ranks 30 sick 8 wounded evacuated 19 sick 5 pounced to duty sent to Caw Co six died 18 P Banks one 1st Kings one both from wounds. Remaining 54 sick five wounded 8 pyrexia 36 sick + five wounded at B section total baths 210	

WAR DIARY
or
INTELLIGENCE SUMMARY

(Erase heading not required.)

Army Form C. 2118.

Hour, Date, Place	Summary of Events and Information	Remarks and references to Appendices
14th August 1915 8 Rue Same billet	Returns for last 24 hrs Admitted 8 sick 5 wounded evac 11 sick three wounded to No.2 & to CCS No 3 Remaining 62 sick seven wounded 3 Diphtheria 40 sick four wounded at B Section Total 10 Deaths 898 Lt JP Charles RAMC TC returned to Base	[signature]
15th August 1915 8 Rue Same billet	Returns for last 24 hrs Admitted Officers one sick Other ranks 23 sick four wounded Evacuated 8 sick one wounded to No.2 & six to CCS No 3 Remaining Officers 10 sick two wounded Other ranks 68 sick & 9 wounded one Pyrexia 38 sick and 4 wounded at B Section took over from No.4 field amb. The Officers Dressing Station 4.9 Faubourg St Amy Capt N L Joynt RAMC (S.R) reported his return from leave. Lt Charles RAMC TC for temporary Duty with 2nd wd moves as sick Lt Black to Duty 8 F.A. Back for temporary Duty	[signature]

WAR DIARY
INTELLIGENCE SUMMARY.
(Erase heading not required.)

Army Form C. 2118.

Hour, Date, Place	Summary of Events and Information	Remarks and references to Appendices
16. August 1915. 8 P.m. Same billet	Returns for last 24 hrs. 1 Officer admitted other ranks 20 sick two wounded evacuated four Officers other ranks 22 sick two wounded 10 duty eight Officers Three. Others ranks 6 Conv Co B/57. Remaining Officers 4 sick three wounded Other ranks 4 sick Seven wounded 4 Cases) Ypres 36 sick & 6 wounded at B section Total no. of batt 382	R Sampson
17. August 1915. 8 P.m. Same billet	Returns for last 24 hrs. Officers admitted other ranks 20 sick 11 wounded evacuated Officers ranks 11 sick 4 wounded 10 duty 2. To Conv Co 4 Remaining Officer 4 sick 3 wounded. Other ranks 4 sick 14 wounded 28 sick & six wounded at B section No. of batts 39	[signature]
18. August 1915. 8 P.m. Same billet	Returns for last 24 hrs Admitted Officers one sick Other ranks 29 sick ten wounded Evacuated 29 duty 3. to Conv Co 6. Died two Remaining Officers 6 other 5 ninety 62 — total Baths 324 Capt S/Sgt Coram R.A.M.C. Joined for light duty. Capt C. J. W. Clayton temp duty 15th F A R.	[signature]

WAR DIARY
INTELLIGENCE SUMMARY.
(Erase heading not required.)

Army Form C. 2118.

Hour, Date, Place	Summary of Events and Information	Remarks and references to Appendices
19th August 1915. 11.a.m. Same Billet	Under instructions from D.M.S. 1st Army, I have to proceed to H Qrs 1st Army for duty at once in return from leave, which I have just done, and I have handed over the Command of the Unit to Capt T. SAMPSON D.S.O. R.A.M.C. Taken over Command	J.H.R. Wickham. Major. Wickham. P Sampson Capt Rawe
19. August 1915. 8 Pm Same billet	Returns for last 24 hrs. Admitted Officers 3, other ranks 17. Sick eight wounded. Evacuated Officers 2, other ranks 27. To duty 5. to Conv Co 9. remaining seven officers other ranks 46 - 30 carts at B Station. Total Batts '19. Capt M.R Joynt R A M C (S R) to H A A.s Co 2nd Did Paid for permanent duty. Major J H R Wickham Rawe reported his departure	[signature]
20. August 1915. 8 Pm Same billet	Return for last 24 hrs. 8 other ranks 30 evacuated Officers 3 other ranks 8. to duty 3. to Conv Co 3 Dect one remaining five officers other ranks 8+9. 29 at B Section Total Batts 32 ?	[signature]

Army Form C. 2118.

WAR DIARY
— or —
INTELLIGENCE SUMMARY.
(Erase heading not required.)

Instructions regarding War Diaries and Intelligence Summaries are contained in F.S. Regs., Part II. and the Staff Manual respectively. Title pages will be prepared in manuscript.

Hour, Date, Place	Summary of Events and Information	Remarks and references to Appendices
21 August 1915 8PM Same billet	Returns Admitted Officers nil Other Ranks 29 Evacuated 15 to duty 4 to Con Co 5 Remaining Officers six other ranks 54 – 32 at B section total Baths 229 Lt G W McKinney RAMC (SC) joined this unit from No 5 field Ambulance Lieut J H Boag RAMC (SC) joined this unit from 29 the field Ambulance T.O. joined two Officers 1MCO two men and two Ambulances 8 joined from No 19 F.A. for temporary duty with advanced dressing station. B.O. to relieve Capt Clayton for temporary duty with 1st K.R.R.	[signature]
22 August 1915 8PM Same billet	Returns Admitted one Officer Other ranks 36 evacuated 13 to duty three Con Co 8 6 Remaining Officers 6 other ranks 9C and AD in 3 unattached Officers unoccupying Capt Clayton RAMC TC transferred from WoI Harley ST to B section at Hunters Farm	[signature]

WAR DIARY
INTELLIGENCE SUMMARY.

Army Form C. 2118.

Hour, Date, Place	Summary of Events and Information	Remarks and references to Appendices
23rd August 1915 8 P.m. Same Billet	Returns for last 24 hrs. Officers one admitted the Ranks 33, evacuated the Ranks 24. Joining Eight to our Co. 14. Remaining Officers 31, other ranks 55 – 36 at B section. Total baths 392. Lt Dixon & Lt Denny 19th Field Ambulance at No 1 Harley St. for temporary duty. Capt Murray Rance returned to No 19 Field Amb.	Sampson
24 August 1915 8 P.m. Same Billet	Returns for last 24 hrs. Officers admitted five, other ranks 45, evacuated one, Officers 34, other ranks Joined 14. To our Co. 5. Remaining 11 Officers 44 other ranks Total Baths 30. Lt Black Rand(?) & Lt returned from temp duty with No 1 Bucks accid and was posted to No 1 Harley St. Lt J.P. Charles RAMC To reported from temporary duty with 2nd Worcesters. Captain E.G.W. Clayton was evacuated sick to Choeques	BL

Army Form C. 2118.

WAR DIARY
—or—
INTELLIGENCE SUMMARY.
(Erase heading not required.)

Instructions regarding War Diaries and Intelligence Summaries are contained in F.S. Regs., Part II. and the Staff Manual respectively. Title pages will be prepared in manuscript.

Hour, Date, Place	Summary of Events and Information	Remarks and references to Appendices
25 August 1915. 8 Pm Same billet	Returns admitted Officers one Other Ranks 84 evacuated Officers nil Other Ranks 13 to duty one Officer 6 other ranks to Conv Co 6 Remaining nine Officers 56 other ranks total no. of baths 189 two nursing sisters arrived for temporary duty	C Sumpter
26 August 1915. 8 Pm Same billet.	Returns admitted one Officer Other Ranks 23 evacuated one Officer Other ranks 8 eleven to duty 10 to Con.co.8 one Remaining 9 Officers 57 other ranks total baths 332 Lt JP Charles RAMC (T.C) went to temporary duty 34th Field Bde R.F.A Lt Wm S Robinson RAMC Joined from No 14 General Hosp for duty	D.S
27 August 1915. 8 Pm Same billet	Returns admitted 3 9 Other ranks to duty five to Con.co three evac 19 remaining 68 total baths 405 Capt A.H. Heslop RAMC (ordered hydropathic leave)	D.S
28 August 1915. 8 Pm Same billet	Returns admitted three three Other ranks evacuation 1 officer 17 other ranks remaining 10 Officers 57 other ranks to duty one Officer 120 other Ranks Remaining no of baths 170. the two nursing sisters returned to No 1 C C Station. C.C. Statiothe	D.S

WAR DIARY
or
INTELLIGENCE SUMMARY.

(Erase heading not required.)

Army Form C. 2118.

Hour, Date, Place	Summary of Events and Information	Remarks and references to Appendices
29th August 1915 6 p.m. Same Billet	Returns admitted 1 Officer 16 Other Ranks sick 2 O.R. wounded. Evacuated 2 Officers 16 Other Ranks to duty, 4 Other Ranks to Conv Co and O.R. Remaining 6 Officers 56 Other Ranks.	[initials]
30th August 1915 6 p.m. Same Billet	Returns admitted 1 Officer 21 Other ranks to duty, 12 to Conv Co 4. Evacuated 13. Remaining Officers 7, Other Ranks 48. Total no. of Battles 367. Lt. E. C. Black R.A.M.C. proceeded on 14 days leave	[initials]
31st August 1915 8 p.m. Same billet :-	Returns admitted 20 Other Ranks to duty five Officers 9 other ranks to Conv Co 3 O.R. Evacuated 25. Remaining 2 Officers 30 Other Ranks total no. of Baths 384. A Section Bearers on being relieved by no.19 F.Amb. returned from hot Harley St + Bedroom. Capt C. J W Clayton Ravid (S.R) to Ordies from Hospital	[initials]

121/7381

Ans

3rd Division
Summaries

6th Field Ambulance

Vol XIII

Aug P. Sep & Oct 15

Army Form C. 2118

WAR DIARY
or
INTELLIGENCE SUMMARY.

(Erase heading not required.)

No instructions regarding War Diaries and Intelligence Summaries are contained in F.S. Regs, Part II. and the Staff Manual respectively. Title pages will be prepared in manuscript.

Hour, Date, Place	Summary of Events and Information	Remarks and references to Appendices
1st September 1915 8 Pm Same billet	Returns admitted 3 Officers 29 Other Ranks sick 1 Officer & other ranks wounded evac 18 OR sick & wounded attached to duty 4 Officers 8 other ranks sick to Conv Co 3 O.R. Baths 440	[signature]
2nd September 1915 8 Pm Same billet	Returns admitted 2 Officers 24 other Ranks evacuated one Officer 16 O.R. to duty 2 Officers 10 other ranks to Conv Officer Remaining 4 Officers other Ranks 30 Capt S.J.A.H. Voylake DSO RAMC reported his departure on leave total no of Baths 410	[signature]
3rd Sept 1915 8 Pm Same billet	Returns admitted 2 Officers 24 other ranks evac 1 Officer 16 other ranks to duty 2 Officers 10 other Ranks Remaining 4 Officers 36 other Ranks no of Baths 312	[signature]
4th September 1915 8 Pm Same billet	Returns admitted one Officer and 29 Other Ranks evacuated two Officers 18 other ranks to duty one Officer 20 other ranks Remaining three Officers 38 O.R. no of baths 54. Lt D P Chilles Rame A(?) returned from leave Lieut Duty with 34 to Base R La Lt J Wilms Kimray temp duty with 1st Kings	[signature]

WAR DIARY
INTELLIGENCE SUMMARY.

Army Form C. 2118.

Hour, Date, Place	Summary of Events and Information	Remarks and references to Appendices
5th Sept 1915 8 PM Same billet	Returns Admitted 2 officers 33 other ranks evacuated 14 other ranks to duty 5 other ranks Remaining 5 officers & 9 other ranks Captain E TALBOT RAMC (SR) reported his departure for duty with 1st KRR and Lt J P CHARLES RAMC (QC) to duty with 1st Kings Liverpools Capt W.A. MILLER RAMC (SR) reported his arrival for duty from 1st KRR and Captain S J CESARI RAMC SR reported his arrival of leave to duty. Lt J W McKinnery RAMC 2C returned from temporary duty with 1st Kings (Capt A H Westop RAMC returned from leave	JS

WAR DIARY
INTELLIGENCE SUMMARY.
(Erase heading not required.)

Army Form C. 2118.

Hour, Date, Place	Summary of Events and Information	Remarks and references to Appendices
6 PM 6th Sept 1915 Same billet	Returns Admissions 36 Other Ranks Evacuations 2 Officers 20 other ranks to duty 2 Officers 11 Other Ranks Remaining one Officer 55 other Ranks Total no of baths 410	[signature]
6 PM 7th Sept 1915 Same billet	Returns Admitted 6 Officers 44 other ranks Evacuated 20 other ranks to duty 1 Officer 14 other ranks Remaining 4 Officers 65 Other ranks Total no of baths 387	[signature]
8 PM 8th Sept 1915 Same billet	Returns Admitted 3 Officers 22 other ranks to duty 21 20 Evacuation 4 Officers to duty Remaining 4 Officers 4 99 Other Ranks Total Baths 340	[signature]
8 PM 9th Sept 1915 Same billet	Returns admitted 20 other ranks Evacuated 2 Officers 13 other ranks remaining two Officers 420R Total no of Baths 394	[signature]

WAR DIARY
INTELLIGENCE SUMMARY.

(Erase heading not required.)

Army Form C. 2118.

Hour, Date, Place	Summary of Events and Information	Remarks and references to Appendices
8 Pm 10 Sept 1915 Scenie billet	Returns admitted 34 other ranks evacuated 40 other ranks to duty 18 other ranks remaining 2 Officers 254 other ranks total no of battles 313	[signature]
8 Pm 11th Sep 1915 Same billet	Admitted 3 Officers 30 other ranks evacuated 22 other ranks to duty 2 officers 10 other ranks remaining 3 Officers 52 other ranks total no of battles 396 Capt S.G.A.H. Walshe D.S.O. R.A.M.C. S.R. reported his arrival of service	[signature]
8 Pm 12th September 1915 Same billet	Admitted 22 evacuated 13 discharged 11 remaining 3 Officers 44 other ranks the G.O.C. II Div and ADMS II Div inspected the field ambulance and officers dressing station	[signature]

Army Form C. 2118.

WAR DIARY
or
INTELLIGENCE SUMMARY.
(Erase heading not required.)

Instructions regarding War Diaries and Intelligence Summaries are contained in F.S. Regs., Part II. and the Staff Manual respectively. Title pages will be prepared in manuscript.

Hour, Date, Place	Summary of Events and Information	Remarks and references to Appendices
8 P.m. 14th 13th Sept 1915 Same billet	Admitted 3 Officers 22 other ranks evacuated 1 Officer 10 other ranks to duty 8 other ranks Remaining five Officers 48 other ranks. Total no. of ranks 66.	[signature]
6 P.m. 14th Sept 1915	Admitted 3 Officers 30 other ranks evacuated 1 Officer 18 other ranks discharged eight Remaining 7 Officers 52 other ranks total baths 308	[signature]
8 P.m. 15th Sept 1915	Admitted one Officer 29 other Ranks evacuated 2 Officers 11 other Ranks discharged to duty Remaining 6 Officers 61 other Ranks total no. of baths 409. Took over the evacuation South of the Canal including A D St Harley Lt. Beatty sent A Section Heavy Subdivision with two Officers Capt Black Rawe reported Capt Black Rawe reported.	[signature]

WAR DIARY
INTELLIGENCE SUMMARY.
(Erase heading not required.)

Army Form C. 2118

Hour, Date, Place	Summary of Events and Information	Remarks and references to Appendices
8 P.M. 16th Sept 1915 8 P.m.	Returns admitted one Officer 28 other ranks evacuated 17 other ranks to duty 2 Officers 13 other ranks Died 1 other ranks remaining five Officers 58 other ranks total 60 5 baths 344	
8 P.M. 17th Sept 1915 8 P.m.	Returns admitted 2 Officers 22 other ranks evacuated 14 to duty 3 Officers 13 other ranks sent one suspected Cerebro Spinal case to No 10 Stationary Remaining 4 Officers 54 other ranks total baths 123	
8 P.m. 18th Sept 1915 8 P.m.	Returns Admitted 3 Officers 35 other ranks evacuated 1 Officer 24 other ranks discharged 1 Officer 9 other ranks remaining 4 Officers 54 other ranks total 60 baths 357	

WAR DIARY
INTELLIGENCE SUMMARY.

(Erase heading not required.)

Army Form C. 2118

Instructions regarding War Diaries and Intelligence Summaries are contained in F.S. Regs., Part II. and the Staff Manual respectively. Title pages will be prepared in manuscript.

Hour, Date, Place	Summary of Events and Information	Remarks and references to Appendices
8 Pm 19th Sept 1915 Same billet	Returns admitted 13 other ranks sick five wounded evacuated 1 Officer 11 other Ranks to duty 8 other ranks. Remaining 3 Officers 520 other Ranks sick 9 wounded other ranks. Total no 3 bath filled	
8 Pm 20th Sept 1915 Same billet	Returns admitted other ranks 20 sick six wounded evacuations 19 other ranks discharged 1 Officer 10 other ranks. Remaining 2 Officers 589 other ranks total Baths 365. 13 Echelon inspected by A.D.M.S. II Division	
8 Pm 21 Sept 1915 Same billet	Returns admitted five Officers 35 other ranks evacuated 1 Officer 30 other ranks to duty 21 O.Ranks Died one. Remaining Six Officers 41 other ranks 4 baths	
8 Pm 22 Sept 1915 Same billet	Returns admitted 15 sick 12 wounded evacuated 14 Discharged 3 Officers 10 other ranks died 2 Remaining 3 Officers 45 other ranks total baths 176	

Army Form C. 2118

WAR DIARY
INTELLIGENCE SUMMARY.
(Erase heading not required.)

Hour, Date, Place	Summary of Events and Information	Remarks and references to Appendices
23 Sept 1915. 8 Pm Same billet	Returns admitted 3 Officers 39 other ranks evacuated 29 discharged 13. Remaining six Officers & 201 other Ranks. 10 baths opening up to relieve 700 patients	[signature]
24th Sept 1915 6 Pm Same billet	Returns one Officer 88 other ranks including wounded evacuated one Officer 36 other ranks discharged to duty 1 Officer 14 other ranks Died two other ranks remaining 5 Officers 78 other ranks 8 Sent. C Bearer Subdivision to Le Quesnoy	[signature]
25 Sept 1915. 8Pm Same billet.	Returns admitted 39 Officers wounded 1340 other Ranks and about 500 other ranks whose names could not be taken before wounded the Cells suffering from Gas poisoning evacuated 26 Officers 750 other Ranks remaining about 11 hundred other ranks - 18 Officers 5 deaths 2	[signature]
26 Sept 1915 8 Pm Same billet	Returns admitted 5 Officers other Ranks about 100 evacuated 10 Officers other ranks 360 + 205 Gm. Co. Deaths one Officer 40 other Ranks remaining 5 Officers about 540 other ranks. C Section Bearer Subdivision returned to Habis	[signature]

Forms/C. 2118/10

Army Form C. 2118.

WAR DIARY
INTELLIGENCE SUMMARY.
(Erase heading not required.)

Hour, Date, Place	Summary of Events and Information	Remarks and references to Appendices
27 Sept 1915. 8 PM Same billet	Returns admitted 45 Officers Other ranks 147 & transfers from No 2 F Amb 156. Evacuated 8 Officers 405 other ranks. Germans 12 to Cor CCS 192. Remaining 42 Officers Other Ranks 265. Germans Three. By orders of DMS 1st Army found up as ACCS in addition to other duties.	G
28. 16 Sept 1915 8 PM Same billet.	Returns admitted 42 Officers Other ranks 96. Transfers 12. Remained Officers 4 & 2 Others & Other ranks thyself arrived for duty. Officers Capt & Black Watch Rd. u/d to 1st Scottish Rifles inclusive.	G
29th Sept 1915 8 PM Same billet	Returns admitted ten Officers. 15 Other ranks Transfers from Other F Amb 28 Officers 158 Other Ranks. Evacuated 31 Officers 385 Other Ranks to duty 115 Other Ranks. Remaining 46 Officers.	G
30th Sept 1915 8 PM Second Billet	Returns admitted the Officers 27 Other Ranks Transfers from other field Amb 2 Officers 23 OR evacuated eleven Officers 4 & Other ranks 673 Germans discharged 4 Soldiers 26 OR and 4 Brit Remaining 38. 88 Other Ranks	G

No. 6.7.0.

WAR DIARY
INTELLIGENCE SUMMARY.
(Erase heading not required.)

Army Form C. 2118.

Hour, Date, Place	Summary of Events and Information	Remarks and references to Appendices
1st Oct 1915 8 P.m. Same billet	Admitted 8 Officers 83 other Ranks transfers from the Field ambulances 4 Officers 11 other Ranks evacuated 139 other Ranks to Infirmary. Strength now only one Officer 140 other Ranks. Died. Serv. other Ranks 1. Remaining 4 Officers 230 other Ranks. C. Section sent to SAILLY LA BOURSE with its Bearer Subdivision to VERMELLES. Handed over greater part of building to 1/O 3/3 C of S including 124 patients	[signature]
2nd Oct 1915 8 P.m. Same billet	Admitted eleven Officers 43 other Ranks evacuated 23 Officers 4 other Ranks as cleared and other Ranks died and Officers. Renumerating 34 Officers 228 other ranks. A Section Bearer Subdivision Harries over Harley S.L. + Bowry returned to HdQrs	[signature]

WAR DIARY
INTELLIGENCE SUMMARY

(Erase heading not required.)

Army Form C. 2118.

Hour, Date, Place	Summary of Events and Information	Remarks and references to Appendices
3rd Oct 1915 8pm Same billet	Admitted sev Officers 35 other ranks evacuated 14 Officers 17 other ranks discharged to duty 2 Officers six other ranks Remaining 22 Officers 34 other ranks Captain S.J.M. CESARI Rance SR killed in action at 6.15 pm at A.D.S. at Vermelles (See hour handed over to no 4 F.A. and returned to H.Q.	[signature]
4th Oct 1915 8pm Same billet	Admitted 4 Officers 31 other ranks evacuated 13 Officers 14 other ranks to duty 9.O.R. Remaining 13 Officers 4 + 2 other ranks The body of Capt. Cesari was buried at Bethune Cemetery grave No 4. Row E.O.10	[signature]

WAR DIARY
or
INTELLIGENCE SUMMARY.
(Erase heading not required.)

Army Form C. 2118.

Hour, Date, Place	Summary of Events and Information	Remarks and references to Appendices
5th October 1915 Same billet	Admitted 5 Officers 28 other ranks evacuated 14 other ranks to duty 1 Officer 3 other ranks. Remaining 17 Officers 53 other ranks	[signature]
6th Oct 1915 Same billet	Admitted Officers 39 other Ranks evacuated 21 other ranks to duty 19 other ranks remaining 23 Officers 52 other Ranks	[signature]
7th Oct 1915 Same billet	Admitted 3 Officers 20 other ranks evacuated 8 Officers 28 other ranks to duty 14 other ranks & remaining 18 Officers 37 other Ranks & Capt A.H.H. Ess 407 RAMC to Hd Qrs 1st Corps for temporary duty	[signature]

Army Form C. 2118.

WAR DIARY
or
INTELLIGENCE SUMMARY.

(Erase heading not required.)

Instructions regarding War Diaries and Intelligence Summaries are contained in F.S. Regs., Part II. and the Staff Manual respectively. Title pages will be prepared in manuscript.

Hour, Date, Place	Summary of Events and Information	Remarks and references to Appendices
8 Pm 8th Oct 1915 Same billet	Admissions 9 Officers 32 other ranks evacuated eleven to duty 17 Remaining 27 Officers 42 other ranks	[signature]
8 Pm 9th Oct 1915 Same billet	Admitted 4 Officers 21 other ranks evacuated 2 Officers 30 other ranks to duty 1 Officer 8 other ranks 2 Officers Remaining 26 Officers 25 other ranks one Officer 2nd Coldstream Guards Died of wounds two above subdivisions were ordered to stand by the ready to move in an hours notice	[signature]
8 Pm 10 Th Oct 1915 Same billet	Returns Admitted 2 Officers 24 other ranks evacuated 1 Officer 15 other ranks to duty 2 Officers 8 other ranks Remaining 25 Officers 26 other ranks	[signature]

WAR DIARY
INTELLIGENCE SUMMARY.
(Erase heading not required.)

Army Form C. 2118.

Hour, Date, Place	Summary of Events and Information	Remarks and references to Appendices
8 P.m. 11th Oct 1915 Same billet	Returns Admitted 3 Officers 27 other ranks evacuated eight Officers 11 other ranks discharged 2 Officers 5 other ranks. Details Remaining 17 Officers 31 other ranks Capt F.A. Osborn RAMC reported his arrival from 10 General Hospital and Capt R.W. Armstrong R.u.C.T.C reported from 7th Division for duty	
8 P.m. 12th Oct 1915 Same billet	Returns admitted three Officers 27 other ranks evacuated 5 Officers 20 other ranks discharged 1 Officer 7 other ranks remaining 14 Officers 31 other ranks One Officer died	
8 P.m. 13th October 1915 Same billet	Returns admitted 50 Officers 18 other ranks evacuated 22 Officers & other ranks to duty 2 Officers & other ranks, Remaining 40 Officers other Ranks 35.	

Army Form C. 2118.

WAR DIARY
or
INTELLIGENCE SUMMARY.
(Erase heading not required.)

Instructions regarding War Diaries and Intelligence Summaries are contained in F. S. Regs., Part II. and the Staff Manual respectively. Title pages will be prepared in manuscript.

Hour, Date, Place	Summary of Events and Information	Remarks and references to Appendices
8 Pm 14th Oct 1915 Same Billet	Returns admitted 11 Officers 18 Other Ranks evacuated 23 Officers 13 Other ranks to duty 6 Officers 12 Other ranks Died one Officer. Remaining 21 Officers 26 Other Ranks	
8 Pm 15th Oct 1915 Same Billet	Returns admitted 2 Officers 25 Other ranks evacuated 2 Officers 4 Other ranks 8 Officers 25 Other ranks to duty Remaining 13 Officers 24 Other Ranks	
8 Pm 16th Oct 1915 Same Billet	Returns admitted 1 Officers 25 Other ranks sick one Officer wounded evacuated 16 Other Ranks discharged to duty one Officer and two wounded Officers one Other ranks Remaining 12 Officers 26 Other ranks	

Army Form C. 2118.

WAR DIARY
or
INTELLIGENCE SUMMARY.
(Erase heading not required.)

Hour, Date, Place	Summary of Events and Information	Remarks and references to Appendices
8 P.m 17th Oct 1915 Same billet	Returns admitted Seven Officers 25 Other Ranks evacuated 20 other ranks to duty 1 Officer, six Other ranks remaining 16 Officers 25 O.R.	[signature]
8 Pm 18 Oct. 1915 Same billet	Returns admitted seven Officers 13 other ranks evacuated four Officers, 8 Other ranks to duty 2 Officers five other ranks remaining 19 Officers 25 other ranks	[signature]
8 Pm 19th Oct. 1915 Same billet	Returns admitted Six Officers 15 other ranks evacuated five Officers 11 other ranks to duty 3 Officers Seven other ranks Died one Sunday. Remaining 16 Officers 28 Other ranks Lt J.W.McKUNE's Rank ie proceeded on 8 days leave	[signature]
8 Pm 20th Oct 1915 Same billet	Returns admitted Six Officers 193 Other Ranks to duty one Officer five Other Ranks Died one Officer Officers 22 O.Rs Ranks Died one Officer one detailed one standard from 84th F.A Lent Kinsity 10 Officers to 84th F.A Sane Sundaved to 84th F.A	[signature]

Forms/C. 2118/10

(49 29 6) W 4141—463 100,000 9/14 H W V

WAR DIARY
INTELLIGENCE SUMMARY.
(Erase heading not required.)

Army Form C. 2118.

Hour, Date, Place	Summary of Events and Information	Remarks and references to Appendices
6 P.m. 21st Oct. 1915 Same billet	Returns Admissions 7 Officers 19 other ranks evacuated 1 Officer 10 Other ranks to duty 6 Officers one other rank. Remaining 14 Officers 30 o.R. D.M.S. 1st Corps visited 8 Sectional mobile stationary	
6 P.m. 22nd Oct. 1915 Same billet	Returns admitted 27 other Ranks evacuated 22 & 23 other ranks. 1 Officer. to duty 6. Remaining 13 Officers 27 other ranks. Col Holt C.B. D.S.O. A.D.M.S. inspected the Ambulance preparatory to departure from the Division	
8 P.m. 23rd Oct. 1915 Same billet.	Returns Admitted 2 Officers 9 other Ranks evacuated 3 other ranks to duty 1 Officer 5 other Ranks remaining 14 Officers 28 other ranks	

Army Form C. 2118.

WAR DIARY
or
INTELLIGENCE SUMMARY.
(Erase heading not required.)

Instructions regarding War Diaries and Intelligence Summaries are contained in F. S. Regs., Part II. and the Staff Manual respectively. Title pages will be prepared in manuscript.

Hour, Date, Place	Summary of Events and Information	Remarks and references to Appendices
8 PM 24th Oct 1915 Same billet	Returns admitted two officers 16 other Ranks evacuated 10 other ranks to duty 9 other ranks. Died two officers. Remaining 14 officers 25 other Ranks	[signature]
8 PM 25th Oct 1915 Same billet	Returns admitted three officers 13 other ranks evacuated five officers 12 other ranks to duty two remaining 12 officers 28 other ranks	[signature] Sampson
8 PM 26th Oct 1915 Same billet	Returns admitted twenty other Ranks evacuated 12 other Ranks discharged to duty 9 other ranks to Conv. Co. 1 other rank. Remaining 12 Officers 26 other ranks Lieut W.M.S. Robinson R.A.M.C. proceeded on leave	[signature]

WAR DIARY
—or—
INTELLIGENCE SUMMARY.
(Erase heading not required.)

Army Form C. 2118.

Hour, Date, Place	Summary of Events and Information	Remarks and references to Appendices
8 pm 24/16 Oct 1915 Same billet	Returns Admitted 13 other ranks evacuated six other Ranks dis charged three officers 4 other Ranks Remaining 9 officers 29 other ranks	
8 pm 26 Oct 1915 Same billet	Admissions two officers 13 other ranks evacuated 6 other ranks to duty two remaining 11 officers 32 other ranks	
8 pm 29 Oct 1915 Same billet	Admitted 1 officer 19 other ranks evacuated two officers 8 others to duty 14 Remaining ten officers 29 other ranks	

Army Form C. 2118.

WAR DIARY
INTELLIGENCE SUMMARY.
(Erase heading not required.)

Instructions regarding—War Diaries and Intelligence Summaries are contained in F. S. Regs., Part II. and the Staff Manual respectively. Title pages will be prepared in manuscript.

Hour, Date, Place	Summary of Events and Information	Remarks and references to Appendices
8 P.m. 30th Oct. 1915. Same billet.	Admitted two Officers & six other ranks evacuated five Officers 30 other ranks to duty one Officer 9 other ranks remaining 9 Officers 21 other ranks Died one Officer	[signature]
8 a.m. 31st Oct 1915 Same billet	Admitted 5 Officers & 60 other ranks Evacuated 8 other ranks to duty one other rank. Remaining thirteen Officers 33 other ranks Capt Osborn R.A.M.C. T.C. departs for temporary duty with 1st Middlesex	[signature]

No. 6 F. Amb.

Nov. 1
XLV

12/
7655

2nd K Braun

Nov 1915

Army Form C. 2118.

WAR DIARY
or
INTELLIGENCE SUMMARY.
(Erase heading not required.)

Instructions regarding War Diaries and Intelligence Summaries are contained in F.S. Regs., Part II. and the Staff Manual respectively. Title pages will be prepared in manuscript.

No. 6 FIELD AMBULANCE

Hour, Date, Place	Summary of Events and Information	Remarks and references to Appendices
8 P.m 1st November 1915 Same billet	Returns admitted one Officer 25 other ranks evacuated one Officer 20 other ranks. Remaining 10 Officers 4 other ranks	GJ
8 P.m 2nd November 1915 Same billet	Returns one Officer 12 other ranks evacuated 6 other ranks to duty one Officer 16 other ranks. Remaining 10 Officers 36 other ranks	GJ
8 P.m 3rd November 1915 Same billet	Admitted three Officers 12 other ranks evacuated 4 Officers 8 other ranks. To duty one Officer 11 other ranks remaining 8 Officers 29 other ranks	GJ
6 P.m 4th November 1915 Same billet	Returns admitted Officers three sick one wounded 13 other ranks evacuated one Officer 1 other rank. To duty 10 O.R. Remaining 11 Officers 31 O.R. Lt Robinson RAMC re reported from leave	GJ

Forms C. 2118/10
(3 29 6) W 4141—463 100,000 9/14 H W V

WAR DIARY
INTELLIGENCE SUMMARY
(Erase heading not required.)

Army Form C. 2118.

Hour, Date, Place	Summary of Events and Information	Remarks and references to Appendices
8 pm 5th Nov 1915 Same billet	Admitted 4 Officers & other ranks evacuated one Officer & and one other rank to duty one Officer 10 other ranks remaining 18 Officers 24 other ranks. Capt. Armstrong proceeded on leave.	G
8 pm 6th Nov 1915 Same billet	Admitted 5 Officers 14 other ranks evacuated one Officer transferred to 11 DS to O.6 (Senior) to duty four Officers five other ranks remaining 13 Officers 27 other ranks	G
8 pm Th 1st Nov 1915 Same billet	Rhyms Admitted two Officers 11 OR ranks evacuated 1 Officer, 8 other ranks to duty 6; remaining 14 Officers 22 other ranks	G

Army Form C. 2118.

WAR DIARY
INTELLIGENCE SUMMARY
(Erase heading not required.)

Hour, Date, Place	Summary of Events and Information	Remarks and references to Appendices
8 a.m. 8th Nov 1915 Same Billet	Admitted eight other ranks. Transferred to No 5 F.A. two other ranks. To duty 2 Officers 11 other ranks. Remaining 12 Officers 24 other ranks. Lt. McKinney R.A.M.C. proceeded for Temp. Duty with R. Boats	RJ
8 P.m. 9th Nov 1915 Same Billet	Admitted four Officers 11 other ranks. 1 Officer two other ranks to duty. One D.I. Remaining 15 Officers 24 other ranks. Capt Clayton to 5th Kings Liverpools for temporary duty. Capt Osborn returned to Unit	RJ
8 P.m. 10 Nov 1915 Same Billet	Returns. Admitted Humphreys 9 other ranks evacuated one other rank to duty two Officers 30 other ranks. Remaining. 16 Officers 24 other ranks	RJ

(9 29 6) W 4141—463 100,000 9/14 HWV Forms/C. 2118/10

WAR DIARY
INTELLIGENCE SUMMARY.
(Erase heading not required.)

Army Form C. 2118.

Instructions regarding War Diaries and Intelligence Summaries are contained in F.S. Regs., Part II. and the Staff Manual respectively. Title pages will be prepared in manuscript.

[Stamp: No. 6 FIELD AMBULANCE]

Hour, Date, Place	Summary of Events and Information	Remarks and references to Appendices
8 p.m. 11th Nov 1915	Return for last 24 hours. Admitted 1 Other rank. Evacuated 1 Other rank. To duty 9 Officers, 6 Other ranks. Remaining 8 Officers & 27 Other ranks. Capt Sandford posted to Brigade on Lieut Colt Mc Gregor's temporary appt.	S. J. H. Webb
8 p.m. 12th Nov 1915	Return for last 24 hours. Admitted 3 Officers 1 O.R. To duty 4° 1 O.R. Remaining 11 Officers & 41 O.R.	S. J. H. W.
8 p.m. 13th Nov 1915	Return for last 24 hours. Admitted 3 Officers & 16 O.R. Evacuated 28 O.R. To duty 1 O.R. Remaining 14 Officers & 25 O.R.	S. J. H. W.
8 p.m. 14th Nov 1915	Return for last 24 hours. Admitted 3 Officers & 11 O.R. Evacuated 4 Officers & 5 O.R. To duty 2 Officers 28 O.R. 6 O.R. Remaining 11 Officers & 28 O.R.	S. J. H. W.

Army Form C. 2118.

WAR DIARY
INTELLIGENCE SUMMARY.
(Erase heading not required.)

Instructions regarding War Diaries and Intelligence Summaries are contained in F.S. Regs., Part II. and the Staff Manual respectively. Title pages will be prepared in manuscript.

No. 9 FIELD AMBULANCE

Hour, Date, Place	Summary of Events and Information	Remarks and references to Appendices
8 a.m. 15th Nov 1915	Report for last 24 hours. Admitted 1 Officer + 17 O.R. Evacuated 1 O.R. To duty 1 Officer. Remaining 11 Officers 42 O.R.	S.J.S.H. Lt.
8 a.m. 16th Nov 1915	Report for last 24 hours. Admitting 13 O.R. Evacuating 13 O.R. To duty 3 Officers 11 O.R. 1 Officer missing. Remaining 7 Officers 31 O.R.	S.J.S.H. Lt.
8 a.m. 17th Nov 1915	Report for last 24 hours. Admitted 1 Officer + 19 O.R. Evac. 10 O.R. To duty 10 O.R. died 1 O.R. Remaining 8 Officers 29 O.R.	S.J.S.H. Lt.
8 a.m. 18th Nov 1915	Report for last 24 hours. Admitted 9 O.R. Evac. 3 Officers 6 O.R. To duty 2 O.R. Remaining 5 Officers 30 O.R.	S.J.S.H. Lt.
8 a.m. 19th Nov 1915	Report for last 24 hours. Admitted 13 O.R. Evac 4 O.R. To duty 1 Officer 8 O.R. Remaining 4 Officers 31 O.R.	S.J.S.H. Lt.

Army Form C. 2118.

WAR DIARY
or
INTELLIGENCE SUMMARY.
(Erase heading not required.)

Instructions regarding War Diaries and Intelligence Summaries are contained in F.S. Regs., Part II. and the Staff Manual respectively. Title pages will be prepared in manuscript.

Hour, Date, Place	Summary of Events and Information	Remarks and references to Appendices
8 a.m. 20th Nov 1915	Return for last 24 hours. Adm 2 Officers 17 OR. Sick 4 OR. Transfd to 10th Remaining 6 Officers 42 OR. Sergt Major & Staff Sergt moved to H.Q. Stationary Hospital for duty. Two to McGurys returned from time duty on with 1st R. Berks Regt	S.J.K.S [signature]
8 a.m. 21st Nov 1915	Return for last 24 hours. Adm 1 Officer 8 OR. Sick 19 OR. Transferred to No. 5 S.H. 1 Or. Transfd O. Command pc 6. I 5th R. Sussex. H.Q. Remaining 7 Officers 13 OR. two Privates Loaned for temporary work as A + S.H.O.A. Cpl A. Gilley returned from 4 [illegible] Hosp recovering of [illegible] acute.	S.J.K.S [signature]
8 a.m. 22nd Nov 1915	Return for last 24 hours. Adm 2 Officers 9 OR. Sick 8 OR. Transfd 1 Officer to 10th Remaining 8 Officers 16 OR. Evacuation of returns [illegible] [illegible].	S.J.K.S [signature]

Army Form C. 2118.

WAR DIARY
or
INTELLIGENCE SUMMARY.

(Erase heading not required.)

Instructions regarding War Diaries and Intelligence Summaries are contained in F.S. Regs., Part II. and the Staff Manual respectively. Title pages will be prepared in manuscript.

Hour, Date, Place	Summary of Events and Information	Remarks and references to Appendices
8 p.m. 23rd Nov 1915	Return for last 24 hours. Born 1 Officer 12 O.R. Sick 7 O.R. To duty 4 O.R. Remaining 9 Officers 169 O.R.	[signature]
8 p.m. 24 Nov 1915	Return for last 24 hours. Born 2 Officers & 9 O.R. Sick 4 O.R. To duty 1 O.R. 1/ Officer & 1 O.R. admitted to hospital. The Major C.O. with 2/C and 4 men attended the funeral of strays from 2nd & 8th hospital up to S.S. Records from 3rd & 8th who the S.S. Barrie from the French Ed Kim hint interment.	[signature]
8 p.m. 25th Nov 1915	Report for last 24 hours. Born 1 Officer 14 O.R. Sick 5 O.R. To duty 1 Officer 1 O.R. Remaining 10 Officers Other Ranks. 12 Officers 25 O.R. Section Brest Cars took on a convoy of wounded from Canadian	[signature]

WAR DIARY
INTELLIGENCE SUMMARY.
(Erase heading not required.)

Army Form C. 2118.

Hour, Date, Place	Summary of Events and Information	Remarks and references to Appendices
10 am 26th Nov 1915 Same billet	Lt P Simpson R.A.M.C. returned from leave this morning.	3 QMS
8am 26th Nov 1915 Same billet	Taken over Command from Capt Ja Hurdle RAMC. Admitted 5 Officers 28 other Ranks 8 evacuated 12 sounds 2 Officers 6 other Ranks Died one accidentally wounded remaining 15 Officers 26 other Ranks.	
8 am 27 Nov 1915 Same billet	Admitted Officers 12 other Ranks 22 evacuated sick Officers 13 other Ranks 20 duty 5 other Ranks Died one Officer remaining 23 Officers 30 other Ranks. Lt McKinney took over keep of bodies Ranks. Lt McKinney took over keep Change of 1st R.R. Regt.	
8am 28 Nov 1915 Same billet	Admitted Officers 16 other Ranks evacuated Y Officers to duty three other Ranks remaining 30 Officers 26 other Ranks. J Davies took over being duty 28 1/7 Field Ambulance	

WAR DIARY

INTELLIGENCE SUMMARY.

(Erase heading not required.)

Army Form C. 2118.

Hour, Date, Place	Summary of Events and Information	Remarks and references to Appendices
8 pm 29. Nov 1915 Same billet	Returns Admitted 4 Officers 30 other ranks evacuated 11 other ranks to duty 4 Officers 2 other ranks Died one other rank wounded remaining 30 Officers 52 other ranks	
8 am 30 Nov 1915 Same billet	Returns Admitted 4 Officers 15 other ranks evacuated 3 Officers 16 other Ranks transfer to No 5 T.o' pure to duty 4 Officers 18 other ranks Died one other rank remaining 27 Officers 33 other ranks	

6th P. Amok.
Sec.
XV

2nd Div
F/15/11

Dec 1915

WAR DIARY
INTELLIGENCE SUMMARY

Army Form C. 2118.

6th Aust

Hour, Date, Place	Summary of Events and Information	Remarks and references to Appendices
8 p.m. 1st December 1915 Same belt	Returns as milled. Three Officers 35 other ranks 8 evacuated 12 other ranks to duty three officers two other ranks remaining. 3rd officers & 51 other ranks Capt H.A. Osborn reported & departure to take over medical charge of 2 W.D.A.C. and to accompany struck off the strength of the Unit	[signature]
8 a.m. 2nd Dec 1915 Same belt	Admissions 9 Officers 20 other ranks evacuated one Officer (wounded) 21 other ranks. trans(f)r to No 5 G.A. 2 other ranks to duty 3 officers 13 other ranks remaining 32 officers 35 other ranks. Lieut C. Cott E.H. Rawle R.E. joined for temporary duty from No 7 F.A. Capt H.T. Marshall Arrived from 1st A Butts Army No 16 F. Fld Ambulance	[signature]

WAR DIARY
INTELLIGENCE SUMMARY
(Erase heading not required.)

Army Form C. 2118.

Instructions regarding War Diaries and Intelligence Summaries are contained in F.S. Regs., Part II. and the Staff Manual respectively. Title pages will be prepared in manuscript.

Hour, Date, Place	Summary of Events and Information	Remarks and references to Appendices
6 pm 3rd December 1915 Same Billet	Admitted 9 Officers 20 other ranks evacuated 1 Officer 21 other ranks. Transfers to duty = 2. To duty 3 Officers 13 other ranks remaining 32 Officers 95 other Ranks	
8 pm 4th Dec 1915 Same billet	Admitted 9 Officers 18 other ranks evacuated 5 Officers 19 other ranks to duty 1 Officer 14 other ranks remaining 36 Officers 30 other ranks	
8 pm 5th Dec 1915 Same billet	Admitted 4 Officers 25 other ranks evacuated 1 Officer 11 other ranks to duty 6 Officers 10 other ranks. Remaining 31 Officers 54 other ranks 1 Officer Returned to unit from 1st Trps L. from	
8 pm 6th Dec 1915 Same billet	Admitted 3 Officers 16 other ranks evacuated 1 Officer 10 OR 2 Special dispg. SI and to duty 3 Officers 10 OR Remaining 29 Officers 48 other Ranks	

Army Form C. 2118.

WAR DIARY
INTELLIGENCE SUMMARY.
(Erase heading not required.)

Hour, Date, Place	Summary of Events and Information	Remarks and references to Appendices
6 P.m. 7th Dec 1915. Same billet.	Admitted 3 Officers 18 Other ranks. evacuated 7 Officers 16 Other ranks to Special Hospt. One to duty five Officers 10 Other Ranks remaining 22 Officers 48 Other Ranks	Thompson
6 P.m. 8th Dec 1915. Same billet.	Admitted one Officer 21 Other ranks evacuated 4 Officers 11 Other ranks to duty 3 Officers 10 Other ranks remaining 16 Officers 48 Other ranks	[signature]
8 P.m. 9th Dec 1915. Same billet.	Admitted 4 Officers 22 Other ranks evacuated 15 Other ranks to Special Hospital one to duty 3 Officers 19 Other ranks remaining 17 Officers 35 Other ranks Capt. Anstey Ranft reported his departure to 100 F.A. for permanent duty. Arrivals:- Lieut. McKinney Rhule C. from temporary duty with 1st K.R.R. Lieut E.J Robinson from temp duty with the A+S H.Y.R	[signature]

WAR DIARY

INTELLIGENCE SUMMARY.

(Erase heading not required.)

Army Form C. 2118.

Instructions regarding War Diaries and Intelligence Summaries are contained in F.S. Regs., Part II. and the Staff Manual respectively. Title pages will be prepared in manuscript.

Hour, Date, Place	Summary of Events and Information	Remarks and references to Appendices
8 AM 10th December 1915. Same billet	Admissions 4 Officers 8 other ranks, evacuated one Officer, five other ranks. To duty 2 Officers 11 other ranks, remaining 18 Officers 229 other ranks. Lieut J.H. Murray R.A.M.C. reported his arrival for temporary duty from No 100 Field Ambulance	[signature]
6 PM 11th Dec 1915. Same billet	Admissions 1 Officer, 27 other ranks, evacuated 8 other ranks, Discharged one Officer to 9 other ranks, remaining 18 Officers 51 other ranks.	[signature]
8 PM 12th Dec 1915. Same billet	Admitted three Officers, 14 other ranks, evacuated one Officer, 13 other ranks. To duty three Officers 12 other ranks, remaining 17 Officers 40 other ranks. Capt. C.J.W. Clayton R.A.M.C. &c. returned to duty.	[signature]

Army Form C. 2118.

WAR DIARY
INTELLIGENCE SUMMARY.
(Erase heading not required.)

Instructions regarding War Diaries and Intelligence Summaries are contained in F.S. Regs, Part II. and the Staff Manual respectively. Title pages will be prepared in manuscript.

Hour, Date, Place	Summary of Events and Information	Remarks and references to Appendices
8 pm 13th Dec 1915 Same billet	Admitted 4 Officers 21 Other Ranks evacuated one Officer 15 Other Ranks to duty one Officer S.S. remaining 19 Officers 41 Other Ranks	
8 pm 14th Dec 1915 Same billet	Admitted 6 Officers 78 Other Ranks evacuated 15 Other to duty one Officer 9 Other Ranks remaining 24 Officers 4 9 Other Ranks. Lt Paine posted to F.D.S. for instruction	
8 pm 15th Dec 1915 Same billet	Admitted 18 Other Ranks evacuated two Officers 9 Other ranks remaining 24 Officers 60 Other Lieut C.E. Steel Rowe RC RAMC joining unit for duty	
8 pm 16th 1915 Same billet	Admitted three Officers 16 Other Ranks evacuated 6 Officers 8 Other Ranks to duty 9 O.R. remaining 19 Officers 59 Other Ranks. Capt S.D. Att Walls RSO RAMC joined unit for duty 1st Corps S.	

WAR DIARY
INTELLIGENCE SUMMARY.
(Erase heading not required.)

Army Form C. 2118

Hour, Date, Place	Summary of Events and Information	Remarks and references to Appendices
8 P.m. 17th Dec 1915 Same billet	Returns admitted 3 Officers 14 other Ranks evacuated one Officer 1 other Rank. Discharged two Officers 9 other Ranks remaining 19 Officers 33 other Ranks	[signature]
8 P.m. 18th Dec 1915 Same billet	Admitted 6 Officers 24 other Ranks evacuated 10 other R. Discharged two Officers 12 other Ranks remaining 23 Officers 35 other Ranks	[signature]
8 P.m. 19th Dec 1915 Same billet	Admitted three Officers 14 other Ranks 8 evacuated 1 Officer 1 other Rank. Discharged 9 other Ranks remaining 21 Officers 38 other Ranks. Lieut G H Murray RAMC T.C. Att. E.G. for temporary duty	[signature]
8 P.m. 20th Dec 1915 Same billet	Admitted 3 Officers 16 other Ranks evacuated two other Ranks today 1 other Rank. 8 Officers 44 other Ranks remaining 24 Officers 24 other Ranks	[signature]

Army Form C. 2118.

WAR DIARY
or
INTELLIGENCE SUMMARY.
(Erase heading not required.)

Instructions regarding War Diaries and Intelligence Summaries are contained in F. S. Regs., Part II. and the Staff Manual respectively. Title pages will be prepared in manuscript.

Hour, Date, Place	Summary of Events and Information	Remarks and references to Appendices
8 Pm. 21st Dec 1915. Same billet	Admitted 8 Officers 25 Other Ranks evacuated 2 Officers 11 Other Ranks discharged 11 Other Ranks. Remaining 30 Officers 47 O.R.	[signature]
9 Pm 22. Dec 1915. Same billet	Admitted four Officers 22 Other Ranks evacuated six Officers 4 Other Ranks Rank's discharged six Officers 14 Other Ranks Remaining 22 Officers 51 Other Rank's.	[signature]
8 Pm 23rd Dec 1915. Same billet	Admitted one Officer 20 Other ranks evacuated 4 Other ranks discharged one Officer 19 O.R. Remaining 22 Officers 48 Other rank's	[signature]
8 Pm 24.th Dec 1915. Same billet	Admitted 4 Officers 23 Other rank's evac 9 Other ranks Discharged One Officer to other Units remaining 20 Officers 58 Other Rank's	[signature]

ns regarding War Diaries and Intelligence Summaries are contained in F. S. Regs., Part II. and the Staff Manual respectively. Title pages will be prepared in manuscript.

Army Form C. 2118

WAR DIARY
INTELLIGENCE SUMMARY.
(Erase heading not required.)

Hour, Date, Place	Summary of Events and Information	Remarks and references to Appendices
8 P.m. 25th Dec 1915. Same billet.	(1) Killed 6 other ranks evacuated two Officers 11 other ranks discharged 6 other ranks. Died one Officer. Remaining 22 Officers 4 & 6. Other ranks	
8 P.m. 26th Dec 1915 Same billet.	(2) Killed two Officers 22 other ranks evacuated 9 Officers five other ranks. Discharged (15 other ranks Remaining 25 Officers 4 & 8 Other ranks	
8 P.m. 27th Dec 1915 Same billet.	(3) Killed two Officers 24 other ranks evacuated 6 other ranks discharged one Officer 14 other ranks. remaining 25 Officers & other ranks	

(9 20 6) W 4141—463 100,000 9/14 H W V Forms/C. 2118/10

WAR DIARY
or
INTELLIGENCE SUMMARY.
(Erase heading not required.)

Army Form C. 2118

Instructions regarding War Diaries and Intelligence Summaries are contained in F.S. Regs., Part II. and the Staff Manual respectively. Title pages will be prepared in manuscript.

Hour, Date, Place	Summary of Events and Information	Remarks and references to Appendices
8pm 24 Dec 1915 Same billet	Admitted five Officers 15 other Ranks less 66 other Ranks Discharged three Officers one Officer rank one Officer died Remaining 29 Officers 110 other Ranks Bearer Subdivision from CAMBRIN rejoined Head quarters Capt. S/H CANUSHE RAO rejoined from leave	
8 Pm 29 H 1915 Same billet	Admitted two Officers 9 other Ranks evacuated Five Officers one other Rank Discharged one Officer Remaining 24 Officers one other Rank two Sections Bye under Command Capt. WALSH DSO proceeded to L/ES HARISOIRS to assist divisions at College St Vaast.	

WAR DIARY
INTELLIGENCE SUMMARY.
(Erase heading not required.)

Army Form C. 2118

Hour, Date, Place	Summary of Events and Information	Remarks and references to Appendices
8 pm 30th Dec 1915 20 Rue de Lillers. BETHUNE	Admitted 4 Officers 11 other Ranks evacuated 6 Officers 12 other Ranks to duty 1 Officer Died one Officer Remaining 23 Officers	[signature]
8 pm 31 Dec 1915 Same billet	Admitted 4 Officers 9 other Ranks evacuated 4 other Ranks Discharged 4 Officers Died one Officer Remaining 25 Officers 2 other Ranks Officers Hospital inspected by D.M.S. 1st Army	[signature]

2ND DIVISION
MEDICAL

NO.6 FIELD AMBULANCE

JAN - DEC 1916.

2.

6. 70th Ambulance
Jain
Vol XVI

2nd Div

F/115/2

11.

Jan 1916

Army Form C. 2118.

WAR DIARY
INTELLIGENCE SUMMARY.
(Erase heading not required.)

6 Found

Hour, Date, Place	Summary of Events and Information	Remarks and references to Appendices
8 P.m. 1.1.16 Rue De Lillers BETHUNE	Admitted 4 Officers, 9 other Ranks evacuated 4 other Ranks to duty 4 Officers Died one Officer 25 Officers 2 O.R. on leave. Remaining Capt Miller, R.A.M.C. S.R. rejoined from leave.	Thompson
8 a.m 2-1-16 Same billet	Admitted five Officers 4 other Ranks evacuated 6 other Ranks. Died one Officer. Remaining 84 Officers 3 other Ranks	
8 P.m 3.1.16 Same billet	Admitted 10. Officers 4 other Ranks evacuated 3 Officers full other Ranks to duty 4 Officers. Died one Officer. Remaining 31 Officers 2 other ranks	evacuated
8 a.m 4.1.16 Same billet	Admitted 3 Officers 6 other Ranks evacuated 4 other Ranks to duty Several Officers 4 other Ranks Remaining 23 Officers	

WAR DIARY
INTELLIGENCE SUMMARY.
(Erase heading not required.)

Army Form C. 2118.

Hour, Date, Place	Summary of Events and Information	Remarks and references to Appendices
8 pm 5.1.16 Same billet	Admitted 10 Officers 8 other ranks evacuated Seven other ranks to duty three Officers 1 O.R. remaining 30 Officers three other ranks	[signature]
8 pm 6.1.16 Same billet	Admitted 4 Officers 6 other ranks evacuated 4 Officers three other ranks to duty 4 Officers 1 other rank's remaining 23 Officers five other rank's. Lt. N.M. Colvin Rouke to S.O.R.Y for temp duty. Lt. H.T. Chatfield Raine joined for duty from 1/4 Royal Fusiliers	[signature]
8 pm 7.1.16 Same billet	Admitted five Officers evacuated one Officer remaining 24 Officers 6 other ranks (6 mules) three evacuated one to duty one remaining other ranks four	[signature]

Army Form C. 2118.

WAR DIARY
INTELLIGENCE SUMMARY.
(Erase heading not required.)

Instructions regarding War Diaries and Intelligence Summaries are contained in F.S. Regs., Part II. and the Staff Manual respectively. Title pages will be prepared in manuscript.

Hour, Date, Place	Summary of Events and Information	Remarks and references to Appendices
8 pm 8.1.16 Same billet	Admitted 4 Officers evacuated two Other Ranks. Nil admission evacuated one to duty, three Officers died one. Remaining 28 Officers three Other Ranks	G
8 Pm 9.1.16 Same billet	Admitted seven Officers 10 Other Ranks 8 evacuated two Officers. Died one Officer to duty five Officers 8. Remaining 21 Officers three Other Ranks 8	G
8 Pm 10.1.16 Same billet	Admitted 8 Officers 7 O.R. evacuated three Officers 4 Other Ranks to duty 4 Officers 1 Other Rank. Five Officers proceeded on leave. Remaining 28 Officers five Other Ranks. Lt McKinney R.a.m.C proceeded on leave	G
8 Pm 11.1.16 Same billet	Admitted 3 Officers Other ranks 1 evacuated five Officers three other Ranks to duty one other Rank. Remaining 26 Officers 4 Other Ranks 8. 30 N.C.O & Men proceeded No 1 Composite Cav. Fd. Amb. of Div.	G

(9 29 6) W 4141—463 100,000 9/14 H W V Forms/C. 2118/10

Army Form C. 2118.

WAR DIARY
INTELLIGENCE SUMMARY.
(Erase heading not required.)

Instructions regarding War Diaries and Intelligence Summaries are contained in F.S. Regs., Part II. and the Staff Manual respectively. Title pages will be prepared in manuscript.

Hour, Date, Place	Summary of Events and Information	Remarks and references to Appendices
8 Pm. 12·1·16 Same billet	Admitted 3 Officers 9 other Ranks evacuated 4 Officers 3 other Ranks to duty 4 Officers 1 other Rank remaining 20 Officers 12 other Ranks	[initials]
8 Pm 13·1·16 Same billet	Admitted 8 Officers five other Ranks evacuated one Officer 4 other Ranks to duty 1 Officer 1 other Rank Remaining 27 Officers 8 other Ranks	[initials]
8 Pm. 14·1·16 Same billet	Admitted See Officers Six other Ranks evacuated 3 Officers 4 other Ranks to duty two Officers 1 OR Remaining 28 Officers 9 OR. Capt Clayton RAMC to be returned to centre Lieut Robinson proceeded to centre	[initials]
8 Pm 15·1·16 Same billet	Admitted two Officers Six other Ranks evacuated Six Officers four other Ranks to duty three Officers 10 OR Remaining 21 Officers 9 OR Capt Clayton C.O. & Same O. to go to No 5 A. for permanent duty	[initials]

Forms/C. 2118/10

Army Form C. 2118.

WAR DIARY
or
INTELLIGENCE SUMMARY.
(Erase heading not required.)

Hour, Date, Place	Summary of Events and Information	Remarks and references to Appendices
6 P.m. 16.1.16 Same billet	Admitted 8 Officers 39 Other Ranks evacuated 6 Officers 42 O.R. To duty 1 Officer 2 O.R. Remaining 24 Officers 43 O.R.	[signature]
8 P.m. 17.1.16 Same billet	Admitted 11 Officers five O.R. evacuated 1 Officer 4 O.R. To duty Nil. Died one Officer Remaining 35 Officers 42 O.R.	[signature]
8 P.m. 18.1.16	Admitted 6 Officers evacuated nine Officers one Other Rank. To duty 3 Officers Remaining 29 Officers 41 O.R.	[signature]
8 PM 19.1.16	Admitted 4 Officers other Ranks Nil. Evacuated Nil. on duty two Officers and 12 O.R. Remaining 31 Officers and 29 O.R. Capt Simpson proceeded on leave.	W.A.M.

WAR DIARY
INTELLIGENCE SUMMARY.
(Erase heading not required.)

Army Form C. 2118.

Instructions regarding War Diaries and Intelligence Summaries are contained in F.S. Regs., Part II. and the Staff Manual respectively. Title pages will be prepared in manuscript.

Hour, Date, Place	Summary of Events and Information	Remarks and references to Appendices
8 P.M. 20.1.16 Same Billet	Admitted 9 Officers. Evacuated two Officers to duty one officer. 11 O.R. Died one officer. Remaining 26 Officers 18 O.R. Sent N.T. E Hatfield to 2nd South Staffs for transfer duty Lieut McKinney referred from same.	To A.M.
8 P.M. 21.1.16 Same Billet	Admitted 6 Officers, two O.R. Evacuated Six Officers and one other rank. O.R. duty five Officers remaining 27 Officers and 19 O.R. Sent Captor Kirkpatrick returned from leave on the 21st.	To A.M.
8 P.M. 22.1.16 Same Billet	Admitted Nine Officers Evacuated Two Officers to duty four Officers, seven other ranks, remaining 28 Officers 12 other ranks. Lieut J.H. Murphy to 1st Hants for two fourths duty. Lieut. ...	To A.M.

Army Form C. 2118.

WAR DIARY
INTELLIGENCE SUMMARY.
(Erase heading not required.)

Instructions regarding War Diaries and Intelligence Summaries are contained in F.S. Regs., Part II. and the Staff Manual respectively. Title pages will be prepared in manuscript.

No 6 FIELD AMBULANCE

Hour, Date, Place	Summary of Events and Information	Remarks and references to Appendices
8.PM. 23.1.16. Same Billet	Admitted three Officers. Evacuated one Officer. To Duty ~~three~~ one Officer, three O.R. Remaining 29 Officers, nine O.R.	A.M.
8.PM. 24.1.16 Same Billet	Admissions six Officers one other rank. Evacuated one officer one other rank. To Duty one Officer one other rank, remaining 33 Officers and eight other ranks	to A.M.
8 PM. 25.1.16 Same Billet	Admissions six Officers, evacuated one Officer and one other rank, to duty 10 Officers 3 other ranks, died one Officer, remaining 27 Officers 4 other ranks	to A.M.
8PM. 26.1.16 Same Billet	Admissions 11 Officers, evacuated one officer, to duty one Officer, remaining 36 Officers 4 other ranks.	W.A.M.

(9 29 6) W 4141—463 100,000 9/14 H W V Forms/C. 2118/10

WAR DIARY
INTELLIGENCE SUMMARY.
(Erase heading not required.)

Army Form C. 2118.

Hour, Date, Place	Summary of Events and Information	Remarks and references to Appendices
8 P.M. 27/1/16 Same Billet	Admitted 5 officers, two other ranks, Evacuated six officers one other rank. To duty five officers remaining 26 officers, 5 other ranks.	W.M.M.
8 P.M. 28/1/16 Same Billet	Admitted two officers, two other ranks. Evacuated three officers to duty two officers two other ranks, remaining 27 officers 5 other ranks.	W.M.M.
8 P.M. 29/1/16 Same Billet	Admitted 10 officers one other rank. Evacuated Nil. To duty one officer, remaining 36 officers six other ranks. Lieut Turner returned from 22nd F.Ps. on completion of temporary duty.	W.M.M

Army Form C. 2118.

WAR DIARY
INTELLIGENCE SUMMARY.
(Erase heading not required.)

No.— Instructions regarding War Diaries and Intelligence Summaries are contained in F.S. Regs., Part II. and the Staff Manual respectively. Title pages will be prepared in manuscript.

Hour, Date, Place	Summary of Events and Information	Remarks and references to Appendices
8 P.M. 30/1/16 Same Billet	Admitted 3 Officers, One other rank. Evacuated 3 Officers. To duty 10 Officers + other ranks. Remaining 26 Officers, 3 other ranks. Lieut Chatfield returned from temporary duty with the 62nd South Staffs	W. A. M.
8 P.M. 31/1/16 Same Billet	Admitted 2 Officers One other rank. Evacuated 3 Officers two other ranks. To duty 21 remaining 29 Officers two other ranks. Lieut Garts proceeded on leave Lieut Otsell to 17 A Flo for temp duty.	W. A. Miller Capt R.A.M.C.

Lord Johnson

No. 6 Feb. Aut.

Feb. J. 1916

D.A.G.
    Base

Herewith War Diary (AFC2118)
for month of February 1916
(six sheets)

P. Sampson
Major R.A.M.C.
O.C. mmdg. No 67 A.

Army Form C. 2118

WAR DIARY
or
INTELLIGENCE SUMMARY.

(Erase heading not required.)

Instructions regarding War Diaries and Intelligence Summaries are contained in F.S. Regs., Part II. and the Staff Manual respectively. Title pages will be prepared in manuscript.

Hour, Date, Place	Summary of Events and Information	Remarks and references to Appendices
8 PM Same Billet 1/2/16	This day handed over Officer's Hospital at 33 Boul Victor Hugo to No 33 C.C.S the Hospital to be transferred by and three R.A.M.C personnel, these being one cook and two nursing orderlies. Returned to leave.	W.A. &M. Thompson
8 Pm 2. 2. 16 Same Billet	Nothing except as Officers Hosp had been handed over	[signature]
8 Pm 3. 2. 16 W.2.a.6.2. Bethune map 1/40000	Reformed B+C Section at this farm. It is being proposed to form a EosD Sahara at this place, Lieut W. Last Carr being detailed. Lt Murray Ross returned from 1st Hghrs	[signature]
8 Pm 4. 2. 15 Same Billet	Reft for temp duty Routine march by Squad Company drill	[signature]

Army Form C. 2118

WAR DIARY
or
INTELLIGENCE SUMMARY.
(Erase heading not required.)

Instructions regarding War Diaries and Intelligence Summaries are contained in F.S. Regs., Part II. and the Staff Manual respectively. Title pages will be prepared in manuscript.

Hour, Date, Place	Summary of Events and Information	Remarks and references to Appendices
8 PM 5.2.16 Same billet	No amusements or discharges. Nothing to note.	GJ
8 PM 6.2.16 Same billet	Carried out Company & Squad & Stretcher drill.	GJ
8 PM 7.2.16 Same billet	Stretcher drill & route march.	GJ
8 PM 8.2.16 Same billet	Pair out to NCOs & men.	GJ
8 PM 9.2.16 Same billet	Lt CHATFIELD RAMC LC proceeded on leave. Overhauling of the equipment. Route march.	GJ
8 PM 10.2.16 Same billet	Lt GAVIN RAMC returned from leave. Capt S.J.A.H. WALSHE DSO RAMC to proceed from tomorrow on 10 days II D. is Capt MILLER RAMC SR 622nd R.F. from tomorrow. Lt O'KELL RAMC rejoined from temp duty 14th M.R.F.	GJ
8 PM 11.2.16 Same billet	Ordinary drills & route march	GJ
8 PM 12.2.16 Same billet	Nothing to note	GJ

Forms/C. 2118/10

WAR DIARY
or
INTELLIGENCE SUMMARY.
(Erase heading not required.)

Army Form C. 2118

Instructions regarding War Diaries and Intelligence Summaries are contained in F.S. Regs., Part II. and the Staff Manual respectively. Title pages will be prepared in manuscript.

Hour, Date, Place	Summary of Events and Information	Remarks and references to Appendices
6 P.m. 13th 2.16	Shelby Mills travelled L.W.S. Robinson R.M.C. I.C. returned from temp duty with 13th Essex Regt	[initials]
8 P.m. 14th. 2.16	Capt R W Mackenzie R.a.m.C. returned for duty from 11 General Hospital BOULOGNE Inspection of Horse transport and harness Mare Reaphon ones	[initials]
8 P.m. 15th 2/16. BUSNES	Unit moved from LES HARISOIRES to BUSNES arrived at noon. Lt Robinson R.a.M.C. reported his departure to BOULOGNE	[initials]
8 P.m 16. 2.16 Same billet.	Rained all day nothing of note Lt C C SKELL proceeded on leave	[initials]

Army Form C. 2118

WAR DIARY
INTELLIGENCE SUMMARY.
(Erase heading not required.)

Instructions regarding War Diaries and Intelligence Summaries are contained in F.S. Regs., Part II. and the Staff Manual respectively. Title pages will be prepared in manuscript.

Hour, Date, Place	Summary of Events and Information	Remarks and references to Appendices
8 pm 17th. 2-16. Same billet.	Nothing to report except fixed up a small nursing station in a barn. The other building being available to other ranks being shipped from there.	PJ
8 pm 18. 2-16 Same billet.	Lt CHATFIELD RAMC shipped from there.	PJ
8 pm 19. 2-16 Same billet.	Admissions 12 Evacuates 8 to No 106 C.C.S. Remained 4. Lt Murray proceeded on leave & Lt Murray (proceeded on leave) & Reviewing	PJ
8 pm 20. 2-16 Same billet.	Admissions 9. Evacuated 9 - 4 Remaining. Inspected by ADMS II Division	PJ
9 AM 21. 2-16 Same billet.	Changed over. Working up the Diary. so as to agree with Lieut Dyble's morning style Dyble. represented A. Murfeld 80 Evacuated 7 to No 106 F.A - 3 to duty two "hard_lines"	PJ
9 AM 22. 2-16	Admitted Six evacuated Six remaining nil. All 1900's and men issued with 1914 pattern Infantry Equipment. Seemed to be much appreciated by the men	PJ

WAR DIARY
or
INTELLIGENCE SUMMARY.

(Erase heading not required.)

Army Form C. 2118

Hour, Date, Place	Summary of Events and Information	Remarks and references to Appendices
9 AM 23.2.16 Same billet	Admitted five evacuated 4, remaining one. Inspected linen with the new equipment. Route march.	PJ
9 AM. 24.2.16 Same billet	Admitted 11. evacuated 11 to Div Co. one Route march. Packed up all equipment. Received orders to stand by to move off at short notice.	PJ
9 AM 25.2.16 Same billet	Admitted 22. evacuated 19. to Div Co. 3. Route march.	PJ
9 AM 26.2.16 Same billet	Admitted 11. evacuated 11. the remaining 21. not proposed to keep patients in this village as the accommodation is very bad. (a Barn) the CCS is quite close. Lt Col. O'Kell Rame RC returned from leave	PJ
9 AM 27.2.16 Same billet	Admitted 16 evacuated 16 remaining nil.	PJ
9 AM. 28.2.16 CHAMBORD Barracks BETHUNE	Unit moved from BUSNES at 3 P.m. on 27th to CHAMBORD Barracks BETHUNE arriving here 6-30 P.m. Did not open out	PJ

Army Form C. 2118.

WAR DIARY
INTELLIGENCE SUMMARY.
(Erase heading not required.)

Hour, Date, Place	Summary of Events and Information	Remarks and references to Appendices
9 A.M. 29.2.16 BRUAY Sheet 36 B 1st Division J 15 & 5.4	Unit moved from BETHUNE at 6 A.M. on 28.II. and arrived at BRUAY at 10.30 A.M. Billet near Cycle Rue ALFRED, LEROY. Have received orders to be Gsar ? BRUAY before 12 hours, + proceed to LA BOUISSIERE	[signature] Thompson Major ? RAMC

6 Ja Amb
Vol XVIII

WAR DIARY
or
INTELLIGENCE SUMMARY.
(Erase heading not required.)

Army Form C. 2118.

Hour, Date, Place	Summary of Events and Information	Remarks and references to Appendices
9 AM. 1.3.16 France Maps 36 C. 30 Edition	Nothing to report. This hospital is very busy and the numbers have been largely occupied in clearing up.	GJ
9 AM 2.3.16 Same billet	Lt Murray RAMC T.C. returned from leave. Boy Scouts Association sent Car Johnson Munt.	GJ
9 AM 3.3.16 Same billet	Inspected by A.D.M.S. Nothing else to report	GJ
9 AM 4.3.16 Same billet	Lieut JAMES LYONS RAMC TC joined for permanent duty. Please weather bad.	GJ
9 AM 5.3.16 Same billet	Nothing to report - named 40 par. Cooks to unit. The cooks at present supplied one of inferior quality. Report from A.D.M.S sent Hospitals recommendations to A.D.M.S	GJ
9 AM 6.3.16 Same billet	Inspection of Clothing 16 new shirts issued. Sunny ready weather	GJ
9 AM 7.3.6 Same billet	Nothing to report weather still bad	GJ

Army Form C. 2118.

WAR DIARY
or
INTELLIGENCE SUMMARY.
(Erase heading not required.)

Hour, Date, Place	Summary of Events and Information	Remarks and references to Appendices
9 AM. 8. 3. 16 Same billet	Horses and transport inspected by O.C. Des Prairie and Vet. Officer all correct	PS
9 AM 9. 3. 16 Same billet	Received instruction to choose billets for ambulance at J 36. Sheet 36.B. h a 1 6 N 14 6 ss RUITZ	PS
9. A.M. 10. 3. 16 J 36 d 1·7 Sheet 36.b.	Unit moved to billets at Ourinent address Billets very dirty village practically wrecked unwashed linen & to sheet inferious	PS
9 AM 11- 3· 16 Same billet	Unit & billets inspected by A.D.M.S. & Dunlop. Nothing also to report - No C.O.S.T. men	PS
Several 9 AM 12- 3· 16	Nothing to note. Snow so sleet in the ground.	
9 AM. 13· 3. 16	Regret to report that Lieut Ned Murphy Grace Rameye was accidentally killed yesterday afternoon whilst exercising his Charger. He was taken to No 18 C o S and died at 8·25 p.m. from fracture of the base of skull and will take place 2/30 pm today	PS

Army Form C. 2118.

WAR DIARY
or
INTELLIGENCE SUMMARY.
(Erase heading not required.)

Hour, Date, Place	Summary of Events and Information	Remarks and references to Appendices
9 AM 14th 3.16 Same billet	Lieut Gavin Rawe RE was buried yesterday at B.E. Kemebery Row 5. Grave + map 36.B.D4.c.66. LAPUGNOY. Court D'enquiry held in re cause of his fatal injuries	
9 AM 15th 3.16 Same billet	B. Section moved to Chateau De COUPIGNY Q.11.c.4.7. map 36.B. 6th Edition + opened up + received sick and wounded. Accommodation 150 lying 100 wounded sitting	
9 AM 16. 3.16 Same billet	"B" sick return cancelled 10 remaining tent sick. Nothing else to report	
9 AM. 17. 3.16	Received instructions to have whole unit to BRUAY J.22.a.2.8. Sheet 36 B Sixth Edit. to be clear of MAISNIL + COUPIGNY at 9 A.M. Sick returned to B. attached one officer 11 O.R. evacuated 1 officer + 15 remaining	

Forms/C. 2118/10

Army Form C. 2118.

WAR DIARY
INTELLIGENCE SUMMARY.
(Erase heading not required.)

Instructions regarding War Diaries and Intelligence Summaries are contained in F. S. Regs., Part II. and the Staff Manual respectively. Title pages will be prepared in manuscript.

Hour, Date, Place	Summary of Events and Information	Remarks and references to Appendices
9AM 18.3.16 J22 a.9-8-36 B Sheet 6th Edition	heard unofficially that position opened up at school MARMATTON accommodation 160 lying up. Sitting Court Enquiry in the late Lieut. N.M. GAVIN Raine & C. confirmed by GOC II Division. (The finding of the enquiry was "The late Lieut. N.M. GAVIN R.A.M.C. was on duty at the time of the accident and that he was in no way to blame")	Empson Major RAMC
9AM. 19.3.16 Same billet	Opened up as a Rest Station also for Scabies for the Division also as a Field Ambulance controlled Rest Station for scabies 16 Remaining 16 Other Cases 8 96 Admitted 1 evacuated remaining 30. Lt. Chatfield R.A.M.C. returned totals.	J
9AM 20.3.16 Same billet	Admitted to Rest Station 22. to duty 88. Remaining 70. Other Cases admitted 9. to duty 11. Remaining 88.	J

WAR DIARY
— or —
INTELLIGENCE SUMMARY.
(Erase heading not required.)

Army Form C. 2118.

Hour, Date, Place	Summary of Events and Information	Remarks and references to Appendices
9 AM 21.3.16 Same billet	89 O.R.'s. B: R.C.H. Reeve proceeded on leave. Admitted Rest Station 26. To duty 24. Remaining 12. 8 O.R.'s Cases. 9 O.R.'s remaining to locality. 3 evacuated. 30 Remaining.	G
9 AM 22.3.16 Same billet	Admitted Rest Station 33. To duty 32. Evac. to Rem. 69. 8 O.R.'s Cases admitted 26 to duty 10 Evac. 1 Rem. 4. 4 Field Amb'l inspected by D.D.M.S. 4th Corps.	G
9 AM 23.3.16 Same billet	Inspector Cap't ADMS E.D.S. who saw all Cases sent to this Unit specially for his inspection. — Admitted to Rest Station one. Discharged to Duty 44. evacuated Three Remaining 22. 8 O.R.'s Cases admitted 9 to duty 7 evacuated one Rem. 45.	G
9 AM 24.3.16	Admitted to Rest Station three locality 9 evacuated one remaining 15. 8 O.R.'s Cases admitted 10 locality one evacuated Remaining 42.	G

WAR DIARY
or
INTELLIGENCE SUMMARY.
(Erase heading not required.)

Army Form C. 2118.

Instructions regarding War Diaries and Intelligence Summaries are contained in F. S. Regs., Part II. and the Staff Manual respectively. Title pages will be prepared in manuscript.

Hour, Date, Place	Summary of Events and Information	Remarks and references to Appendices
9 AM 25-3-16 Same billet	Nothing to report, weather very bad, snow & sleet	G
9 AM 26-3-16 Same billet	Rest Station admitted two today 2 Remaining 15 Other Cases admitted 9 to duty 7 Evacuated 4 Remaining 4 - O Capt R.W. McKenzie R.A.M.C. posted to Bn. as Bn. M.O. for duty	G
9 AM 27-3-16 Same billet	Rest Station admitted two today two evacuated one Remaining 14 Other Cases admitted 7 to duty 11 Evacuated two D Remaining 34	G
9 AM 28-3-16 Same billet	Rest Station admitted 4 to duty 14 Remaining 5 Other Cases admitted 23 to duty 24 Others evacuated 4 Remaining 31.	G
9 AM 29-3-16 Same billet	Rest Station admitted 10 to duty 8 Remaining 17 Other Cases 13 admitted five to duty evacuated three Remaining 36. Lieut B.J. BAILEY RAMC joined from No 26 General Hospital for duty	G

Army Form C. 2118.

WAR DIARY
or
INTELLIGENCE SUMMARY.
(Erase heading not required.)

Instructions regarding War Diaries and Intelligence Summaries are contained in F.S. Regs., Part II. and the Staff Manual respectively. Title pages will be prepared in manuscript.

Hour, Date, Place	Summary of Events and Information	Remarks and references to Appendices
9 AM 30.3.16 Same billet	Rest Station admitted two to duty three unmarked three Remaining 13 Other Cases admitted 9 to duty three Evacuated Three Remaining 89	
9 AM 31.3.16 Same billet	Rest Station admitted two to duty three evacuated one Remaining eleven Other Cases admitted 15 to duty 10 o.R. to duty No 6 evacuated via officers 2 O.R. Remaining 41 Received orders to close down Rest Station and hand over patients from No 100 F.A.	

2nd. Div.

No. 6 F. Amb.

April 1916.

6 7d Amb.

Vol XIX

WAR DIARY
INTELLIGENCE SUMMARY

Army Form C. 2118.

(Erase heading not required.)

Hour, Date, Place	Summary of Events and Information	Remarks and references to Appendices
9.A.M. 1.4.16 J 22 a 2.8	Admitted 16 to duty 9 Evacuated one Remaining 57. Rest Station to duty 3 Remaining 8	
9.A.M. 2-4-16 Same billet	Admitted one Officer 10 O.R. to duty 13 Evacuated one Officer 4 O.R. Remaining 49 Rest Station 1 Adm. 2 admitted to duty 1 to be remaining five. All Officers went to lecture by G.O.C. 7th Corps.	
9.A.M. 3.4-16 Same billet	Admitted 7 to duty 13 evacuated two remaining 41. Rest Station 8 to duty 3. Remaining 2 10 Stokes to 2nd Div. T.B. for temp duty.	
9.A.M. 4.4.16 Same billet	Admitted one O.R. - 14 O.R. to duty 8 Evac 1 Off 3 O.R. Remaining 44. Rest Station 1 to duty. Lieut. Murray proceeded to temp duty with mine Rescue School. - Two Officers to Aire for 3 days course.	
9.A.M. 5-4-16	Admitted Officers 17 O.R. to duty 4 Evac 1 Off 3 O.R. Remaining 54. Rest Station closed Unit unrelieved infantry	

WAR DIARY

INTELLIGENCE SUMMARY.

(Erase heading not required.)

Army Form C. 2118.

Instructions regarding War Diaries and Intelligence Summaries are contained in F.S. Regs, Part II. and the Staff Manual respectively. Title pages will be prepared in manuscript.

Hour, Date, Place	Summary of Events and Information	Remarks and references to Appendices
9 AM 6. 4.16 Same Billet	Admitted 16 Duty 6 evacuated 5 remaining 57	GS
9 AM 7. 4.16 Same Billet	Admitted 5 Duty 12 Evacuated 9 Remaining 41 Nothing to report otherwise	GS
9 AM 8. 4.16 Same Billet	Admitted 4 Duty 9. Evacuated five Remaining 33	GS
9 AM 9. 4.16 Same Billet	Admitted 7 duty, 10 evacuated one Remaining 29	GS
9 AM 10. 4.16 Same Billet	Admitted 6 duty 2 evacuated 3 Remaining 30. Car waggons are being Painted & lettering Bayonets this duty	GS
9 AM 11. 4.16 Same Billet	Admitted one Officer 14 other ranks 8 duty 6 evacuated 10 Officer 3 O.R. Rank 8 remaining 35. Capt. S. W. A H and L. D.O. Ranie S.R. (on leave) one letain	GS

Forms/C. 2118/10

Army Form C. 2118.

WAR DIARY
INTELLIGENCE SUMMARY.
(Erase heading not required.)

Instructions regarding War Diaries and Intelligence Summaries are contained in F.S. Regs, Part II. and the Staff Manual respectively. Title pages will be prepared in manuscript.

Hour, Date, Place	Summary of Events and Information	Remarks and references to Appendices
9 A.M. 12.4.-16 Same billet	Admitted to duty 5 evacuated 11 Remaining 42. Weather very bad interfering with the Retraining	GP
9 A.M. 13.4.-16 Same billet	Admitted 28 duty 11 evacuated 10. Remaining 56. The majority of cases admitted are mild cases of influenza	GP
9 A.M. 14.4.-16 Same billet	Admitted eight 8 duty 6 evacuated five 5 remaining 51. Eight R.A.M.C. reinforcements posted to this unit for duty	GP
9 A.M. 15.4.16 Same billet	Admitted 14 to duty 11 evacuated 16 Remaining 38	GP
9 A.M. 16.4.-16 Same billet.	C section complete went to R.8 Central hop 36.5 "Fosse ten" with advanced Dressing Stations at BULLY GRENAY (R.11 a.4.1 hop 36 B) with advanced Post at PONT GRENAY M.1.D.4.1 hop 36 B and Bearers at CIté CALONNE	GP

Army Form C. 2118.

WAR DIARY
INTELLIGENCE SUMMARY.
(Erase heading not required.)

Instructions regarding War Diaries and Intelligence Summaries are contained in F.S. Regs., Part II. and the Staff Manual respectively. Title pages will be prepared in manuscript.

No 6 FIELD AMBULANCE
No.
Date

Hour, Date, Place	Summary of Events and Information	Remarks and references to Appendices
9 AM 16.4.16 continued	One Section of No 40 F.A. arrived by an advance party to take over these schools. Admitted 8. to duty 19. evacuated 1. Remaining 20	
9 AM 17.4.16 12 noon 17.4.16 R.B. Central Map 36 B "Fosse Ten"	Am on lines of march to R.B. Central. Arrived at R.B. Central. There are Buildings 3 blocks with accommodation for Sisters. 300 lying and 300 sitting. Handed over Ecole intermediare to No 40 F.A. Brought our own patients with us.	J.G.
9 AM 18.4.16 Same billet	Admitted wounded 1 officer 1 OR sick 1 OR to duty Nil evacuated 1 officer and 1 OR. Remaining 6 wounded 3 9 sick Capt. SJA Hurleston D.S.O. Returned by leave. Weather very hot 80	J.G.

Army Form C. 2118.

WAR DIARY
or
INTELLIGENCE SUMMARY.
(Erase heading not required.)

Instructions regarding War Diaries and Intelligence Summaries are contained in F.S. Regs., Part II. and the Staff Manual respectively. Title pages will be prepared in manuscript.

Hour, Date, Place	Summary of Events and Information	Remarks and references to Appendices
9 A.M. 19-4-16 Same Billet	Admitted 22 sick 1 Officer sick. To duty three evacuated 3 wounded 23 sick 1 Officer sick. Remaining one Officer sick - 38 sick 3 wounded. Lieut. J. H. M. Fay R.A.M.C was admitted to No. 69 Field Ambulance at 8.15 P.M. 16th Inf. and was marked on for offensive.	J
9 A.M. 20.4.-16 Same Billet	Admitted 1 Officer 23 Other Ranks sick. To duty three Evacuated one Officer 9 O.R. sick three wounded. Remaining 48 sick six wounded. Inspected the A.D. Stations went to R.A. Posts. Leave not quite central. Up intend to interview the A.D.M.S	J
9 A.M. 21.4.-16 Same Billet	Admitted 1 Officer 8 O.R. wounded 14 sick. To duty six evacuated 9 wounded 13 sick to Rest Station four wounded. Remaining 1 Officer sick wounded 39 sick	J

WAR DIARY
INTELLIGENCE SUMMARY.
(Erase heading not required.)

Army Form C. 2118.

Hour, Date, Place	Summary of Events and Information	Remarks and references to Appendices
9 AM 22-4-16 Same held	Admitted 1 Officer & 8 O.R. wounded 2 Officers 15 O.R. sick. Jodbuty 1 Officer & 7 O.R. evacuated 1 Officer 18 O.R. sick. One O.R. wounded Revd Statr. two. Remaining 1 Officer 10 O.R. wounded 1 Officer 32 O.R. sick	[signature]
9 AM 23-4-16 Same billet	Admitted one Officer 2 O.R. wounded, two Officers 11 O.R. sick. Jodbuty 1 evacuated one Officer. Two Officers 9 O.R. wounded. Remaining 2 Officers 3/ O.R. sick 3 O.R. wounded	[signature]
9 AM 24-4-16 Same billet	Admitted 20 sick 4 wounded. O.R. Jodbuty 8 sick one wounded evacuated 4 sick. Three wounded O.R. – Revd. Station 3 Remained 2 Sick Officers 47 O.Ranks. 3 O.R. injured Pt Barley Rayne JC reported his departure to 15 O.R. Beds as per manual entry	[signature]

Army Form C. 2118.

WAR DIARY
or
INTELLIGENCE SUMMARY.
(Erase heading not required.)

Instructions regarding War Diaries and Intelligence Summaries are contained in F. S. Regs., Part II. and the Staff Manual respectively. Title pages will be prepared in manuscript.

Hour, Date, Place	Summary of Events and Information	Remarks and references to Appendices
9 A.M. 25.4.16 Same billet	Admitted 8 wounded 22 sick. To duty one wounded two sick. Evacuated 4 wounded 4 sick Rest Station two. Remaining 3 sick 2 Officers 6 wounded 53 sick O.R. Instructions have been received to strike Batt. Strength Batt. Return from 19th Batt.	
9 A.M. 26.4.16 Same billet	Admitted 3 Officers 10 wounded T/17 sick O.R. To duty one Officer 8 O.R. evacuated 4 Officers 9 wounded 7 sick O.R. to Rest Station 3. Remaining 7 wounded 50 sick O.R.	
9 A.M. 27.4.16 Same billet	Admitted one Officer 13 wounded 16 sick O.R. To duty two Evacuated one Officer 8 wounded 7 Sick O.R. Remaining 12 wounded 4 (Sick O.R. Capt D W. Kelmey (proceded) on 15 days leave	

Forms/C. 2118/10

WAR DIARY
INTELLIGENCE SUMMARY.
(Erase heading not required.)

Army Form C. 2118.

Hour, Date, Place	Summary of Events and Information	Remarks and references to Appendices
9 AM 28.4.16 Some bullet	One Officer to wounded 9:22 sick D.R. admitted to duty 8 Evacuated sick wounded two sick D.R. Known my one Officer 7 wounded 752 O.R. sent D.R. Capt H.C. Chatfield R.A.M.C. O.R. Proceeded on duty to 15th Group Hosp. Artillery Reserve	[signature]
9 AM 29.4.16 Some bullet	Admitted one Officer 6 wounded 91 sick D.R. to duty two Evacuated 7 wounded six sick D.R. (Rail Station in Reuwing two Officers 8 wounded 44 sick D.R. Received Slight wound today while pressing A.D. Station 1 Officer)	[signature]
9 AM 30.4.16 Some bullet	Admitted one Officer six wounded 9 sick D.R. to duty 4 wounded two Officer two wounded 8 sick D.R. Reuwing 866 Officers 2 wounded D.R. sick D.R.	[signature] E. Sampson Major RAMC

2nd Div

N.B. to F. Amb.

May 1916.

COMMITTEE FOR THE
MEDICAL HISTORY OF THE WAR
Date 26 JUN 1916

WAR DIARY
INTELLIGENCE SUMMARY.
(Erase heading not required.)

Army Form C. 2118

Hour, Date, Place	Summary of Events and Information	Remarks and references to Appendices
9 AM 1-5-16 Josse Fm R 8 Central M36B	Admitted 12 wounded 22 sick DR. on duty 4 evacuated 6 wounded 5 sick DR to DRS. Remaining 1 sick Officer, 14 wounded 55 sick OR. 11 Remaining 1 sick Officer	[signature] Jan 21 Dr hosp Rouen
9 AM 2-5-16 Same billet	Admitted 1 Officer wounded 8 wounded 14 sick OR. on duty 1 evacuated 11 wounded 11 sick OR to DRS. 16 Remaining 2 Officers wounded 45 sick OR.	[signature]
9 AM 3-5-16 Same billet.	Admitted 1 Officer wounded 11 wounded 18 sick OR. to duty one died one evacuated one officer five wounded five sick OR to DRS 16 Remaining one Officer 10 wounded 43 sick OR Lieut KEITH Kane/Esq died from Bar.	[signature]
9 AM 4-5-16 Same billet	Admitted 7 wounded 15 sick OR. one evacuated 7 wounded 12 sick OR to DRS. Remaining ...	[signature]

6 Field Ambulance

WAR DIARY
or
INTELLIGENCE SUMMARY.
(Erase heading not required.)

Army Form C. 2118.

Hour, Date, Place	Summary of Events and Information	Remarks and references to Appendices
9AM 5.5.16 Same billet	Admitted 2 Sick Officers 5 O.R wounded and 13 Sick O.R Totally two admissions one Officer seriously wounded and 4 Sick O.R & O.R Strength 5 Running and Officers five wounded 74.5 Sick O.R	[signature]
9AM 6.6.16 Same billet	Admitted 7 wounded 16 Sick O.R 7 doubtful case evacuated 12 to D.R.S & Remaining Officers Sick 7 wounded 41 Sick O.R Capt Chatfield RAMC. to Posted to 15th Group H.Battery	[signature]
9AM 7.5.16 Same billet	Admitted one Officer 9 wounded 23 Sick O.R Twenty 8. O.R evacuated 1 Officer Sick 7 wounded 73 Sick O.R to D.R.S five Remaining 1 sick Officer six wounded 60 Sick O.R Capt Chatfield RAMC S.R rejoined Mult instructed on 6.6.16 by D.D.M.S. 10 Corps and Col ENSOR	[signature]

WAR DIARY
INTELLIGENCE SUMMARY
(Erase heading not required.)

Army Form C. 2118.

Hour, Date, Place	Summary of Events and Information	Remarks and references to Appendices
9.A.M. 8.5.16 Same billet	Admitted five wounded 3.3 sick OR. Injury 4. Evacuated 13 to DRS 4. Remaining 15 sek & Officers 5 pte wounded. one by Sgt OR. Capl Bain Rame joined for temp duty only from wod F A	G
9.A.M 9.5.16 Same billet	Admitted one sick, Officer 4 wounded and 19 sick OR. To duty 8 Evacuated 21 to DRS 7. Remaining 25 sek. 3 wounded & 37 sick OR.	G
9.A.M 10.5.16 Same billet	Admitted Officers 1 sek OR. 19 wounded 4 sek. To duty 8 OR. Evacuated Officers 25 sek OR 13 wounded 1 sek. Remaining Officers one & wounded 79 sek OR. Lt J B STEVENSON RAMC the joined from Base for duty.	G

WAR DIARY
—or—
INTELLIGENCE SUMMARY.
(Erase heading not required.)

Army Form C. 2118.

Hour, Date, Place	Summary of Events and Information	Remarks and references to Appendices
9 AM 11-5-16 Same billet	Admitted Officers one wounded 37 sick, OR 22 wounded 65 sick to duty Officers one OR 8 Evacuated OR 12 wounded 38 sick to DRS. OR 1 Remaining Officers two OR 19 sick wounded 71 sick	[signature]
9 AM 12-5-16 Same billet	Admitted Officers two OR sick wounded 22 sick to duty Off 18 Evacuated Officers two OR 11 wounded 23 sick. Returning 2 Offrs 8 wounded 55 sick. Capt J W McKinney rejoined from leave one section to 6 FA. Arrived to take over (part) the building 8	[signature]
9 AM 13-5-16 Same billet	Admitted one wounded OR 9 wounded 22 sick to duty One Officer OR 3 sick Evacuated Wn Officers 10 wounded 7 25 sick OR (Includes 15 Evac transferred to No 69 FA to DRS 15. Remaining 6 wounded OR. Handed over post of BUY GRENAY to 67 FA	[signature]

WAR DIARY
INTELLIGENCE SUMMARY

Army Form C. 2118.

Hour, Date, Place	Summary of Events and Information	Remarks and references to Appendices
9 AM 14.5.16 Same billet	Admitted 1 wounded. 72 sick O.R. four wounded & 7 sick O.R. to duty. four 2 evacuated 14 O.R. to DRS. 4 Remaining 8 Officers 7 wounded 28 O.R. sick	G. Thompson
9 A.M. 15.5.16 Same billet	Admitted 7 wounded 13 sick O.R. to duty five O.R. evacuated 3 Officers 8 6 O.R. to DRS. Five Remaining 8 wounded + 21 sick + sick O.R.	G.
9 A.M. 16.5.16 Same billet	Admitted 2 sick Officers 10 wounded 73 sick O.R. to duty six O.R. evacuated two Officers 10 wounded 12 sick O.R. to DRS 11 O.R. Remaining one Officer S. sick + one wounded. 14 sick O.R. Capt Hoff Chatfield RAMC S.R. R.E.H. for duty	G.
9 AM 17.5.16 Same billet	Admitted 9 wounded 65 sick O.R. to duty two O.R. Died two wounded evacuated 4 wounded Five sick O.R. Evan Remaining 10 Officer sick 3 wounded 13 sick O.R. Capt Walshe DSO RAMC as DADMS temp duty	G.

Army Form C. 2118.

WAR DIARY
or
INTELLIGENCE SUMMARY.
(Erase heading not required.)

No 6 FIELD AMBULANCE

Instructions regarding War Diaries and Intelligence Summaries are contained in F. S. Regs., Part II. and the Staff Manual respectively. Title pages will be prepared in manuscript.

Hour, Date, Place	Summary of Events and Information	Remarks and references to Appendices
9AM 18.5.16 Same Billet	Admitted six wounded 17 Sick OR. Evacuated two wounded 10 Sick OR to DRS 11. Remaining 1 Officer two wounded and 14 Sick OR	
9 AM 19.5.16 Same Billet	Admitted four wounded and one Sick OR. On duty. evacuated three wounded six wounded six sick OR to DRS 9. Remaining nil. Unit moved from Josse to R & Central & NAISNIL to ES RUITZ arriving there at 10.15 AM. Handed over Running Buildings to 6 g F Z Amb	
9AM 19.5.16 MAISNIL les RUITZ J 36 c 8 6 36. B	Arrived at 10.15AM on 19th Billeted in field and proceed at 7 AM 6 MONNEVILLE M5a.4 Y 36. B Sent on transport sheet from Josse Em to Monneville also advanced Party to Clean out Stables and Billets Weather fine	

Army Form C. 2118.

WAR DIARY
or
INTELLIGENCE SUMMARY.
(Erase heading not required.)

Instructions regarding War Diaries and Intelligence Summaries are contained in F.S. Regs., Part II. and the Staff Manual respectively. Title pages will be prepared in manuscript.

Hour, Date, Place	Summary of Events and Information	Remarks and references to Appendices
9 AM 21-5-16 MONNEVILLE N 5 a 4.4 36.B.	Arrived at noon. Day very warm and men much fatigued from lengthy march. Part of this is to be small Decay in reaching water supply	[signature]
9 AM 22-5-16 Same billet	Nothing to report. Unit forming itself up in billets. Require lorries at 1 AM. to be ready to proceed at an hours notice	[signature]
9 AM 23-5-16 FRESNICOURT Q.19.d.4.3 Sheet 36B	Received orders at 3.45 PM to have to hospital address arrived there at 10 PM. Took over a field hospital of 3 wards & 50 sick & wounded. HD motor ambulance cars & 16 bearers arrived both from huts 6 and 100 FA. Received instructions from ADMS. to have here Bearers Subdivns dressing ready to move out at a moments notice had Unfurniture not arrived A Section opened up to receive 500 wounded Bearers very chilly on arrival	[signature]

Forms/C. 2118/10

WAR DIARY
or
INTELLIGENCE SUMMARY.

Army Form C. 2118.

Hour, Date, Place	Summary of Events and Information	Remarks and references to Appendices
9 A.M. 24.5.16 Same billet	Lt. O'Kell and 36 bearers and four ambulance Cars reported at billets an Boris at X.19.b.5.6. Sheet 36 c & 4 N.C.Os proceeded via Point G over X.16.d.9.3. 36 sheet 36 c to S.13.d.7.7. sheet 36 c then collected wounded from our E. VALLEY carried them to A.D.S. 75th Division Field Ambulance. This bearer subdivision supply aid bearer work.	[signature]
9 A.M. 25.5.16 Same billet	Sent a bearer subdivision with Lts. Lyons & Keith to assist at Point G and Calais Rouge (S.13.d.7.7. sheet C)	[signature]
9 A.M. 26.5.16 ESTREE-CAUCHIE W.2.a.4.6.	Unit minus two bearer subdivisions moved to Magnicourt address and also LES 4 VENTS W.9.a.1.9 sheet 36S and took over the premises from 5th Indian field ambulance. Also took over Evacuees dressing station at Point G. Capt. Cunningham and 20 men to left of line from 4 Feb. now Fat. S. 25. C. 5.8. and N. St. ELOI. F.8.d central map 51 C	[signature]

WAR DIARY
—or—
INTELLIGENCE SUMMARY.
(Erase heading not required.)

Army Form C. 2118.

Hour, Date, Place	Summary of Events and Information	Remarks and references to Appendices
9 A.M 27.5.16 Same billet.	51 patients were taken over from 5th London Field Ambulance. 7/6 Wheelden R.A.M.C. was wounded on 24th. Admitted 2 Officers – 14 wounded. 33 sick OR today. 7 evacuated. 2 wounded + 2 no sect to DRS. 12 wounded + 17 sick. Remaining 2 Officers 19 wounded 41 sick OR	[signature]
9 A.M 28.5.16 Same billet.	Admitted 9 wounded Officers, 25 wounded + 20 sick OR to duty 9 wounded two Officers, 5 wounded 7 sick. Remaining 10 Officers 3 wounded + 43 sick OR. Inspected the Divisional Front – The Reg¹ in action were 13th Essex, 2nd & S. Staffs, 22 and 23 R. Fusiliers. No wounded from the line must come down through Cabaret Rouge Pont G	[signature]
9. A.M 29.5.16 Same billet.	Admitted one Officer, 9 wounded, 15 sick OR to duty 14 evacuated two Officers, 14 wounded + 7 sick OR to DRS 11. Remaining 10 Officers, 15 wounded + 51 sick OR. Lieut. KEITH went to Jeune Essone School, Bethune	[signature]

WAR DIARY
INTELLIGENCE SUMMARY.
(Erase heading not required.)

Army Form C. 2118.

Hour, Date, Place	Summary of Events and Information	Remarks and references to Appendices
9 A.M. 30.5.16 Same billet	Admitted two Officers 25 wounded 12 sick OR. To duty one evac. 6 wounded 8 sick OR to HQ RE 13. Remaining two Officers 24 wounded 30 sick OR. Visited Point G. CABARET ROUGE	[signature]
9 A.M. 31.5.16 Same billet	Admitted 8 wounded 18 sick OR to duty two evacuated two Officers 14 wounded and 4 sick OR to DRS Fu OR. Remaining 13 wounded 73 sick OR. Par. Pts Rauc (bearer wounded) tracked route with ADMS II Divs usz.	C Newport Major RAMC

2nd Division

No 6 Field Ambulance

June 1916

WAR DIARY
or
INTELLIGENCE SUMMARY.

(Erase heading not required.)

Army Form C. 2118

6 2a Ccent [Vol 2]

Hour, Date, Place	Summary of Events and Information	Remarks and references to Appendices
En Quatre Vents W 9 Central Sheet 36 E. 9AM. 1-6-16	Admitted 1 Officer 14 wounded 20 sick OR. To duty one wounded. Evacuated eight to DRS 5. Remain upon Officer 2 16 wounded 49 sick OR.	Sampson
Same billet 9AM. 2-6-16	Admitted seven Officers 103 wounded 25 sick OR. To duty three Evacuated two Officers 34 wounded and 8 sick OR. to DRS 15. Remaining 5 Officers 17 wounded 46 sick OR. Received instructions to send 24 stretcher bearers to Pont Yaures to 4th HUNTER RANCE (bearers) wounded surely	
9AM 3-6-16 Same billet	Moved H# OS 3 luit from ESTREE CAUCHIE to hospital Bddns Div Admitted 3 Officers 64 wounded 25 sick OR. To duty one evacuated 7 Officers 108 wounded H.Q. 55 sick OR. to DRS 45 Remain 2 officers six wounded and 7 sick OR.	

Forms/C. 2118/10

WAR DIARY
INTELLIGENCE SUMMARY
(Erase heading not required.)

Army Form C. 2118.

Hour, Date, Place	Summary of Events and Information	Remarks and references to Appendices
Somme billet 9 AM 4.6.16	Admitted two sick, 14 wounded and 14 sick O.R. to duty. Three evacuated. Three officers, 1 wounded sick O.R. Remaining on Effec. 10 wounded and 8 sick	Champion Major Rand
Somme billet p.m. 5/6/16	7th men temporarily attached to this unit. Major Sampson reported on sick. Admitting 8 O.Rs. 14 wounded, 27 sick Evacuated 1 to 8 F.A. S. 2 F.Rs. 8 O.Rs. 13 wounded & 4 sick. To 8 F.A. S. 2 F.Rs. Remaining Officers 1 sick. Men gunners 8 355 sick	St J.H. Walker Capt R.A.M.S.
Somme billet a.m. 6/6/16	R.A.M. Officers 1 attending 8 f.Rs 13 wounded 18 sick Injury to 1 sick f.Rs 2 sick Evac. to 1 wounded f.Rs 5 wounded 12 sick To D.R.S. — — f.Rs 2 wounded 3 sick Remaining — f.Rs 14 do 31 do.	St J H W

WAR DIARY
INTELLIGENCE SUMMARY.
(Erase heading not required.)

Army Form C. 2118.

Hour, Date, Place	Summary of Events and Information	Remarks and references to Appendices
Same billet 9 a.m. 2/6/16	Adm. Officers + 1 man / 1 NCO. The gunners 15 cwt. — 3 cars. Lorry — 1 — do 8 runners 11 do E.T. — 1 — do 2 do 11 do L.P.S. — 1 — do 8 do 23 do. Runners — do — 1 NCO do 8 do —	Stanley
Same billet 9 a.m. 3/6/16	Adm. Officers / 1 NCO / 1 runner. The S.M.O. Gunners 15 cwt. — 1 — Duty — 1 — " — " 3 " 4 " E. + R. — " 1 " — " 1 NCO " 2 " 6 " L.P.S. — 1 " — " — " 8 " 26 " Runners — " — " — " Capt. R.D. MCGEAGH returned from leave + is taken on this unit for furnish and duty. Capt. H.T. CHATFIELD + horse from 1st K.E.H. in completion of Establishment. Lieut. Adm. Stanley Sh. + do Rts in the afternoon.	Stanley

Army Form C. 2118.

WAR DIARY
INTELLIGENCE SUMMARY.
(Erase heading not required.)

Instructions regarding War Diaries and Intelligence Summaries are contained in F.S. Regs., Part II. and the Staff Manual respectively. Title pages will be prepared in manuscript.

No 6 FIELD AMBULANCE

Hour, Date, Place	Summary of Events and Information	Remarks and references to Appendices
Somewhere 9 a.m. 9/6/16	R.A.M. Officers — 3 F.M.4, 21 Officers & 119 O.Ranks 1 " Staff — 1 " " " " " F.P.S. — — " 15 " " " D.R.S. — — " " " 14 " " " Running — — " " " 27 " " " Lieut J. R. BOYD R.A.M.C. F.S. attached for duty with 36th Brigade R.F.A. Duty with 36th Brigade R.F.A. B/4 B Cavalry — 1 F.R. Rejoins. Wounds.	Sgd H.H.
Somewhere 9 a.m. 10/6/16	R.A.M. Officers 1 1 Officers & 7 O.Ranks 15 sick Staff — 1 " 1 " " " " F.P.S. — — " 8 " " & sick D.R.S. — — " 1 " " 5 " " Running " 1 " 1 " Oths 11 " 31 "	Sgd H.H.

WAR DIARY
INTELLIGENCE SUMMARY.
(Erase heading not required.)

Army Form C. 2118.

Hour, Date, Place	Summary of Events and Information	Remarks and references to Appendices
Spanbroek 9 a.m. 11/6/16	R.A.M. officers 2 nursers O.R.s 2 wounded 20 sick Batty — 1 " " 1 " 2 " B — 1 " " 5 " 10 " B.R.S. — " " 5 " — " Remaining — 2 " 1 sick " 3 " 33 "	S/g.H.S.
Spanbroek 9 a.m. 12/6/16	R.A.M. officers O.R.s 5 wounded 21 sick Batty — " " 1 " 2 " B — 1 wounded 1 sick " 3 " 16 " B.R.S. — " " 1 " 1 " Remaining — 1 " 1 " 3 " 35 "	S/g.H.S.
Spanbroek 12/6/16	Handed over to Major G.A. KENPTHORNE. on his taking command of the unit. Taken over — galenpthortane Maj. R.a.e	S/g.K.KK

Army Form C. 2118.

WAR DIARY
INTELLIGENCE SUMMARY.
(Erase heading not required.)

Hour, Date, Place	Summary of Events and Information	Remarks and references to Appendices
Same Billet 9 AM 13.6.16	Admitted - Officers one sick O.R. 4 W. 23.S To duty — 1 W. one sick OR — 2 S. Evacuated — — OR. 3W. 13 S. To DRS OR — 2 S. Remaining 1.S. OR 4 W 41 S.	Gallentstone Major Rose.
Same Billet 9 AM 14.6.16.	Adm - off. 1.S. OR. 5W. 27.S. Duty. — — 4.S. Evac. — 1S. 5W 19 S. DRS — — 8 S. Remaining 1 S — 4W 37 S. Visited ADS during afternoon of 13/6/16. and arranged for relief of Officers & Bearers as under- Capt McGeagh & Capt Chatfield in relief of Lt O'Kell & Lt Stevenson. Lt Lyons remained. 2 NCO's and 16 Bearers A Sec. in relief of same no. of B Sec Bearers	Gen.

Battle Casualty. 75894 Pte Peele slightly wounded hand & thigh.

Army Form C. 2118.

WAR DIARY
or
INTELLIGENCE SUMMARY.
(Erase heading not required.)

Hour, Date, Place	Summary of Events and Information	Remarks and references to Appendices
Same billet 9 AM 15.6.16	Adm. Offs 3S — OR 1W. 22.S. Duty — 1S. 1W. 1.S. Evacuated — — 2W. 19.S. To DRS — 3S. — 4.S. Remaining — — 2W. 35.S. Lt Lyons to 1st R. Berks for temp duty.	gan.
Same billet 9 AM 16.6.16	Adm. Offs. 1W. OR 17W. 32.S. Duty 1W. 1S. ╪ 3.S. Evac — — 4W. 9.S. DRS — — 1W. 4.S. Remaining — 2S 14W. 51.S.	gan.
Same billet 9 AM 17.6.16	Adm Offs 2W. 2.S. OR 19W 23.S. Duty — — 1W. 3.S. Evac — — 17W. 21.S. DRS — — — 8.S. Remaining 2W. 4S. 15W 42.S.	gan.

WAR DIARY
INTELLIGENCE SUMMARY.

(Erase heading not required.)

Army Form C. 2118.

Hour, Date, Place	Summary of Events and Information	Remarks and references to Appendices
Same billet 18.6.16.	Admitted Off 2S. Duty Evac. Off 2W. 2S. D.R.S. Rem. Offs 4S OR W5 - 30 S. W4 - S5. W5 - S15. W2 - S10 W9 - S 42. Lt. BOYD from 36 Brig RFA to med insp room VILLERS AU BOIS. Maj. SAMPSON returned off leave, handed over permanent charge. Inspected ADS and Regimental Aid Posts. Also the detatchment at VILLERS AU BOIS.	goat. goat.
Same billet 19.6.16.	Adm. Off 1 W Duty Offs - 2S. Evac Offs - 2S DRS Rem 1W OR W5 S.19. OR W1 S 5. OR W4 S10. OR W2 S13. OR W7 S 33. Major SAMPSON proceeded to report to DDMS ETAPLES and struck off strength	goat.

Army Form C. 2118.

WAR DIARY
INTELLIGENCE SUMMARY.
(Erase heading not required.)

Hour, Date, Place	Summary of Events and Information	Remarks and references to Appendices
Some billet 20/6/16	Adm. offs 1S. OR 6W. 15S. Duty - - OR - 1S. Evac. offs 1W. OR 3W. 11S. DRS - - OR 1W. 7S. Rem. offs 1S. OR 9W. 29S. 1st LYONS reported for duty at CABARET ROUGE yesterday	Jas ⎯
Same billet 21.6.16	Adm. off. nil OR. 4W. 22S. Duty - - 1S. Evac. - - 5W. 12S. DRS off S1. 2W. 6S. Rem. - - 6W. 32S.	Jas
" 22.6.16	Adm. offs 1S. OR 5W. 23S. Duty - - OR 1W. 1S. Evac. offs 1S. OR 1W. 17S. DRS - - OR 3W. 33S. Rem. offs 1S. OR 2W. - OR 4W. 35S. Lt. Col. OKELL to 2/4 L.F. for temporary duty. DDMS 4th Corps inspected hospital.	Jas.

No. 6 FIELD AMBULANCE

Instructions regarding War Diaries and Intelligence Summaries are contained in F.S. Regs., Part II. and the Staff Manual respectively. Title pages will be prepared in manuscript.

Army Form C. 2118.

WAR DIARY
INTELLIGENCE SUMMARY.
(Erase heading not required.)

Instructions regarding War Diaries and Intelligence Summaries are contained in F. S. Regs., Part II. and the Staff Manual respectively. Title pages will be prepared in manuscript.

Hour, Date, Place	Summary of Events and Information	Remarks and references to Appendices
Same Billet 23.6.16	Adm. off. nil Duty " " Died " 1 S. Evac " 1 DRS " 1 Rem " 1	O.R. 15 W. 30 S. O.R. — 1 S. O.R. 1 W. O.R. 6 W. 9 S. O.R. 1 W. 4 S. O.R. 11 W. 51 S.	gan.
24.6.16	Adm. off. nil Duty Evac DRS Rem Inspected ADS. Roofing of dug outs proceeding satisfactorily	O.R. 5 W. 22 S. 1 W. 4 S. 4 W. 16 S. 1 W. 9 S. 10 W. 44 S. 6	gan.
25.6.16	Adm. off. nil Duty Evac DRS Rem Surg. gen. W.G. MACPHERSON inspected the Lipitz yesterday.	O.R. 6 W. 18 S. 3 S. 2 W. 14 S. 2 W. 9 S. 12 W. 36 S.	gan.
26.6.16	Adm. off. nil Duty Evac DRS Rem L/LYONS to VILLERS AUX BOIS and L/BOYD to ADS.	O.R. 11 W. 19 S. O.R. 1 S. O.R. 7 W. 7 S. O.R. 3 W. 9 S. O.R. 13 W. 38 S.	gan.

WAR DIARY

INTELLIGENCE SUMMARY.

(Erase heading not required.)

Army Form C. 2118.

Hour, Date, Place	Summary of Events and Information	Remarks and references to Appendices
27.6.16.	Adm. Off 4 W. OR 56 W. 18 S. Duty OR 1 W. 1 S. Evac. 2 W. OR 13 W. 14 S. DRS 3 W. 9 S. Rem. 2 W. 52 W. 32 S. Of these cases 1 Off. 31 OR were the result of a raid by the 1st R Berks.	gan.
28.6.16.	Adm. Off nil OR 2 W. 23 S. Duty 3 W. 2 S. Evac. 1 W. 35 W. 11 S. DRS 1 W. 7 W. 9 S. Rem. 9 W. 33 S. Surg. Gen. Pike visited the hospital yesterday afternoon. Inspected ADS yesterday. All correct.	gan.
29.6.16	Adm. Off 1 S OR 8 W. 20 S. Duty 1 W. 2 S. Evac. 1 W. 1 W. 8 S. DRS 1 S 4 W. 7 S. Rem. 11 W. 36 S. Inspected detachment at VILLERS AU BOIS yesterday	gan.

WAR DIARY
INTELLIGENCE SUMMARY.
(Erase heading not required.)

Army Form C. 2118.

Hour, Date, Place	Summary of Events and Information	Remarks and references to Appendices
Same billet 9AM 30.6.16	Adm. Off 1S. OR 7W 22S Duty 1S. - 1S Evac 1S. 7W 11S DRS 4W 10S Rem. 1S 7W 36S Various works have been completed since taking over the buildings at QUATRE VENTS from the 5th London FA. Ground has been levelled, gravel for paths laid down. A kitchen with cement floors – a much wanted improvement – has been built, and a proper ablution room has been erected. Tables and benches has also been made for the improvised dining room. The latrine arrangement has also been much improved and are still in hand. All the work has been done by the personnel of the hospital with the assistance of two skilled workmen supplied by the RE. At the ADS parties of men supplied by the ADMS have much improved the existing dug-outs, and men of the unit have been patching shell holes with success in the CARENCY road	G. Wemysthorne Lt Col. RAMC OC. 6 FA

2nd Division

No. 6 Field Ambulance

July 1915

July 1915

COMMITTEE FOR THE
MEDICAL HISTORY OF THE WAR
Date 13 SEP. 1915

Army Form C. 2118.

Vol 22

WAR DIARY
INTELLIGENCE SUMMARY.
(Erase heading not required.)

No 6 FIELD AMBULANCE

Instructions regarding War Diaries and Intelligence Summaries are contained in F.S. Regs., Part II. and the Staff Manual respectively. Title pages will be prepared in manuscript.

Hour, Date, Place	Summary of Events and Information	Remarks and references to Appendices

Quatre Vents – 1/7/16	Adm. off. S.1.
	Duty
	Evac
	DRS
	Rem. S.2.
		OR W.19. S.21.
		          S.1.
		     W.8 S.19.
		          S.3.
		     W.18. S.35.
			Quatemptine
			Lt.Col RAMC

2/7/16	Adm. off W.3
	Duty 1S.
	Evac W1· S.1.
	DRS
	Rem. W.2
	Inspected ADS yesterday and the advanced posts in the Zouave Valley.
		OR W.49 S.21
		          S.1.
		    W.22 S.11.
		    W.1. S.12
		    W.44 S.32.
			gan.

3/7/16	Adm. off.
	Duty
	Evac 2W.
	DRS
	Rem.
	
	DDMS 4th Corps inspected hospital yesterday
		OR. W.11 S.16.
		          S.4.
		     W.35 S.11.
		     W.5 S.4.
		     W.15 S.29.
			gak.

Army Form C. 2118.

WAR DIARY
INTELLIGENCE SUMMARY.
(Erase heading not required.)

No 6 FIELD AMBULANCE

Instructions regarding War Diaries and Intelligence Summaries are contained in F. S. Regs., Part II. and the Staff Manual respectively. Title pages will be prepared in manuscript.

Hour, Date, Place	Summary of Events and Information			Remarks and references to Appendices
QUATRE VENTS 4.7.16	Adm - Off Duty Died. Evac DRS Rem.	W.2 W.1. W.1	OR W.27 S.14. S.3.	
	OC Divl train inspected horse transport.			gak.
5.7.16	Adm. Off Evac DRS Rem.	W.1.	OR W5 S.30. W17 S.7. W.8 S.8. S.47.	gak.
6.7.16	Adm. Off Duty Evac DRS Rem.	S.1. S.1.	OR W.2 S.22 W.1 S.3 W.3 S.18. W.4 S.16 W.2 S.38	gak.

Forms/C. 2118/10

Army Form C. 2118.

WAR DIARY
INTELLIGENCE SUMMARY.
(Erase heading not required.)

Instructions regarding War Diaries and Intelligence Summaries are contained in F. S. Regs., Part II. and the Staff Manual respectively. Title pages will be prepared in manuscript.

No. 6 FIELD AMBULANCE

Hour, Date, Place	Summary of Events and Information	Remarks and references to Appendices
QUATRE VENTS 7.7.16	Adm. Off W.3 S1 Duty – – Evac. – W.1 S1. DRS – – Rem – W.2 S1.	OR W.17 S.24 – S.4 W.8 S.8. W.2 S.1. W.9 S.49	J.a.K.
8.7.16.	Adm. Off nil Duty – Evac. W.1. DRS W.1 S1. Rem – Inspected advanced dressing station with Col. Meek DDMS 4th C.	OR W.8 S.18. W.1 S.3. W.4 S.22 – S.9 W.12 S.33	J.a.K
9.7.16	Adm. Off nil. Duty – Died – Evac. – DRS W.1 S1 Rem. –	OR W.21 S.31. – S.5. W.1 S.16. W.12 S.6. W.1 S.37. W.19	J.a.K.
10.7.16	Adm. Off W.1 S1 Duty – Evac. – DRS W.2 S.2.	OR W.7 S.23. OR – S.2 W.10 S.10 W.4 S.6. W.12 S.42	J.a.K.

Army Form C. 2118.

WAR DIARY
or
INTELLIGENCE SUMMARY.

(Erase heading not required.)

Instructions regarding War Diaries and Intelligence Summaries are contained in F. S. Regs., Part II. and the Staff Manual respectively. Title pages will be prepared in manuscript.

Hour, Date, Place	Summary of Events and Information	Remarks and references to Appendices
QUATRE VENTS. 11.7.16.	Adm. Off IS. OR W.14 S.31. Duty — — — Evac. IS 1W. W7 S.14 DRS — 1W. W4 S.4 Rem. — — W15 S.55.	gen.
12.7.16	Adm. Off IS 1W OR W19 S19 Duty — — — W1 S2 Died — — — — Evac — — — W17 S15 DRS IS. — — N1 S12 Rem. — — — W15 S45 Capt McKINNEY in relief of Capt CHATFIELD to ADS. 11.7.	gen.
13.7.16	Adm. Off W1 S1 OR W20 S22 Duty — — — W4 S2 Died — — — W1 — Evac W1 S1 — W7 S4 DRS — S1 — W3 S9 Rem. — — — W20 S52 Lt O.KELL admitted Rob - synovitis Knee Pt REYNOLDS Steel stuck. Lt BOYD, Sgt. B.J. JOHNSTON E, and Pt V. REYNOLDS escorted 3 men RE buried at ADS, under heavy steel fire.	gen.

WAR DIARY or INTELLIGENCE SUMMARY.

Army Form C. 2118.

(Erase heading not required.)

Hour, Date, Place	Summary of Events and Information	Remarks and references to Appendices
QUATRE VENTS. 14/7/16	Adm. Off S1 Duty OR W11 S28 Evac W1 S2 DRS W6 S11 Rem S2 W6 S55 W18 S62	gak
15.7.16	Adm. Off S1. Duty OR W2 S20. Died W2 S3 Evac W1 S8. DRS W3 S11 Rem S3 W13 S60 Inspected all advanced posts yesterday - all correct.	gak.
16.7.16.	Adm. Off Duty OR W6 S27 Evac S1 W7 S31. DRS W5 S18. Rem S2 - - W7 S38. Inspected VILLERS AO BOIS inspection room. The sanitation of the place has been much improved under the supervision of Lts BOYD & LYONS. 2 p.m. One Section 5th London FA arrived to take over ADS.	gak.

Army Form C. 2118.

WAR DIARY
— or —
INTELLIGENCE SUMMARY.
(Erase heading not required.)

Instructions regarding War Diaries and Intelligence Summaries are contained in F.S. Regs., Part II. and the Staff Manual respectively. Title pages will be prepared in manuscript.

No. 9 FIELD AMBULANCE

Hour, Date, Place	Summary of Events and Information	Remarks and references to Appendices
17.7.16 QUATRE VENTS.	Admitted Off. W1 S1. O.R. W3 S15. Duty S1. W3 S10. Evac. S 18. Rem. W1 S2 W7 S25.	ganl
18.7.16 Q19.d.7.1 FRESNICOURT	Adm. Off — O.R. S4. Duty W1 S2 S5. Evac nil W7 S.24 Rem. nil FA moved from last billet on 17th 11.30 AM and proceeded to the marginally named billet. Lt J Lyons to 13th Essex for duty. 5th London FA took over the hospital at QUATRE VENTS on departure of unit.	ganl
19.7.16 FERME D'ESTRAYELLE	Adm 10 sick OR and evacuated to 22 CCS Unit moved out to marginally named billet at 10.30 AM arriving 2 o'clock, yesterday. Lt C.C. OKELL evacuated to 22 CCS, Synovitis Knee. Capt J R HARRACK RAMC (TC) joined from 13 Sta Hp for duty. Lt Qmr C. DUNGLISON arrived from England for duty in relief of Lt BIRCH.	ganl

Army Form C. 2118.

WAR DIARY
or
INTELLIGENCE SUMMARY.
(Erase heading not required.)

Instructions regarding War Diaries and Intelligence Summaries are contained in F.S. Regs., Part II. and the Staff Manual respectively. Title pages will be prepared in manuscript.

No. 6 FIELD AMBULANCE

Hour, Date, Place	Summary of Events and Information	Remarks and references to Appendices
FERME D'ESTRAELLE. 20/7/16	Sick state nil. Ambulance closed 1st E.BIRCH proceeded to No 18 Ad. Sep MS. yesterday	G.A.K
SALEUX 21/7/16.	Unit entrained at PERNES CHATELAIN at 11 PM last night. Owned at SALEUX 10 AM.	G.A.K
CORBIE 22/7/16	Remained in a field near the station until 5 PM yesterday then marked to present billet arriving at 11.30 PM.	G.A.K
MAIN DRESSING STN. DIVE.CORSE J24 B Sheet 62d 23/7/16.	Tent subdivisions proceeded to this Camp yesterday arriving at 4.30 PM. Unit placed under orders of the Commandant to work with other F.A's as a section of the whole. Bearer subdivisions under Capt MCGEAGH remained with orders to follow 5th Brigade when they march.	G.G.K.
do. 24.7.16.	Bearer Subdivisions spent last night at CORBIE.	G.A.K.
do. 25.7.16.	Bearer Subdivision bivouacked in HAPPY VALLEY with 5th Bryg. Visited them there.	G.A.K
do. 26.7.16	Bearers took over posts at CARNOY and BERNAFAY WOOD last evening. Horse amb. waggon & forage carts and water cart remained at SAPPER CORNER.	G.A.K.

WAR DIARY
INTELLIGENCE SUMMARY.
(Erase heading not required.)

Army Form C. 2118.

Place	Date	Hour	Summary of Events and Information	Remarks and references to Appendices
MAIN DRESSING STATION		1916		
	27.7		Battle Casualty. Pte WADE. GSW arm (slight) evacuated. Arranged to send up rations daily to SAPPER CORNER, to be carried up thence by forage cart. S.S. Major BURDELL ASC reported for duty.	
	28.7		Battle Casualties - Pte MILLER C. and CLARK N. GSW Scalp (slight) - evacuated Pte ROEBUCK. ASC MT. GSW R. Leg & Shell Shock (slight) - not evacuated. ADS under heavy shell fire, especially goo shells. The PH G helmet is found to be ample protection against the latter.	
	29.7		Battle casualty Pte BLOWERS.W. GSW L. Thigh (slight) The work at the ADS is extremely arduous and the position under constant shell fire. Three extra ASC drivers applied for and obtained. Visited reserve dressing post at BRONFAY FARM which has been occupied by reserve bearers in place of CARNOY (evacuated with approval of ADMS.)	
	30.7		Battle casualties Pte KERR R. W. skull stock. Pte WAYNE. W. GSW R. side. Pte COTTER W.F. GSW R arm & leg (slight) Pte WARREN.C. mumps. Believed Killed. All 6 FA Bearers returned to BRONFAY FARM much exhausted. By order of ADMS the ADS is being worked by each FA Bearer divn. alternately in 4 day reliefs, reinforcements being sent up on demand from the others at BRONFAY FARM. Lt BOYD awarded MC for gallantry on 13.7.16.	

J.A Hampton
Lt Col R.A.M.C

Army Form C. 2118.

WAR DIARY
INTELLIGENCE SUMMARY.
(Erase heading not required.)

Place	Date	Hour	Summary of Events and Information	Remarks and references to Appendices
DIVE COPSE	31.7		Battle casualties - P/Hampson W.B, Shuter W, Heel I.R, Owen E.J, Scott W.B, Duggan T, Crees A.H, Petre W, Kemble N.H, Jeffery A. all evacuated wounded yesterday. Capt. J.B. Matthews reported for duty.	J. Kempthorne Lt Colonel OC 6 FA

No. 6. Field Ambulance.

2nd Div

Aug. 1916

COMMITTEE FOR THE
MEDICAL HISTORY OF THE WAR
Date 26 OCT 1915

Confidential.

A.A.M.S.
    2nd Division

Herewith War Diary
(A.F. C2118) for the month
of August 1916.

J.W. Templeton
Lt Col RAMC
OC N°6 F.A.

Army Form C. 2118.

6th F.A.

WAR DIARY
INTELLIGENCE SUMMARY.
(Erase heading not required.)

Place	Date	Hour	Summary of Events and Information	Remarks and references to Appendices
DIVE COPSE.	Aug 1916 1.		Sent up 30 men from the tent division to reinforce Bearers at BRONFAY FARM and Capt CHATFIELD. A quiet day yesterday. The remainder of the tent division continues to work at the main dressing station	
	2.		Visited BRONFAY FARM - Capt J.B.MATTHEWS and 9 O.R. attached to Wooling Dressing Station at this place.	
	3.		All Bearers and Bearer officers went up to BERNAFAY WOOD A.D.S. last night.	
	4.		10 Reinforcements joined yesterday	
	5.		Battle Casualty. Pte McDONNELL.N. Shell abrasion back. 25 Bearers lent from tent division returned to H.Q. Visited BRONFAY FARM - all correct. Relief proceeding satisfactorily. Two A.S.C. horse transport reinforcements arrived for duty.	
	6.		Six reinforcements R.A.M.C.	
	7.		Visited BRONFAY FARM - all satisfactory	
	9.		Battle Casualty yesterday. Sgt. JENKINS W.E. GSW. R. Heel slight. to duty. Sgt ROBIN.SON G.F. A.S.C. Shoulder (slight) to duty. Lt BOYD to temp. med. charge 1st Kings	
	10		Six reinforcements RAMC arrived for duty yesterday. Orders received for Bearer Divn. to proceed to Sandpits near MEAULT on relief of 24th Divn. to day. Visited BRONFAY FARM yesterday.	JAM.

Army Form C. 2118.

WAR DIARY
INTELLIGENCE SUMMARY.
(Erase heading not required.)

Instructions regarding War Diaries and Intelligence Summaries are contained in F. S. Regs., Part II. and the Staff Manual respectively. Title pages will be prepared in manuscript.

Place	Date	Hour	Summary of Events and Information	Remarks and references to Appendices
	1916.			
YDIVE COPSE	11.9	9 PM	Beaver moved yesterday to SANDPITS.	
VILLE-SUR-ANCRE.	12.9		Tent division moved yesterday evening to this place. Bivouacs in open by river. All transport proceeded under OC Div. train to DAOURS - including water carts	
	13.9		Here all yesterday - flies, mosquitos, water difficult to arrange for owing to absence of Carts. Beaver joined yesterday.	
PICQUIGNY	14.9		Marched to MERICOURT 5 PM. Last evening. Tactical train 6.45 PM - arrived SALEUX 9 PM. Lorry for carrying packs - marched 9.30 PM - arrived here 1 AM.	
	15.9		Billets excellent. Opened in a Château. Adm. 9 sick OR, Duty 2, Rem 7. Six reinforcements arrived.	
	16.8		Adm. Off. W.1, OR S.15, W.i. Duty OR S.1. Rem. Off. W.1. OR S.21, W.1.	
FRESSELLES.	17.8		Marched 4.30 PM. arrived here yesterday 7.30 PM. Adm. Off S.1, OR S.28 Evac. Off 15. 1 W. OR S 46 W.1. Duty ORs 2. Rem O.R. S.1.	
GORGES.	18.9		Arrived yesterday 1.30 PM - small dirty village 70 inhabitants. 1st BoyD to 1st King's for duty, 4th STEVENSON to temp. duty yesterday to 22 R.F. Capt. MILLER DSO joined FA for temporary duty. Adm. Off S.1, OR S.37 Evac Off S.1 OR S.37 Duty 1.	

WAR DIARY
or
INTELLIGENCE SUMMARY.

Army Form C. 2118.

(Erase heading not required.)

Place	Date	Hour	Summary of Events and Information	Remarks and references to Appendices
BUSLES ARTOIS	19.8		Arrived here yesterday 6.30 PM - 20 mile march. In barns. Not open.	
	20.8	9 AM.	Yesterday took over evacuation of S.a Central sectors from no.s 3 x 4 FAs. ADS at COUIN CAMPS. Admitted QS. Rem QS.	
	21.8	12 AM	Moved into hutments yesterday vacated by no. 16 FA. Adm. off 32, OR S.16 W.6. Evac. off S.2 OR S.35. W.1, died 1 acc. wounded - duty OR S.1. Rem OR S.18 W.5	
	22.8		Adm OR S.13, W.13, Evac OR S.12, W.8. Died OR W.1. Duty OR S.16. W.9	
	23.8		Yesterday Capt J. METURK [TC] joined from no.2 General Hospital. Went round S. sector trenches and aid posts. Ad. off W.2, OR S.22, W.14. Evac of W.2, OR S.10, W.13, DRS - OR S.3, W.2 Died OR W.2. Rem OR S.25. W.6.	
	24.8		Adm Off. S.1, OR S.8, W.8 Evac Off. S.1 OR S.14, W.5 DRS S.6 W.2. Rem OR S.13. W.7 Three reinforcements joined leaving personnel 2 short	
	25.8		Adm. OR S.21, W.26 Evac OR S.9, W.13. Died OR W.2 Duty OR S.2 W.1 Rem OR S.23. W.17.	
	26.8		Adm. OR S.19, W.10. Evac S.10. W.12. DRS. S.6. W.4. Duty OR S.2 Rem OR S.24 W.11.	
	27.8		Adm. OR S.13. W.7 Evac OR S.8. W.8 DRS. OR S.6. W.5. Died OR W.1. Duty OR S.1 Rem OR S.22 W.14	
	28.8		Visited ADS and went round R.Bat. Central Sector evacuation area. Adm. OR S.10. W.11. Evac OR S.12. W.7. DRS. OR S.2. W.1. Died OR W.1. Duty OR S.2. Rem OR S.16 W.6.	

WAR DIARY

INTELLIGENCE SUMMARY.

Army Form C. 2118.

Place	Date	Hour	Summary of Events and Information	Remarks and references to Appendices
	1916			
COIGNEUX	29.8		Took over 6 indifferent and leaky huts here with a view to making a hospital. Village recently blown up by accidental explosion. Adm. OR S.11. Evac. OR S.4. W.3 DRS OR S.10. W.3 Rem. OR S.13. Heavy rain.	
	30.8		Adm. OR S.21 W.2 Evac OR S.6. Duty OR S.2 W.1. Rem. OR S.26 W.1. Capt J R MARRACK and 10 OR for temporary duty 29th CCS. More heavy rain - bog.	
	31.8		Adm. OR S.30 W.8. Evac S.17. W.3. Rem. OR S.39 W.6. The personnel at HQ we had at work trying to improve the ground, road making etc. with the help of the RE.	

J A Kempthorne
Lt Col RAMC
OC 6 FA

140/1466

No. 6 F.A.
2nd Division

COMMITTEE FOR THE
MEDICAL HISTORY OF THE WAR
Date -2 DEC. 1915

R6/6

Herewith "War Diary"
(A.F. C 2118) for this unit for
month of September 16 please.

J A Hempthorne
Lt Col RAMC
O.C. No 6 F.A.

[Stamp: No 6 FIELD AMBULANCE No. 3/10/16]

Army Form C. 2118.

Vol 24

WAR DIARY
— or —
INTELLIGENCE SUMMARY.
(Erase heading not required.)

Instructions regarding War Diaries and Intelligence Summaries are contained in F. S. Regs., Part II. and the Staff Manual respectively. Title pages will be prepared in manuscript.

No 6 FIELD AMBULANCE

Place	Date	Hour	Summary of Events and Information	Remarks and references to Appendices
COIGNEUX	Sept. 1916 1	Noon	Admitted OR S.30. W.8. Remaining OR S.39 W.6. Five OR of unit awarded military medal.	2nd DRO 202 29/8
	2		Admitted OR S.26. W.7. Remaining OR S.45 W.6.	
	3		Admitted OR S.31. W.6. Remaining OR S.51 W.5.	
	4		Inspected Advanced dressing station at COLINCAMPS and advanced posts. All satisfactory	
	5		Admitted OR S.22. W.6. Remaining OR S.55 W.7	
	6		Adm. OR S.26 W.11 Remaining OR S.56 W.6. A path has now been constructed and a large amount of roadway made so an approach to the hospital.	
	7		Adm. OR S.28 W.22 Remaining OR S.63 W.18.	
	8		Adm. OR S.17 W.16 Remaining OR S.55 W.25. Lt STEVENSON reported in relief of Capt. MILLER D.S.O.	
	9		Adm. OR S.28 W.6. Remaining OR S.53. W.24. GOC 2nd Divn visited hospital yesterday.	
	10		Adm. OR S.21 W.6 Remaining OR S.46 W.17. Proceeded on leave to England. Handed over to Capt. WALSHE D.S.O.	

T2134. Wt. W708—776. 500'000. 4/15. Sir J. C. & S.

Army Form C. 2118.

WAR DIARY
INTELLIGENCE SUMMARY
(Erase heading not required.)

Place	Date	Hour	Summary of Events and Information	Remarks and references to Appendices
Same Billet	10/9/16	noon	CR proceeded on leave to England this morning. 1 officer & 10 others from temp duty at 35 C.C.S. Adm. 20 sick, 2 wounded. Remaining 43 sick, 9 wounded. Took over command from Lt Weatherston	S/Smith
Same Billet	11/9/16	noon	Adm. 19 sick 4 wounded. Remaining 42 sick, 8 wounded	S/Smith
Same Billet	12/9/16	noon	Adm. 19 sick 12 wounded. Remaining 43 sick, 13 wounded	S/Smith
Same Billet	13/9/16	noon	Adm. 27 sick 15 wounded. Remaining 27 sick, 15 wounded. Capt Walsh attached 38th Hants C.W.	S/Smith
Same Billet	14/9/16	noon	Handover to Capt Weatherston on receiving orders to proceed to the 38th Division. Taken over from Capt Walsh DSO. Adm. O.R. S.19. W.10. Remaining O.R. S.53. W.18.	S/Smith P.R.Stafford
Same Billet	15/9/16	noon	1 N.C.O. 14 Men proceeded to 35 C.C.S. for temporary duty on evening 14th. Capt S./. Lt Walsh DSO proceeded to 38th Div. to take up appointment as D.A.D.M.S. Adm. O.R. S.34. W.10. Remaining O.R. S.59. W.14.	P.R.Stafford

WAR DIARY or INTELLIGENCE SUMMARY

Army Form C. 2118.

(Erase heading not required.)

Place	Date	Hour	Summary of Events and Information	Remarks and references to Appendices
Same Billet	16/9/16	noon	Visited H/EBUTERNE area with D.A.D.M.S. to inspect site for F.A. in event of an advance. Adv'd O.R. S.28. W.5. Remaining O.R. S.72. W.13.	9.R.F.B.
Same Billet	17/9/16	noon	Work of improvement of present billet progressing satisfactorily. Permission & Road Metal obtained from paths etc. made. Adv'd Officers S.1. O.R. S.32. W.6. Remaining O.R. S.73. W.15.	9.R.F.B.
Same Billet	18/9/16	noon	Very wet all day but drains which have been made on Hospital premises proved adequate, water being carried away satisfactorily. Adv'd Officers W.1. O.R. S.19. W.31. Dist. O.R. 1. Remaining O.R. S.54. W.28.	9.R.F.B.
Same Billet	19/9/16	9.00a	Adv'd Officers W.1. O.R. S.22. W.1. Remaining Officers W.1. O.R. S. 47.W./5.	9.R.F.B.
Same Billet	20/9/16	9.00a	Advance party under Capt Inreadale to take M.I. Room at SARTON. H.18.a.3.5. Shot 57D. Advanced Dressing Station COLINCAMPS & outposts handed over to 132 F.A. correct. Adv'd O.R. S.17. W.12. Remaining O.R. S.46. W.28. Lt Col G. Arkenthorne returned from leave.	9.R.F.B.

WAR DIARY

INTELLIGENCE SUMMARY.

(Erase heading not required.)

Army Form C. 2118.

Place	Date	Hour	Summary of Events and Information	Remarks and references to Appendices
COIGNEUX	1916. Sept 21		Resumed command of Field Ambulance yesterday. Adm. Off. W.3. OR s.17. Rem. ORs. 49. W.3.	
	22		Capt J. McTURK to temp. charge 2nd Ox.L.I. Capt H.T. CHATFIELD to temp. charge 1st KRR yesterday. Adm. OR s. 22. Rem. OR s. 46 W.3.	
	23		Adm. Off. S.1, OR S.39. Rem. OR S. 56 W.2. Inspected det. at SARTON	
	24		Adm. OR s. 28. Rem. OR s. 66 W.1. Sgt E. HARDY and Pte C.A. SASSE awarded military medal. dated Gazette 14.9.16.	
	25		Adm. OR S. 25 Rem OR S. 61	
	26		Adm. OR S. 28 Rem. OR S. 53 Much has been done to improve the site of the Field Ambulance. Roads made. Bath room, pack store, officers mess, and horse standings are nearly finished and place made generally habitable.	
	27.		Adm. OR S. 40 Rem. OR S. 56	
	28.		Adm. OR S. 25 Rem OR S. 53. Capt S.H. NATHAN joined from the base	
	29.		Adm. OR S. 30 Rem OR S. 61. Five orders & GROs 1295 & 1436 read out at 2 PM parade	
	30		Adm. Off. S1. OR S. 21 Rem OR S 54	

J Hempsthorne
Lt.Col RAMC

R6/31

ADMS

Herewith "War Diary" (A.F.C 2118) for the month of October please.

J A Kempthorne
LIEUT-COL. R.A.M.C.
O.C. No. 2 FD. AMBCE.

[Stamp: No. 2 FIELD AMBULANCE / 2-11-16 / ORDERLY ROOM]

Army Form C. 2118.

WAR DIARY
INTELLIGENCE SUMMARY.
(Erase heading not required.)

6th F.A.

Vol 23

Place	Date	Hour	Summary of Events and Information	Remarks and references to Appendices
COIGNEUX	1916 Oct. 1st	8 PM	Admitted O.R. S.6. Rem. O.R. S.61. Holding party of 1 officer and 10 O.R. to CLAIRFAY F.M.	
	2		Capt NATHAN to temporary duty Divisional Train. Capt CHATFIELD rejoined from 1st R.N.R.	
	3		Adm. O.R. S.19. Rem. O.R. S.30.	
	4		Adm. O.R. S.13. Rem. O.R. S.11.	
	5		Sent out 1 section to take over E. CLAIRFAY. Adm. O.R. S.3 Off. S.1. Rem. O.R. S.8. 7 Reinforcements joined	
			Unit moved to huts at VARENNES P.25.d.2.6. Sheet 57d. Section at CLAIRFAY handed over to 2nd F.A. R.N. Divn. Capt McTUCK rejoined from 2nd/2nd L.I. Adm O.R. S1 W1.	
	6		Rem. O.R. S.2 W.1. Opened as hospital for scabies & sick	
			Adm. O.R. S.11 Rem. O.R. S.11.	
	7		Adm. Off. S1, O.R. S.10. Rem. O.R. S.15. Sent out a working party of 5 O.R. to MAILLY.	
	8		Adm. O.R. S.12 Rem O.R. S.22. Working party rejoined	
	9		Took over the complete F.A. site, half having been occupied by Infantry. Adm. Off. S1 O.R. S.24. Rem. O.R. S.38.	
	10		Adm. O.R. S.29 Rem O.R. S.47. Lt STEVENSON to temp. duty 1st Kings Regt.	
	11		Adm. Off. S.1 O.R. S.33. Rem. O.R. S.50. Capt C.N. COAD joined for temp duty.	

Army Form C. 2118.

WAR DIARY

INTELLIGENCE SUMMARY

(Erase heading not required.)

Place	Date	Hour	Summary of Events and Information	Remarks and references to Appendices
VARENNES	1917 Oct 12	8 PM	Adm. Off. si. ORs. 44 Rem Off si. ORs. 65	
	13		Adm. OR s 39 Rem Off si ORs 57	
	14		Adm OR s. 25 Rem Off si. OR 38	
	15		Adm OR s 19 Rem Off si OR 28	
	16		Adm OR s 30 Rem Off si ORs 25	
	17		Adm OR s 17 Rem Off si ORs 21. Since taking over the men have been actively employed improving the site and making it fit for a Divisional Main Dressing Station. Huts were all in very poor condition and have all been made water tight. Much gravel has been carted to improve the paths. Kitchen has been reconstructed and dining hall built. A scabies department has been opened and worked most successfully. The site, which was filthy on taking over, has been generally cleaned up.	
BERTRANCOURT J33.a.5.3	18		Order to pack up and do the same at BERTRANCOURT, which proceeded to do. Adm. off. si, ORs 28 WS. Rem OR s 36. Hospital opened at J 33 a.5.3. Readys for reception of all sick & Wounded from the division. 11 Reinforcements joined.	
	19		Adm Off s. 2 ORs 46 W1 Rem OR s. 27 Capt NATHAN rejoined from 2nd Divl. Train.	

Army Form C. 2118.

WAR DIARY

INTELLIGENCE SUMMARY.

(Erase heading not required.)

Instructions regarding War Diaries and Intelligence Summaries are contained in F. S. Regs., Part II. and the Staff Manual respectively. Title pages will be prepared in manuscript.

Place	Date	Hour	Summary of Events and Information	Remarks and references to Appendices
	Oct	PM		
BERTRANCOURT	20	8	Adm. Off. S1. OR.S 50. W1. Rem. Off. S1. OR.S 45. W1.	
	21		Adm. Off. S1. OR.S 23. W11. Rem. Off. S1. OR.S 21. W9.	
	22		Adm. Off. S3. OR.S 45. W4. Rem. Off. S2. OR.S 47. W1.	
	23		Adm. Off. OR.S 33. W17. Rem. OR.S 60. W.15.	
	24		Adm. Off. S3. OR.S 45. W16. Rem. Off. S1. OR.S 58. W13	
	25		Adm. OR.S 41. N. 20. Rem. OR.S 46. W.14.	
	26		Adm. OR S 42. W13. Rem. OR.S 44. W12.	
	27		Adm. Off. S3. W1. OR.S 31. W.14. Rem. Off. S3. W1. OR.S 32. N10.	
	28		Adm. Off. S1. W1. OR.S 55. W2. Rem. OR.S 48. W3. Handed over 4 Ambulance cars to Div Supply Column in exchange for 4 Daimler cars	
	29		Adm. Off. S2. OR.S 40. W5. Rem. Off. S1. OR.S 59. W6. Capt NETURN to permanent duty 2 NZ. 2. 1.	
	30		Adm. Off. S1. OR.S 63. N3. Rem. Off. S1. OR.S 81. W5	
	31		Adm. Off. S1. OR.S 66. W2. Rem. Off. S1. OR. 366. Since the unit has been here the weather has been vile. The whole place is inches deep in mud. In addition to the farm buildings & huts 5 large hospital marquees have been erected for extra accommodation for wounded if required.	

140/1649.

2nd Div.

No. 6. Field Ambulance.

COMMITTEE FOR THE
MEDICAL HISTORY OF THE WAR
Date −3 JAN. 1917

R6/44.

A.D.M.S.

Herewith "War Diary" (A.F. C2118) for the month of November '16. please.

J.A.Kempthorne
LIEUT-COL. R.A.M.C.
O.C. NO.6 FD-AMBCE.

30/11/16

Army Form C. 2118.

WAR DIARY
INTELLIGENCE SUMMARY.
(Erase heading not required.)

Instructions regarding War Diaries and Intelligence Summaries are contained in F. S. Regs., Part II. and the Staff Manual respectively. Title pages will be prepared in manuscript.

6 3a Amb Vol 26

Place	Date	Hour	Summary of Events and Information	Remarks and references to Appendices
BERTRANCOURT	1916 Nov. 1	8 PM	Adm. OR S.32 N1. Rem. Offs S.1. OR S.56	
	2		Adm OR S.48. N.4. Rem OR S.69. N.2	
	3		Adm. OR S.45. N.7. Rem. OR S.61. N.2	
	4		Adm. Off. S.3, OR S.47. N.1. Rem Offs S.3. OR S.67. W.1	
	5		Adm. Offs.O. OR S.34 N.10. Rem Offs S.3. OR S.62 W.S. GOC 2nd Divn visited hospital	
	6		Adm Offs S.1, OR S.40, N.3. Rem Offs S.1. OR S.70. N.1	
	7		Adm Offs S.1, OR S.37. Rem. Offs S.1, OR S.70. N.1	
	8		Adm. Offs S.2, OR S.39, N.12. Rem Offs S.1. OR S.63, N.9.	
	9		Adm. Offs S.2, OR S.40, N.5. Rem Offs S.3, OR S.69 N.13. Surg gen SKINNER DMS 5th Army visits hospital.	
	10		Adm. Offs S.1. OR S.42, N.6. Rem Offs S.2, OR S.63, N.6.	
	11		Adm. Offs N.1 OR S.38 N.25. Rem. Offs S.2 OR S.54.N.5. There is little to record during the period but persistent rain and mud. The sick are mostly PUO. Fever brought on by the inclemency of the weather. Some of these cases are not certainly of the relapsing type known as Trench Fever. The unit has been taking most of the sick and wounded of the Division, a few total sick going to no 100 who are doing corps collecting stn.	

Army Form C. 2118.

WAR DIARY

~~INTELLIGENCE SUMMARY.~~

(Erase heading not required.)

Place	Date	Hour	Summary of Events and Information	Remarks and references to Appendices
BERTRANCOURT	1916 Nov. 12	8 P.M.	at ACHEUX. 5 F.A. is parked and managing the ADS at MAILLY MAILLET. All their Bearers are up.	
			This is "y" day. Bearers are to go up this afternoon to evacuate part of the line under Nos. F.A. Cars to be at disposal of 5 F.A. Ambulance-waggons to go up to Divl. Collecting Stn. at BEAUSSART this evening, evacuating to ACHEUX under orders of Nos 5 F.A. Capt. MARRACK Mc and Capt CHATFIELD with Bearers. Capts McGEAGH, NATHAN, COADE, and McKINNEY at H.Q. Three officers 2/5 Midland F.A. and 100 men arrived in the evening under Capt JAMIESON	
	13		20 more Bearers. Admitted Offs. 11 OR. 551 WB Rem. OR 531 N.S. Active operations commenced at 5.45A.M. Admitted up to 12 noon Offs. 32 NS OR. 373 N.S.9 Am. OR 313 WS4. 38th M.A.C. arrived in village. Battle Casualties MATHARIS, CAMPBELL, SCHRODER slightly wounded. A steady stream of wounded came in during the day Up to 5 P.M. 2nd Divn. Offs. 9 OR 111. Other divisions Offs. 5. OR 52. Germans 17. All walking cases had been struck and posted by the large number of cases admitted 2. 16. 4 F.A. sent orderlies and officers [?] to Capt JAMIESON. By 8 o'clock P.M. all wounded cleared.	

Army Form C. 2118.

WAR DIARY
INTELLIGENCE SUMMARY
(Erase heading not required.)

Instructions regarding War Diaries and Intelligence Summaries are contained in F.S. Regs., Part II. and the Staff Manual respectively. Title pages will be prepared in manuscript.

Place	Date	Hour	Summary of Events and Information	Remarks and references to Appendices
BERTRANCOURT	1916 Oct. 14	8 PM	Admitted to 6 A.M. Wounded Officers 14 OR 150. To 5 PM Officers 8 OR 97. Prisoners 1. Battle casualties – Killed 1909. Pte J.SMITH. buried at Q.14.B.0. Sheet 57d. Wounded Ptes GIBBONS, LESTER, PHILLIPS, DANCE. A cold day but fine.	
	15.		Wounded to 6 A.M. Officers 6. OR 92. To 5 PM Officers 6. OR 93. Prisoners 2. Battle Casualty 1st STEVENSON Lt. 1st Kings. (GSW head and shock) Pte DALE & RICH (slight, both to duty) Weather frosty.	
	16.		Wounded to 6 A.M. Officers 6. OR 76. Prisoners 4. To 5 PM Officers 2. OR 63. 1st STEVENSON evacuated last night and struck off the strength. 6 Reinforcements arrived. Beaux came in for a days rest and Capt CHATFIELD relieved by Capt COAD. Advanced Party 90th FA arrived.	
	17.		Wounded to 6 A.M. Officers 4. OR 53. Prisoners 1. Admitted to 2 P.M. Officers 0 OR 37. Germans 4. The Main Dressing Station was handed over at 2 P.M. to 90th FA with 1 officer sick, 90R and 3 S.I. wounded. The unit parked for the night. The DDMS on saying goodbye to the unit expressed the entire satisfaction with the work of the Field Ambulance. The total casualties passing though the Main Dressing Station during the last 5 days has been Off. 45. OR 874. Germans 49. Sick 73. Total 1041. All ranks worked splendidly. The conditions in the trenches owing to the cold, rain, and mud was the worst ever experienced during the campaign.	

T2134. Wt. W708—776. 50C000. 4/15. Sir J. C. & S.

Army Form C. 2118.

WAR DIARY
~~INTELLIGENCE~~ SUMMARY.
(Erase heading not required.)

Instructions regarding War Diaries and Intelligence Summaries are contained in F. S. Regs., Part II. and the Staff Manual respectively. Title pages will be prepared in manuscript.

Place	Date	Hour	Summary of Events and Information	Remarks and references to Appendices
BERTRANCOURT	1916 Nov. 18.	8 PM	Field ambulance closed. Marched out under orders for ACHEUX at 9.30 AM in the rain. Orders were cancelled en route and the unit returned to spend a night of intense discomfort in the mud outside the village	
BRETEL	19.		Marched at 9.30 AM coming under orders of S.W. Brigade group. Reached the village (1m from DOULLENS) at 4 PM. Capt MARRACK remained behind to endeavour to bring in a party of wounded believed to be still out	
	20		Capt COAD for temporary duty with 22.23. The unit rests today. Capt MARRACK rejoined	
LE MEILLARD	21		Marched to billet as per margin. Arrived 3.30. Good billets. Sick collected 11. Evacuated to no. 19 C.C.S. (Doullens)	
	22.		Remained at same place. Sick collected from brigade 10. Capt J.G.HIGGINS for duty	
RIBEAUCOURT	23		Marched as per margin about 7 miles. Satisfactory billets in village. Sick collected 8. 9 reinforcements joined	
FROYELLES	24		Marched as per margin. About 13 miles. Arrived very wet. Very few billets left and those bad. Admitted and evacuated 10 patients	
NEVILLY L'HOPITAL	25 26		Satisfactory accommodation for unit here. Off. 1. OR 3 admitted and evacuated. Weather very wet. Same billet. Capt CHATFIELD proceeded on leave. Admitted 3. Remaining 3	

WAR DIARY

INTELLIGENCE SUMMARY

(Erase heading not required.)

Army Form C. 2118.

Place	Date	Hour	Summary of Events and Information	Remarks and references to Appendices
YVRENCHEUX	1916 Nov 27	P.M.		
		8.	Marched to day to marginally named billet. Capt HIGGINS to temporary duty with 17 A.Mk. Admitted sick OR 10 Offs 2. As there was no accomodation for sick in the village I accompanied the ADM to inspect a new site at MAISON ROLLAND.	
MAISON ROLLAND	28	8	Moved as per margin. Hospital opened in a large empty house. Good billets for the men. Admitted 2 Sick. Remaining 3. A Scabies department was opened	
	29		Admitted 16. Remaining 19. Three reinforcements joined.	
	30		Adm 13. Remaining 29.	

J Monkstone
Lt Col RAMC
OC 63A

16/1900

2nd Res.

No. 6. Field Ambulance

COMMITTEE FOR THE
MEDICAL HISTORY OF THE WAR
Date 31 JAN. 1917.

Rb/46

A.D.M.S.

Herewith "War Diary"
(A.F. C 2118) for the month of
December 1916 please.

G. R. B...
Capt. for.
LIEUT-COL. R.A.M.C.
O.C. NO. 6 FD. AMBCE.

1/1/17

Army Form C. 2118.

WAR DIARY
or
INTELLIGENCE SUMMARY.
(Erase heading not required.)

Instructions regarding War Diaries and Intelligence Summaries are contained in F. S. Regs., Part II. and the Staff Manual respectively. Title pages will be prepared in manuscript.

Place	Date	Hour	Summary of Events and Information	Remarks and references to Appendices
MAISON ROLLAND	DEC 1	8 PM.	Admitted OR S 5. Remaining OR 26. Capt MARRACK to 2nd S. Staffs. temporary duty	
	2		Adm. Offs SI. OR S. 15 Rem. Off SI OR 30	
	3		Adm. OR S 19 Rem. OR S 45	
	4		Adm OR S 6. Rem. OR S. 39. Capt McKINNEY went on leave. A scheme of work incl. Res. Corps drills & exercises and lectures has been started. The inclement weather causes difficulties. Rev WEMORGAN Byt, time expired.	
	5		Adm. OR S 7. Rem OR S. 34	
	6		Adm. OR S 18. Rem OR S 40	
	7		Adm. OR S 11. Rem OR S. 39. Capt McGEAGH & Lt DUNGLISON went on leave. DDMS 2nd Corps inspected hospital	
	8		Adm OR S 12. Rem OR S. 40. The hospital continues to collect and treat the sick of the 6th Brigade and scabies. Weather very damp and foggy. Inoculations with the mixed typhoid & paratyphoid vaccine are being commenced. 30 in all were completed. Adm. OR 13. Rem. 42.	
	9		Adm OR 15. Rem. 42. Capt CHATFIELD returned off leave	
	10			
	11		Adm. OR 5 Rem 37. Inspection by Surg Gen SKINNER. DMS S. Army. A party of 40 men were sent to LANNOY to unload RE stores.	

T2134. Wt. W708—776. 50000. 4/15. Sir J. C. & S.

Army Form C. 2118.

WAR DIARY
or
INTELLIGENCE SUMMARY.
(Erase heading not required.)

Instructions regarding War Diaries and Intelligence Summaries are contained in F. S. Regs., Part II. and the Staff Manual respectively. Title pages will be prepared in manuscript.

Place	Date	Hour	Summary of Events and Information	Remarks and references to Appendices
	Dec	PM		
MAISON ROLAND	12	8	Adm. Off 1. OR 12. Rem. Off 1 OR 32.	
	13		Adm. OR 11. Rem. Off 1. OR 32. 20 men & 2 NCO's additional to LANNOY	
	14		Adm. OR 10. Rem. Off 1. OR 29. Capt MARRACK rejoined	
	15		Adm. Off 1. OR 6. Rem Off 2. OR 26. Capt McKINNEY returned from leave.	
	16		Adm. Off 1. OR 6. Rem OR 20. Capt NATHAN for duty to 2nd H.L.I. Lanney party rejoined.	
	17		Adm 1 OR. Rem 24 OR. Capt MARRACK went on leave. A regimental coffee bar was opened.	
	18		Adm 12 OR. Rem 32 OR. Lt DUNGLISON rejoined from leave. Drills, route marches and foot-ball were being continued, the former a good deal interfered with by the wet. A good football ground has been built for the men	
	19		Adm. OR 11. Rem OR 37.	
	20		Adm. Off 51. OR 515. Rem OR 37.	
	21		Adm. OR S 23. Rem OR 49. Working Party started filling in trenches near DOMVREUR.	
	22		Adm. OR S10. Rem OR S 36.	
	23		Adm. OR S8 Rem OR S 33. Three men surplus sent to 18th Divn.	
	24		Adm OR S11. Rem OR S 25. No.5 FA closed. Half patients transferred to no 6.	
	25		Adm Off S2. OR S21 Rem Off S1. OR S 24 Christmas Day. Capt MCGEAGH returned off leave	J.O.K.

T.134. Wt. W708—776. 500000. 4/15. Sir J. C. & S.

WAR DIARY

INTELLIGENCE SUMMARY.
(Erase heading not required.)

Army Form C. 2118.

Place	Date	Hour	Summary of Events and Information	Remarks and references to Appendices
MAISON ROLAND	26	P.M. 8	Admitted O.R.S. 4. Remg. O.R.S. 22. Lt.Col KEMPTHORNE proceeded on leave. Capt. SGGEAGH took over command temporarily	G.R.Sh?gh
	27	8	Adnd O.R.S. 6. Remg O.R.S. 25.	
	28	8	Adnd O.R.S. 11 Remg. O.R.S. 25. CAPT. H.T. CHATFIELD to 2nd Div.Am.Col. for temp duty.	
	29	8	Adnd Officers S.2. O.R.S. 20. Remg Officers S.1. O.R.S. 40. CAPT. S.H. NATHAN returned from completion of temporary duty with 2 H.L.I.	
	30	8	Adnd Officers S.1. O.R.S. 16 Remg O.R.S. 45	
	31	8	Adnd Officers S.2. O.R.S. 19. Remg Officers S.2. O.R.S. 41. CAPT. S.H. NATHAN proceeded with but hindered to course at Div² Gas School. Training being proceeded with but hindered by almost continuous rain. Health of Unit very good.	

G.R.Sh?gh.
Capt R.A.M.C.
for O.C. 6 F. Amb.

2nd Division
War Diaries
6th Field Ambulance

January, To 31st December
1917

6th Field Ambulance

Army Form C. 2118.

Vol 25

WAR DIARY
or
INTELLIGENCE SUMMARY

(Erase heading not required.)

Place	Date	Hour	Summary of Events and Information	Remarks and references to Appendices
MAISON ROLLAND	1917 Jan 1	8 p.m.	Adm Offrs S.3, O.R. S.24. Rein Officers S.2. O.R.S.36.	O.R.B Stoff Capt Rouse
	2		Adm Officers S.2. O.R.S.32. Rein Officers S.2. O.R.S.52.	SR&f
	3		Capt. J.R. MARRACK.M.C. returned from leave. Adm Officers S.1. O.R.S.16. Rein Officers S.1. O.R.47. CAPT. S.H. NATHAN returned from course at GAS School.	Capt. S.H. NATHAN QR&f
	4		Adm O.R.S.18. Rein Officers O.R.S.46. CAPT.J.R.MARRACK M.C. to 23.R.F. for temporary duty. CAPT.S.H. NATHAN to 1.R.BERKS for temporary duty. Inspection of Horse transport by Col. BROOKE.D.S.O. of 2nd Div Train	SR&f
	5		Adm O.R. S. 14. Rein O.R. S.44. G.O.C. 2nd Div. paid a visit to Hospital QR Stof	
			† Billets	
	6		Adm Offrs S.3, O.R S.18. Rem Offrs S.3, O.R S.37.	
	7		Adm Offrs S.1, O.R S.24. Rem Offrs S.2, O.R S.36. Returned off leave	Gallenshlin 2nd Lieut.
	8		Adm Offrs S.1, O.R S.19. Rem Offrs S.1, O.R S.17.	
VACQUERIE	9		Adm Offrs S.2, O.R S.16. Rem Offrs S.1, O.R S.15. Marched to magnuelly named Billet about 9 miles.	
	10		Adm O.R S.23. Rem O.R.S.12. Capts NATHAN and MARRACK rejoined.	

WAR DIARY
or
INTELLIGENCE SUMMARY.
(Erase heading not required.)

Army Form C. 2118.

Place	Date	Hour	Summary of Events and Information	Remarks and references to Appendices
VAL-DE-MAISON	Jan 11	PM	Adm. OR 30 Rem OR 14. A long march to magnally named billet with the 5th Brigade. Capt NATHAN went on leave.	
SENLIS	12	8.	Ad. OR 11, Rem OR 14. Took over in the evening the evacuation of the 2nd Divn Front near COURCELETTE. ADS at SUNKEN R and CRICHTON'S POST. Amb. Advance moved at one hours notice to most unpleasant billet at SENLIS.	
OVILLIERS HUTS	13.		Took over huts as magnally named from 2/1 Highland FA. HQ field amb to hospital. All cases from Civil sent to MDS (100 FA) at AVELUY. Capt C.N.COAD struck off strength on posting to 22nd RF. Capt McKINNEY to 22nd RF on temporary duty. Inspected ADS at SUNKEN ROAD	
	11		Lt DN KNOX posted for permanent duty. Capt McGEAGH moved to ADS at CRICHTON'S POST, Capt MARRACK remained at SUNKEN ROAD. Inspected former ADS with DDMS. A car transfer has been taken over in POSIÈRES and a dug out at TRAMWAY CROSSING. It's FA is also letting mat-guns formerly used for walking wounded at TARA HILL.	
	14		Capt McGEAGH and Capt MARRACK both sick. Evacuated to officio hospital GEZAINCOURT	
	18.		Lt KNOX to CRICHTON'S POST.	

Army Form C. 2118.

WAR DIARY
or
INTELLIGENCE SUMMARY.
(Erase heading not required.)

Place	Date	Hour	Summary of Events and Information	Remarks and references to Appendices
OUILLIERS HUTS	Jan. 19		Capt CHATFIELD reported. Sent up to SUNKEN ROAD. Capt J.M.HILL joined for duty.	
	20		A hard frost has now set in and the weather is icy cold. The men at HQ have put up 2 extra Nissen Huts. Horse lines with overhead cover have been made and a kitchen and oven built. Watering party is engaged on deep dug out at CREIGHTON'S POST.	
	22		Sgt SANDERS struck off the strength on being granted a Temporary Commission	
	24		Capt MARRACK returned from hospital. Corps Commander visited huts and expressed his approval.	
	25		DDMS visited the unit	
	26		Capt MARRACK returned to SUNKEN ROAD. Capt HILL relieved Capt KNOX at CREIGHTON'S POST.	
	27		Capt McGEAGH returned from hospital	
	28		Capt McKINNEY reported. Capt NATHAN came back off leave. Posted permanently to D.A.C. Owing to alterations in the regimental aid posts and the occupation of RED CHATEAU by troops the teams have been redistributed. The ALBERT-BAPAUME road is blocked by a fallen down lorry and under heavy shell fire. Evacuations previously by CREIGHTON'S POST to which the Bihem officers have moved. One NCO and 17 men remain in reserve at SUNKEN ROAD.	

Army Form C. 2118.

WAR DIARY
or
INTELLIGENCE SUMMARY.
(Erase heading not required.)

Place	Date	Hour	Summary of Events and Information	Remarks and references to Appendices
OVILLERS.	Jan. 29		Lt. QM DUNGLISON in arrest for drunkenness. FGCM applied for. The intense cold and hard frost continues. There are few casualties from the line but there is considerable artillery activity and almost daily casualties from the POSIÈRES road. The hospital huts have not been shelled at present. The car drivers all having the greatest difficulties with their cars owing to the frost.	
	30		Lt. DUNGLISON evacuated sick with myalgia and dyspepsia	

J.R. Kempthorne
Lt-Col
OC 6 FA

URGENT

O.C.
No 6 Field Ambulance

Please inform me at once number
of Volume of War Diary for January
1917.

[signature]
Colonel A.M.S.
A.D.M.S. 2nd Division.

ADMS-

The volumes have never been numbered since the beginning of the war. As the unit mobilised in Aug 14. this will presumably be vol iv. I regret I am unable to give any further information as I did not understand that this was necessary.

6/2/17

Gayempthorne
Lt Col.
OC 6 FA

Army Form C. 2118.

WAR DIARY
or
INTELLIGENCE SUMMARY.
(Erase heading not required.)

War Diary
N° 6 Field Ambulance
February 1917
Vol. 31.

Army Form C. 2118.

WAR DIARY
or
INTELLIGENCE SUMMARY.
(Erase heading not required.)

Instructions regarding War Diaries and Intelligence Summaries are contained in F. S. Regs., Part II. and the Staff Manual respectively. Title pages will be prepared in manuscript.

Place	Date 1917	Hour	Summary of Events and Information	Remarks and references to Appendices
OVILLIERS HUTS	Feb. 1	PM 8	L⁺ D M⁺ KNOX proceeded in temporary medical charge of 2ⁿᵈ Div⁺ train	
	3.		Col HERRICK, having ceased as A.D.M.S. inspected the unit	
	5		Capt⁺ HILL to temporary duty with 24ᵗʰ R.F. Weather continues intensely cold. Evacuation of sick continues uninterruptedly. Work at the CRICHTON'S post dug out continues. Anti air craft shells continue to drop about	
	8		Neighbourhood of hospital shelled for half an hour with a 12 in howitzer. Three huts slightly damaged. No casualties. Took refuge in old trenches.	
	10		Court martial on Lt DUNGLISON. Had to adjourn in the middle on account of shell fire. Two more huts damaged. Capt MᶜGEAGH evacuated sick	
	13.		Nothing to note. Line is quiet. Much disturbed by bombs and machine gun fire from hostile aeroplanes at night. Health of men is fair. Several have bad colds.	
	14		L⁺ KNOX returned from duty with divisional train.	
	16		Detailed a tent sub-division and 6 climbs to walking wounded post at CABSTAND near AVELUYE to be under orders of no 5 F.A. Beaw to complete 100 wer sent up the line and L⁺ KNOX and Capt CHATFIELD posted to A.D.S SUNKEN ROAD Capt MARRACK	

A5834 Wt.W4973/M687 750,000 8/16 D. D. & L. Ltd. Forms/C.2118/13.

WAR DIARY or INTELLIGENCE SUMMARY

Army Form C. 2118.

Place	Date	Hour	Summary of Events and Information	Remarks and references to Appendices
OVILLERS HUTS	Feb. 20.		and Capt HILL to CRICHTON'S POST. Horse Ambulances and Sanitary Lorry Well posted at TRAMWAY CROSSING, 6 F.A. transport being augmented by that from the other ambulances. A collecting post for walking wounded will an officer was established at the Same place and the Zone transport used for convoy of walking wounded to GAUSTAND. The Divisional coffee bar adjoining was brought into the scheme. The motor ambulance post at POZIERES POST was reinforced by the Cars of other F.A's, the whole being regulated by Sgt. ROBINSON. Capt G.R.D. McGEAGH reported sick from CCS and struck off the strength. Sentence of F.G.C.M. severely reprimanding Lt DUNGLISON promulgated	
	17		Thaw Rain commenced Ground very heavy Active operations commenced 5.45 A.M. On visiting SUNKEN ROAD at 10 o'c found evacuations proceeding satisfactorily the ALBERT-BAPAUME road having been met successfully patched by the motor drivers and Car orderlies the previous day. Cars were running to regiment. Removal of wounded from both this sector and the Eft sector was enormously facilitated by the dense mist. On visiting L sector at 10.30 Capt Hancock who had been out early	

A5834 Wt. W.4973/M687 750,000 8/16 D.D. & L. Ltd. Forms/C.2113/13.

Army Form C. 2118.

WAR DIARY
or
INTELLIGENCE SUMMARY.
(Erase heading not required.)

Instructions regarding War Diaries and Intelligence Summaries are contained in F. S. Regs., Part II. and the Staff Manual respectively. Title pages will be prepared in manuscript.

Place	Date	Hour	Summary of Events and Information	Remarks and references to Appendices
	1917 Feb.		posting his Bearers was found to be entirely unfit for duty owing to severe tonsilitis and fever. He was sent in at once to hospital. The officer placed and determination in keeping at work and even assisting personally to carry stretchers under heavy fire in his condition was noteworthy. He had in the previous days in company with Capt McKENZIE M.C. (DADMS) worked hard at the preliminary arrangements, going forward over jobs etc. at the post, reinforcements of bearers were found to be necessary in the course of the day. The A.D.M.S. sent up the bearer divisions of the 3 Field Amb. Bearers and a company of the 17th R.F. Capt BOURNE PRICE M.C. was ordered to CRICHTON'S POST as senior Bearer (100 FA) officer with the duty of arranging relief as required. These duties he carried out with great efficiency.	
OVILLERS HUTS	18		Dense mist continues, all proceeding satisfactorily. Conditions most arduous owing to heavy ground, long carry, and bad roads. Up to 9 A.M. this morning 117 cases have been evacuated from CRICHTON'S POST and 18 from SUNKEN ROAD. A large number of walking wounded have passed through. Numbers are only approximate as records are kept at Main Dressing Station AVELUYE POST.	

Army Form C. 2118.

WAR DIARY
or
INTELLIGENCE SUMMARY.
(Erase heading not required.)

Place	Date	Hour	Summary of Events and Information	Remarks and references to Appendices
	1917 Feb 18.		The following Casualties have occurred - 2360 Pte ROBERTS J. } Killed in action 75389 " PROCTOR L. } 57495 " FARMERY G.A. } died of wounds. 72927 " PILGRAM P.W. } 64951 " BARLOW W. severely wounded 605 " FITZGERALD J. " 22243 " ORMEROD C. slightly wounded 81654 " WARDELL S.H. " 6924 L.C. ROBBINS A.C.J. "	
	19		Capt J. VALLANCE reported for duty from Calais following slightly wounded 76614 Pte PULFORD R, 22814 Pte PEARSON R.	
	20		Bearers of 6th F.A. were relieved from L Sector. Bearers of no 5 tank over R rest companies to be run by Capt CHATFIELD and 8 F.A. Bearers OC 6 F.A. continues to be in charge of Evacuations and supplies cars	
ALBERT W.28.c.5.6	22		The F.A. HQ. moved to marginal address opening a divisional main dressing station in the ECOLE DES JEUNNES FILLES cellars and a walking Wounded dressing station in the building opposite. Detachment from 5th F.A. returned	
	23		Trench feet coming in in large Nos. owing to bad weather conditions and want of shelter in the line	

A.5834 Wt.W4973/M687 750,000 8/16 D.D.&L.Ltd. Forms/C.2118/13.

Army Form C. 2118.

WAR DIARY
or
INTELLIGENCE SUMMARY.
(Erase heading not required.)

Place	Date	Hour	Summary of Events and Information	Remarks and references to Appendices
ALBERT	1917 Feb. 25		Memorial service for men of the unit killed in the recent active operations. Senior Chaplain conducted service. ADMS present.	
	26		Capt HIGGINS for duty to CALAIS.	
	28		Lt DUNGLISON evacuated sick. The OC 6 FA is still in charge of the line. Bearers of 5 FA with ADS at RED CHATEAU are doing forward evacuation. Part of No 6 FA bearers assisting. The Car evacuation is also carried out by No 6. There is plenty of work doing in ALBERT. About 70 evacuations are carried out per day by the MAC Cars and about 50 local sick dealt with.	

J. Hempstone
Lt Col RAMC
OC 6 FA

Army Form C. 2118.

WAR DIARY
or
INTELLIGENCE SUMMARY.
(Erase heading not required.)

Instructions regarding War Diaries and Intelligence Summaries are contained in F. S. Regs., Part II. and the Staff Manual respectively. Title pages will be prepared in manuscript.

Place	Date	Hour	Summary of Events and Information	Remarks and references to Appendices
ALBERT Ecole des jeuns gens	1917 March 1.	PM 8	The unit remains in the same billet acting as a main dressing station. About 200 local sick are also seen and disposed of daily. Bearers remain in the line.	
	2.		Capt CHATFIELD on 10 days special leave to England.	
	3.		Fatigue parties sent to keep the 2 Field Ambulances constant working wounded and main dressing stations at POZIERES.	
	4.		The Headquarters of the Bearers under Capt. ELLIS. S F.A. have moved into RED CHATEAU COURCELETTE. About 30 of 6th F.A. Bearers remain working Dug Sap of F.A. Capt. HILL & KNOX Bearer officers. Our cars continue to evacuate the line. Lt. A. HOLDEN assumes duties of Qm. vice Lt. DUNGLISON granted sick.	
	6.		Following awarded military medals – Pte A.E. FRENCH R.A.M.C. Dr. A. HALL A.S.C.(MT) Dr. E. RICHARDSON A.S.C.(MT). a Sergeant & 7 men arrived as reinforcements.	
	7.		Capt. R.J. TAIT reported for duty from Cavalry Division.	
	8.		Capt J.R. VALLANCE transferred to 100 F.A. Capt T.H. JAMES joined from 12th division.	
	9.		Bearers to complete 75 went up to RED CHATEAU and also a dressing party. This place is now called advanced main dressing station and during the following day was open for admission of cases which were cleared by MAC cars.	

A8834 Wt.W4973/M687 750,000 8/16 D. D. & L. Ltd. Forms/C.2118/13.

Army Form C. 2118.

WAR DIARY
or
INTELLIGENCE SUMMARY.

(Erase heading not required.)

Instructions regarding War Diaries and Intelligence Summaries are contained in F. S. Regs., Part II. and the Staff Manual respectively. Title pages will be prepared in manuscript.

Place	Date	Hour	Summary of Events and Information	Remarks and references to Appendices
ALBERT	Mar 10	8 PM	Active operations resulting in capture of GREVILLERS TRENCH. An A.D.S. was established at the Quarry on the Quesnoy Road near LE SARS from which cases were carried to CHALK ROAD - ALBERT-BAPAUME road junction. Almost all the cars were evacuated the long direct to main M.D.S. and cars work was done in RED CHATEAU. The F.A. cars there did practically all the advanced work. The Ant Subdivision returned in the evening and the Chateau ceased to be an A.D.S.	
	11		Capt. MARRACK M.C. rejoined from hospital	
			All Ford ambulances and 3 G.S. waggons employed during the night bringing in stragglers of the Brigade coming in. They were not all right between ALBERT and POZIERES	
	12		Lance Sgt. H.A. HOLT mortally wounded, a most gallant act efficient N.C.O. The following was also wounded. PTES S. BOSTOCK, A. BAILEY, S.J. SCHOFIELD, J. TATLOCK, W. ANSELL, T.J. ALLEN (slight)	
	13		The enemy having retreated beyond LOUPART WOOD things all unsettled and new schemes for evacuation are been up pending orders for the Division. All no. 3 and 6 bearer remain up. The RED CHATEAU party not moving to QUARRY and an attempt is being made to get a Ford car up through LE SARS to the new ADS.	
	14		Ford car proving of no use, a horse ambulance was substituted	
	15		Handed over evacuation of line to O.C. 100 F.A. QMS F.W. COUPLAND to 49 CCS as acting S. Major	

Army Form C. 2118.

WAR DIARY
or
INTELLIGENCE SUMMARY.
(Erase heading not required.)

Instructions regarding War Diaries and Intelligence Summaries are contained in F. S. Regs., Part II. and the Staff Manual respectively. Title pages will be prepared in manuscript.

Place	Date 1917	Hour	Summary of Events and Information	Remarks and references to Appendices
ALBERT	Mar 16	PM 8	Bearers of Nos 5 and 6 F.A returned to HQ 6 F.A.	
	18		One officer and 25 Bearers of 5 & 6 F.A returned to line post. Enemy retiring. Sent a tent subdivision under Capt McKinney to Corbet AVELUY CHATEAU into a corps scabies station and 50 bearers to keep five bags mattresses were filled with out thistle bristles. C.O. & staff and Medic. element met and 100 patients were taken over in the afternoon. A lorry and 10 waggon loads of medicine and being collected from the old hospital at VADENCOURT. Handed over cellars in School to No 34. AD Vet Stores and sent 'Burying party' and waggons to move them in.	
	19		A tent subdivision detailed to No 3 C.C.S. Bearers came in BAPAUME occupied. Enemy still retiring. Infantry at of Irish Cavalry Brigade out. The division is being relieved to stay and concentrating behind Awaiting orders. Continue to deal with large numbers of sick sent at ALBERT. There at 150 Scabies cases at AVELUY still collecting staff from	
	20		VADENCOURT. Tent subdivision returned to HQ.	
	21		Capt JAMES to temporary duty 23rd R.F.	
	23.		22 Bearers returned to HQ from AVELUY.	

A5834 Wt. W4973/M687 750,000 8/16 D. D. & L. Ltd. Forms/C.2118/13.

Army Form C. 2118.

WAR DIARY
or
INTELLIGENCE SUMMARY.
(Erase heading not required.)

Instructions regarding War Diaries and Intelligence Summaries are contained in F. S. Regs., Part II. and the Staff Manual respectively. Title pages will be prepared in manuscript.

Place	Date	Hour	Summary of Events and Information	Remarks and references to Appendices
VADENCOURT	March 25th	PM 8	Evacuated premises at ALBERT and marched to marginally named billet with 99th Brigade Group. Holding party left at AVELUY.	
DOULLENS.	26th		Marched to DOULLENS	
BEAUVOIS.	27th		Marched to BEAUVOIS. Holding Party rejoined from AVELUY having handed over to 2nd Anzac Divn.	
BLANGERMONT	28th		Marched to BLANGERMONT.	
	29th		Halt. Heavy rain.	
SACHIN.	30th		Marched to SACHIN. Transport marched via S.POL Hospital remained Closed. Roads hilly and bad, but no casualties in horses	
	31st		11 O.R joined as reinforcement	

J.W.Templetone
Lt. Col. R.Wne
OC 6 7 A

B.E.F.

SUMMARY OF MEDICAL WAR DIARIES FOR 6th F.A. 2nd Divn. 13th Corps, 1st Army
7th Corps, 3rd Army from 10/4/17.
13th Corps from 13/4/17.

WESTERN FRONT April- May. '17.

O.C. Lt. Col. G.A. Kempthorne.

SUMMARISED UNDER THE FOLLOWING HEADINGS.

Phase "B" Battle of Arras- April- May. 1917.

1st Period Attack on Vimy Ridge April.
2nd Period Capture of Siegfried Line May.

B.E.F.

6th F.A. 2nd Divn. 13th Corps 1st Army.   WESTERN FRONT
O.C. Lt. Col. G.A. Kempthorne.   April. '17
17th Corps, 3rd Army from 10/4/17.

Phase "B" Battle of Arras- April- May. 1917.
1st Period Attack on Vimy Ridge April.

1917.	Headquarters. at Sachin.
April. 1st-6th.	Operations R.A.M.C. Unit closed sick of 99th Bde. collected and passed on to 100th Field Ambulance Pernes.
7th.	Moves: To Rocourt En L'Eau. "The place does not belie its name".
10th.	Moves: To Y. Huts near Duisans. Transfer. 17th Corps, 3rd Army.

B.E.F.

6th F.A., 2nd Divn. 17th Corps. 3rd Army.   WESTERN FRONT
O.C. Lt. Col. G.A. Kempthorne.
13th Corps from 13/4/17.

Phase "B" Battle of Arras- April- May. 1917.
1st Period Attack on Vimy Ridge April.

1917.
April. 10th.   Transfer. 17th Corps, 3rd Army.
    12th.   Moves: to Maroeuil.
            Moves Detachment: T.S.D. to walking wounded post, Anzin. Rejoined 13th.
    13th.   Transfer. 13th Corps.

B.E.F.

<u>6th F.A., 2nd Divn. 13th Corps.</u>   WESTERN FRONT
<u>O.C. Lt. Col. G.A. Kempthorne.</u>   April. '17.
<u>3rd Army.</u>

<u>Phase "B" Battle of Arras- April- May. 1917.</u>
<u>1st Period Attack on Vimy Ridge April.</u>

1917.
April 13th.   <u>Transfer.</u> 13th Corps.

14th.   <u>Moves:</u> To Ecoivres and took over mixed School and French huts from 2nd Can. F.A. and commenced to convert it into 13th C.R.S.

16th.   <u>Operations R.A.M.C.</u> Work hampered by rain and mud. <u>Casualties.</u> Many local sick, 60 admitted.

27th.   <u>Moves Detachment:</u> 1 and Brs. to Lille Post in reserve.

30th.   <u>Operations R.A.M.C. Health of Troops.</u> C.R.S. satisfactory. Most cases in R.S. sore feet, large number from 63rd Divn. Diarrhoea also common, and s several cases of ? trench fever.

B.E.F.   1.

6th F.A. 2nd Divn. 13th Corps 1st Army.   WESTERN FRONT
O.C. Lt. Col. G.A. Kempthorne.   April. '17
17th Corps, 3rd Army from 10/4/17.

Phase "B" Battle of Arras- April- May. 1917.
1st Period Attack on Vimy Ridge April.

1917.	Headquarters. at Sachin.
April. 1st-6th.	Operations R.A.M.C. Unit closed sick of 99th Bde. collected and passed on to 100th Field Ambulance Pernes.
7th.	Moves: To Rocourt En L'Eau. "The place does not belie its name".
10th.	Moves: To Y. Huts near Duisans. Transfer. 17th Corps, 3rd Army.

B.E.F.

6th F.A., 2nd Divn. 17th Corps. 3rd Army.   WESTERN FRONT

O.C. Lt. Col. G.A. Kempthorne.

13th Corps from 13/4/17.

Phase "B" Battle of Arras- April- May. 1917.
1st Period Attack on Vimy Ridge April.

1917.
April. 10th.   Transfer. 17th Corps, 3rd Army.
    12th.   Moves: to Maroeuil.
          Moves Detachment: T.S.D. to walking wounded post, Anzin. Rejoined 13th.
    13th.   Transfer. 13th Corps.

B.E.F.

6th F.A., 2nd Divn. 13th Corps.　　　WESTERN FRONT
O.C. Lt. Col. G.A. Kempthorne.　　　April. '17.
3rd Army.

Phase "B" Battle of Arras- April- May. 1917.
1st Period Attack on Vimy Ridge April.

1917.
April 13th.　Transfer. 13th Corps.
14th.　Moves: To Ecoivres and took over mixed School and French huts from 2nd Can. F.A. and commenced to convert it into 13th C.R.S.
16th.　Operations R.A.M.C. Work hampered by rain and mud. Casualties. Many local sick, 60 admitted.
27th.　Moves Detachment: 1 and Brs. to Lille Post in reserve.
30th.　Operations R.A.M.C. Health of Troops. C.R.S. satisfactory. Most cases in R.S. sore feet, large number from 63rd Divn. Diarrhoea also common, and several cases of ? trench fever.

WAR DIARY
or
INTELLIGENCE SUMMARY

Army Form C. 2118.

Place	Date	Hour	Summary of Events and Information	Remarks and references to Appendices
SACHIN	April 1917 1	8 PM	Ambulance remains closed. Sick of 99th Brigade are collected and delivered at 100 FA who are open at PERNES.	
	3		Heavy snow last night which drifted into all the mens billets causing great discomfort. Inspection of gas masks.	
	4		Capt HILL and 10 O.R. proceeded to 22 CCS BRUAY for temporary duty. Bearers practised First Aid and Stretcher drill.	
	5		Gas drill.	
	6		Instruction in First Aid.	
ROCOURT EN LEAU	7		Moved as per margin. The place does not belie its name.	
	9		Bearers trained in Scout duties.	
Y. HUTS nr. DIVSANS	10		Moved as per margin. Violent snow storms en route.	
	11		Heavy snow.	
MAROEUIL	12		Billetted at MAROEUIL. Foot subdivision proceeded to walking wounded post at ANZIN.	

Army Form C. 2118.

WAR DIARY
or
INTELLIGENCE SUMMARY.
(Erase heading not required.)

Instructions regarding War Diaries and Intelligence Summaries are contained in F. S. Regs., Part II and the Staff Manual respectively. Title pages will be prepared in manuscript.

Place	Date April	Hour	Summary of Events and Information	Remarks and references to Appendices
MARDEUIL	13		Tent subdivision rejoined	
ECOIVRES	14		Moved to majority named billet and took over the mixed school run by the 2nd Canadian FA as a main dressing station with orders to convert it and the French huts in rear into a Rest Station for 13th Corps. The latter were in a filthy condition.	
	15.		Lt KNOX to temporary duty with 1st KRR.	
	16		Hard at work. Much hampered by rain and mud. Lots of local sick.	
	17		Have admitted about 60 sick of various corps.	
	19.		Working party of 20 men sent to LILLE POST.	
	21		Capt JAMES rejoined	
			Capt TAIT left for permanent duty with xxxivth Brigade RFA. Divisional Band reported for duty	
	22		Lt KNOX rejoined	
	23		Working party rejoined	
	25		Lt J MARTIN arrived for duty from no 9 General Hospital ROUEN. Admitted 92 Evacuated 57 To duty 35. Remaining 304 patients. The hardest part of the work is now completed and the patients seem comfortable. A satisfactory dining room has been arranged with a stage. Band plays every afternoon. Carpenters are still hard at work.	

A5834 Wt.W4973/M687 750,000 8/16 D. D. & L. Ltd. Forms/C.2118/13.

Army Form C. 2118.

WAR DIARY
or
INTELLIGENCE SUMMARY.
(Erase heading not required.)

Instructions regarding War Diaries and Intelligence Summaries are contained in F. S. Regs., Part II. and the Staff Manual respectively. Title pages will be prepared in manuscript.

Place	Date	Hour	Summary of Events and Information	Remarks and references to Appendices
ECOIVRES	April 1917 26		Patients remaining in hospital 311	
	27		Bearers under Capt MARRACK MC went up in reserve to LILLE POST. Remaining in hospital 304.	
	28		Remaining in hospital 350.	
	29		" " " 360	
	30		" " " 425	
			The Rest Station is now running satisfactorily. The whole site has been properly cleaned up and the wards are comfortable. The greater part of the cases consist of sore feet of which the 63rd division contains a large number. Virulent has also been common and there have been a good many cases of what appears to be trench fever.	

J.A. Kempstone
Lt Col
OC 6 FA

A5834 Wt. W4973/M687 750,000 8/16 D. D. & L. Ltd. Forms/C.2118/13.

B.E.F.

SUMMARY OF MEDICAL WAR DIARIES FOR 6th F.A. 2nd Divn. 13th Corps, 1st Army
7th Corps, 3rd Army from 10/4/17.
13th Corps from 13/4/17.

WESTERN FRONT April- May. '17.

O.C. Lt. Col. G.A. Kempthorne.

SUMMARISED UNDER THE FOLLOWING HEADINGS.

Phase "B" Battle of Arras- April- May. 1917.

1st Period Attack on Vimy Ridge April.
2nd Period Capture of Siegfried Line May.

B.E.F.

6th F.A. 2nd Divn. 13th Corps.   WESTERN FRONT.
O.C. Lt. Col. G.A. Kempthorne.   May. '17.
3rd Army.

Phase "B" Battle of Arras- April- May. '17.
2nd Period Capture of Siegfried Line May.

1917.
May. 3rd.   Moves : Operations R.A.M.C. Brs. returned to Headquarters. Good work had been done in clearing line Oppy- Arleux On 29th April Capt. Marrack and Sgt. Johnstone did particularly good work in clearing front line and No Man's Land.

4th.   Casualties. C.R.S. dealt with sick of 15 Divisions 360 in Hospital.

16th.   Moves Detachment: T. Sub. Sect. returned from 22nd C.C.S.

21st.   Health of Troops. Diarrhoea had been prevalent among troops but decreased after rain had laid dust. "P.U.O.", a low fever of relapsing type has been fairly marked especially in Royal Artillery. Considerable number of admissions had septic sores on legs and bodies especially 63rd Division. Appeared to be due to infected bug bites. The same occurred as complication of Scabies, but many cases sent in as such appeared to be entirely due to pediculosis.

22nd-31st.   Nothing of note.

B.E.F.

6th F.A. 2nd Divn. 13th Corps.   WESTERN FRONT.
O.C. Lt. Col. G.A. Kempthorne.   May. '17.
3rd Army.

Phase "B" Battle of Arras- April- May. '17.
2nd Period Capture of Siegfried Line May.

1917.
May. 3rd.   Moves : Operations R.A.M.C. Brs. returned to Headquarters. Good work had been done in clearing line Oppy- Arleux On 29th April Capt. Marrack and Sgt. Johnstone did particularly good work in clearing front line and No Man's Land.

4th.   Casualties. C.R.S. dealt with sick of 15 Divisions 360 in Hospital.

16th.   Moves Detachment: T. Sub. Sect. returned from 22nd C.C.S.

21st.   Health of Troops. Diarrhoea had been prevalent among troops but decreased after rain had laid dust. "P.U.O.", a low fever of relapsing type has been fairly marked especially in Royal Artillery. Considerable number of admissions had septic sores on legs, and bodies especially 63rd Division. Appeared to be due to infected bug bites. The same occurred as complication of Scabies, but many cases sent in as such appeared to be entirely due to pediculosis.

22nd-31st.   Nothing of note.

Army Form C. 2118.

WAR DIARY
or
INTELLIGENCE SUMMARY.
(Erase heading not required.)

Vol 31

Vol 35
N° 6 Field Ambulance
May 1917

Army Form C. 2118.

WAR DIARY
or
INTELLIGENCE SUMMARY.
(Erase heading not required.)

No. 6 FIELD AMBULANCE

Instructions regarding War Diaries and Intelligence Summaries are contained in F. S. Regs., Part II. and the Staff Manual respectively. Title pages will be prepared in manuscript.

Place	Date 1917	Hour	Summary of Events and Information	Remarks and references to Appendices
ECOIVRES	May 1		Remaining in the Rest Station — 417 patients	
	2		" " 381 "	
	3		Bearers returned to HQ. All had done good work in conjunction with the other Bearer airisions. The line to be cleared was the Béden O.P.O.V and ARLEUX. On April 29th Capt MARRACK and Sgt JOHNSTONE did particularly good service in clearing out front line and no mans land. The Field ambulance had no Casualties. Work at the Rest Station continues to be heavy. The seat of 15 American Field Ctes way in. The place has been much improved. In hospital 360.	
	4		Remaining 342	
	5		" 384	
	6		" 374	
	7		" 396. Lt MARTIN to temporary duty with 10th DCLI.	
	8		" 437	
	9		" 470	
	10		" 404. Capt J R MARRACK proceeded on 10 days leave to England.	
	11			

Army Form C. 2118.

WAR DIARY
or
INTELLIGENCE SUMMARY.
(Erase heading not required.)

No. G
FIELD AMBULANCE

Place	Date	Hour	Summary of Events and Information	Remarks and references to Appendices
ECOIVRES	May 12 1917		Remaining in hospital 371.	
	13		" " " 425.	
	15		" " " 373.	
	16		" " " 375. Capt J.McA.HILL and tent subsection returned from 22 CCS	
	17		" " " 380.	
	18		" " " 385.	
	19		" " " 444.	
	20		" " " 492. Capt CHATFIELD admitted to hospital with P.U.O.	
	21		" " " 434.	
			Diarrhoea has been prevalent among the troops but has decreased lately since the dust has been laid by the rain. Bacteriological investigation has revealed nothing of interest. P.U.O., a low fever frequently of a relapsing type, has been fairly marked. It is noticed that a number of the patients admitted are very lousy, especially the Royal Artillery. A considerable number of the admissions have septic sores on the legs and bodies especially in the 63rd Division. These appear to be due to infected bug bites. The same occur as a complication of scabies but many of the cases sent in as such appear to be due entirely to pediculosis. The Labour Companies afford interesting examples of pathological conditions hitherto unknown in the army.	

Army Form C. 2118.

WAR DIARY
or
INTELLIGENCE SUMMARY.
(Erase heading not required.)

No. 6
FIELD AMBULANCE

Instructions regarding War Diaries and Intelligence Summaries are contained in F. S. Regs., Part II. and the Staff Manual respectively. Title pages will be prepared in manuscript.

Place	Date May	Hour	Summary of Events and Information	Remarks and references to Appendices
ECOIVRES	22	8 AM	Lt KNOX admitted to hospital. Remaining 389	
	23		Remaining 365	
	24		„ 360	
	25		381. Capt MALLACK rejoined after leave.	
	26		379. Capt McKINNEY proceeded on leave	
	27		382. Lt MARTIN rejoined	
	28		391. Capt CHATFIELD discharged hospital	
	29		390. Inspection of H.T. by O.C. Divl Train	
	30		395	
	31		410. Inspection of Hospital by G.O.C. 2nd Divn. Capt JAMES admitted to hospital. Capts J.R. MARRACK and J. McKINNEY mentioned in despatches	

J. Humphstone
Lt Col.
O C 6 FA

Army Form C. 2118.

WAR DIARY
or
INTELLIGENCE SUMMARY.
(Erase heading not required.)

Instructions regarding War Diaries and Intelligence Summaries are contained in F. S. Regs., Part II. and the Staff Manual respectively. Title pages will be prepared in manuscript.

No. 6 FIELD AMBULANCE

Place	Date 1917	Hour PM	Summary of Events and Information	Remarks and references to Appendices
ECOIVRES	June 1	8	Capt HILL to Temporary duty 1st KRR. A successful Sports meeting was held in Rest Stn. 390 Remaining	
	2		Lt KNOX on leave to England. Remaining 380.	
	3		Following awarded military medals for recent operations Sgt. J. CRAIG, Pte A. DALE. H.G.H. ENOCK. Remaining 376.	L.G.31.17
	4		Capt CHATFIELD to Temporary duty with H.Q. R.E. Capt MARRACK M.C. awarded D.S.O. Capt JAMES discharged hospital. Remaining 369	L.G.31.17
	5		" 393	
	6		" 422	
	7		Capt JAMES to temporary duty with 1st Kings. Remaining 453. A working party of 1 NCO + 10 men sent to work on filter at ECURIE.	
	8		Remaining 476.	
	9		" 461. Working party returned.	
	10		Capt McKINNEY returned off Past. Rem. 425	
	11		Rem. 389. Inspected and reported on new site for Rest Stn. at MINGOVAL.	

Army Form C. 2118.

WAR DIARY
or
INTELLIGENCE SUMMARY.
(Erase heading not required.)

No. 6
FIELD AMBULANCE

Place	Date 1917 June	Hour	Summary of Events and Information	Remarks and references to Appendices
Ecoivres	13	8 P.M.	Took over from C.O. who proceeded to England on leave. Remaining in Rest. Stn 206	
	14		Lieut Knox returned from leave. Capt Hill proceeded on leave to England. Remaining in Rest. Stn 198	
	15		Remaining 135	
	16		" 122 Sgt. B.O. Johnstone awarded M.S.M.	
	17		" 115 Capt. Chatfield returned from temporary duty Capt Chatfield & 3 O.R. proceeded as advance party under instructions from D.H.Q. Remaining 100.	
	18		Sgt Craig & 5 O.R. proceeded to Annezin-les-Bethune with orders to report to Capt Chatfield Remaining 89.	
	19		Lieut Martin returned from leave. XIII Corps Rest Stn handed over, with 96 patients to 94th Field Ambulance. Orders received to move tomorrow under 5th Bde.	
Rob'Estainc Bethune	20		Transport moved off at 5:15 A.m by road - Personnel at 10:20 by Motor Bus - arrived at 2.5 P.M at Lillers	
	21		moved under orders of A.D.M.S to Main Dressing Stn in School shown in margin.	
Annezin-les Bethune	22		Took over M.D.S from 8/2 East Lancs Fd Amb. - accomodation for 150 patients (con(t))	

A5834 Wt. W4973/M687 750,000 8/16 D. D. & L. Ltd. Forms/C.2118/13.

Army Form C. 2118.

WAR DIARY
or
INTELLIGENCE SUMMARY
(Erase heading not required.)

No. 6 FIELD AMBULANCE

Place	Date	Hour	Summary of Events and Information	Remarks and references to Appendices
Annequin les Bethune	22 contd June	8 P.M.	Capt Hanrack to S.O. M.C. with Lieut Marlin and 40 O.R. Took over posts at Vermelles — Capt Chatfield with 30 O.R. took over A.D.S. & Post at Cambrin took from 2/2 East Lanc Field Amb Capt Hanrack in evacuating part of 6th our front, in addition to part of our own front.	
	23.		Patients remaining 20 —	
	24.		Patients remaining 7 —	James D McKinney Revd Ractine
	25.		Returned off leave Capt JAMES went on leave.	G. McEmpister Lt Col R.amC
	26.		Inspected ADS's and advanced posts	
	27. 28. 29.		Capt KNOX for temporary duty to 2nd Div. Train 18 Reinforcements received Capt D DUNCAN reported for temporary duty.	

G McEmpister
Lt Col R.amC
OC 6 FA

CONFIDENTIAL

WAR DIARY
or
INTELLIGENCE SUMMARY.
(Erase heading not required.)

Army Form C. 2118.

No. 6 FIELD AMBULANCE.

Vol 3

War Diary
for
July 1917
"Vol. 36"

N° 6 Field Ambulance

Army Form C. 2118.

No. 6
FIELD AMBULANCE.

WAR DIARY
or
INTELLIGENCE SUMMARY.
(Erase heading not required.)

Instructions regarding War Diaries and Intelligence Summaries are contained in F.S. Regs., Part II. and the Staff Manual respectively. Title pages will be prepared in manuscript.

Places	Date 1917	Hour	Summary of Events and Information	Remarks and references to Appendices
ANNEZIN.	July 2	8 PM	Evacuation of 60th division aid posts at S. MARYS, WINGS WAY, OBI handed over to 17th field ambulance. Dressing station at VERMELLES remains under command of OC 6 FA and the evacuation from BARTS ALLEY. SUSSEX POST is also being held on the line. In the left of the sector dressing station at CAMBRIN and evacuation from GUYS, HARTFORD ST, and WILSONS WAY is continued. HARLEY ST. dressing station is held	
	3		Capt DUNCAN to temporary charge 2nd HLI, and struck off attached strength	
	7		Capt JAMES returned off leave.	
	9		Capt CHATFIELD proceeded on leave. Headquarters of bearers moved to CAMBRIN - Capt HILL took over VERMELLES	
	11		Inspection room at LE QUESNOY taken over. DDMS Corps inspected the hospital.	
	13		Lt MARTIN to temporary charge 13th ESSEX. Capt J.LYONS reported for temporary duty. Gas attack in Cambrin sector (Hell) twenty cases admitted. 3 died at FA. 3 more at CCS.	
	14		GOC 2nd Div. inspected hospital.	

Army Form C. 2118.

No. 6
FIELD AMBULANCE.

WAR DIARY
or
INTELLIGENCE SUMMARY.
(Erase heading not required.)

Instructions regarding War Diaries and Intelligence Summaries are contained in F. S. Regs., Part II. and the Staff Manual respectively. Title pages will be prepared in manuscript.

Place	Date 1917	Hour	Summary of Events and Information	Remarks and references to Appendices
ANNEZIN	July 15	8 PM	Battle casualties [T.M.] Pte POSTON J slightly wounded – evacuated. Pte VENABLES W.J. remaining slightly wounded in hospital	
	16		Capt J MARRACK DSO. MC. Sent to Special Co. RE 1st Army for duty, in accord once with orders from GHQ	
	20		Ambulance car At 19224 was run into in ANNEZIN by a flying car Lorry and badly smashed. It was evacuated. Full report sent in	
	21		Capt CHATFIELD returned off leave. Sick at now being seen daily at EENSE LA-VALLÉE (XI Corps Cyclists)	
	22		Capt LYONS to 22 CCS on relief by Capt B.L.HUTCHENCE. Capt CHATFIELD took over ADS CAMBRIN	
	23		Capt KNOX relieved Capt HILL at VERMELLES. The 17th FA at the post has now been relieved by the 1/2 N Midland FA	
	25		Capt JAMES to temporary duty 5th Army. Sgt J. BURNS i/c ANNEQUIN baths at-mitted with shell contusions. His baths were destroyed	
	26		Capt HUTCHENCE to duty ADS CAMBRIN. Lines continue pretty quiet	
	28		Lt MARTIN to permanent medical charge of 2nd HLI	

Army Form C. 2118.

No. 6 FIELD AMBULANCE.

WAR DIARY
or
INTELLIGENCE SUMMARY.
(Erase heading not required.)

Instructions regarding War Diaries and Intelligence Summaries are contained in F. S. Regs., Part II. and the Staff Manual respectively. Title pages will be prepared in manuscript.

Place	Date	Hour	Summary of Events and Information	Remarks and references to Appendices
ANNEZIN	1917 July 31st	8 PM	Heavy rain to day. Bearers at ADS practised in marching in gas helmets at night.	

JW Hemptonne
Lt Col RAMC
OC 6 FA.

Army Form C. 2118.

WAR DIARY
or
INTELLIGENCE SUMMARY

(Erase heading not required.)

Instructions regarding War Diaries and Intelligence Summaries are contained in F. S. Regs., Part II. and the Staff Manual respectively. Title Pages will be prepared in manuscript.

Place	Date 1917	Hour	Summary of Events and Information	Remarks and references to Appendices
ANNEZIN.	Aug 1	9 PM	Heavy rain continues.	
	4		Inspector of catering visited hospital on which he reported favourably.	
	6		Capt. J. McD MATHESON reported for duty	
	8		Capt. B.L. HUTCHENCE for temporary duty with 2nd H.L.I.	
	9		Capt. D DUNCAN returned from CCS (sick) and taken on supernumerary strength. Capt. J. McA. HILL rejoined HQ.	
	10		D.M.S. 1st Army inspected hospital.	
	11		Capt. MATHESON for temporary duty with 2nd Batn. Oxford L.I. Weather has cleared up.	
	13		Work was commenced on the defences of the A.D.S. at HARLEY St. and the revetting of the french trench leading to it, which is getting out of repair.	
	17		Capt. DUNCAN proceeded on temporary duty to no. 1 C.C.S.	
	18		Establishment of Riding horses reduced to Eight.	
	20		Capt. B.L. HUTCHENCE returned from temporary duty with 2" H.L.I.	
	23		C.O. (Lt. Col G.A KEMPTHORNE) proceeded to Hqrs 2nd Div as Acting A.D.M.S. during absence on leave of Col H HERRICK on same day Capt. CHATFIELD was evacuated sick to 7 General Hospital	

Army Form C. 2118.

WAR DIARY
or
INTELLIGENCE SUMMARY

(Erase heading not required.)

Instructions regarding War Diaries and Intelligence Summaries are contained in F.S. Regs., Part II. and the Staff Manual respectively. Title Pages will be prepared in manuscript.

Place	Date	Hour	Summary of Events and Information	Remarks and references to Appendices
ANNEZIN	26.8.17	8 P.M.	Capt J. MED MATHESON proceeded to 17th MIDDX REG'D for duty. A.D.S. CAMBRIN with posts handed over to 1/3 NORTH MIDLAND FIELD AMBULANCE. A.D.S. HARLEY ST with post opened.	
	27.8.17		BEARER POST at VERMELLES handed over to 1/1 North Midland Field Ambulance. Capt. KNOX and bearers returned to H.Q. Horse Transport inspected by O.C. 2nd DIV TRAIN	
	28.8.17		Capt. HUTCHENCE proceeded on leave to U.K.	
	31.8.17		Capt A.G. WINTER RAMC(TS) joined for duty from 14 GENERAL HOSPITAL	

James W. McKinney.
Capt. RAMC
A.D.C. 63 Field Ambulance.

Army Form C. 2118.

WAR DIARY
or
INTELLIGENCE SUMMARY

(Erase heading not required.)

Instructions regarding War Diaries and Intelligence Summaries are contained in F. S. Regs., Part II. and the Staff Manual respectively. Title Pages will be prepared in manuscript.

Place	Date	Hour	Summary of Events and Information	Remarks and references to Appendices
ANNEZIN	1.9.17	8 P.M.	10 P.B. BATMEY arrived from 39 Infy Base Depot for duty.	
	2.9.17		10 Category "A" A.S.C. H.T. Drivers proceeded to HT & S Base Depot HAVRE	
	4.9.17		Returned from temporary duty as ADMS and resumed command of unit once perform than	
	5.9.17		Withdrew stay part at Wigmore St. Inspected and arranged the evacuation etc. of th temporary aid post at Woburn Abbey.	
	7.9.17		Capt KNOX to temporary duty with 1st K.R.R.	
	8.9.17		Capt WINTER " " " 2nd R.F.	
			Lt H.DLIN and Lt G.O'NEILL US Army attached for duty. Capt DUNCAN to 52d General Hosp.	
	9.9.17		Capt KNOX returned to HQ.	
	10.9.17		Inspection of Water Carts. Men practised in application of Thomas Splints which are to be universally adopted for fractured thighs in RAPs and ADSs.	
	13.9.17		Capt HUTCHENCE returned off leave	
	14.9.17		Capt KNOX relieved Capt. HILL at CAMBRIN. Capt O'NEILL attached to ADS for duty.	
	15.9.17		Capt HUTCHENCE for temporary duty with 2nd S.STAFFS.	
	17.9.17		1st Lt FOLIN to duty with 57th division.	

WAR DIARY
OR
INTELLIGENCE SUMMARY

Army Form C. 2118.

No. 6 FIELD AMBULANCE

Place	Date	Hour	Summary of Events and Information	Remarks and references to Appendices
ANNEZIN	Sept. 1917 18.		Capt HILL for temporary duty with 2nd HLI	
	19.		Capt J PATON transferred from 5 FA for duty	
	20.		Took over duties at Medical Inspection Room ECOLE CATORIVE Capt PATON temp. to 17th MX CAMBRIN. ADS and posts at TBRAY KEEP and GUYS were taken over from 1/3 NM Field Ambulance. Party sent to BARTS evacuating the extreme left of the front to the 1/1 NMidland FA at BREWERY. ADS. VERMELLES. The main ADS of the ambulance remains at No I. HARLEY ST. Lectured by Col. CUTHBERT WALLACE at ECOLE CATORIVE on Thomas Splint	
	24		Capt A WRIGHT reported his arrival and taken on the strength	
	25.		Capt PATON rejoined. Capt HILL posted to 2nd HLI for duty	
	26		Capt CHATFIELD rejoined from hospital	
	27		Capt WRIGHT for duty to 1st Kings. Capt CHATFIELD to temporary duty 1st Roy. Berks. Capt McKINNEY proceeded on leave.	
	28		No events of importance have occurred during the month. Work has been unusual on the ADS which is crumbling with age. A party has been employed in cleaning up and painting the ECOLE CATORIVE Horse Lines have been completed. The contours of the gas respirators are all being renewed. Capt HUTCHENCE rejoined.	

J.A. Kempthorne
Lt. Col. OC 6 FA

Army Form C. 2118.

WAR DIARY
or
INTELLIGENCE SUMMARY

(Erase heading not required.)

No. 6 FIELD AMBULANCE.

Place	Date Oct 1917	Hour PM	Summary of Events and Information	Remarks and references to Appendices
ANNEZIN	1.	8	Capt HUTCHENCE to 2nd Oxford LI for permanent duty. Capt WINTER rejoined HQ.	
	3		Capt KNOX proceeded on leave. Capt WINTER to charge of ADS.	
	5		Handed over ECOLE CATORIVE and evacuation of CAMBRIN sector to 75 H.F.A. O'NEILL and 40 Bearers returned to HQ	2L
	6		Handed over No 1 HARLEY ST and remainder of the evacuation of the line as above to Capt WINTER and remaining Bearers returned to HQ. The division moved to AUCHEL area. F.A. remains at ANNEZIN which belongs to the new Corps (1st) DDMS 1st Corps visited Hospital.	
	9		Field Ambulance Remains at ANNEZIN. Sick are collected from units at MINES, LA PUGNOY, and LA BEUVRIÈRE. Teaming Wind and heavy rain the last 2 days. Proceeded on leave. Capt McKinney returned from leave.	J.A.Kempthorne Lt Col O.C. 6 F.A.
	10		Took over temporary command of unit	
	14		Capt WINTER to 22nd R Fus Temporary duty. Opened for reception of Scabies of 3rd Divn.	
	15		Capt Knox returned from leave.	
	22		Handed over to C.O. on his return from leave.	James W. McKinney Capt R AMC 6 Fd Amb.

Army Form C. 2118.

WAR DIARY
or
INTELLIGENCE SUMMARY

(Erase heading not required.)

No. 6 FIELD AMBULANCE.

Place	Date 1917	Hour PM	Summary of Events and Information	Remarks and references to Appendices
ANNEZIN	Oct 23rd	8.	The division remains in rest. Route marches and Coy and Sqn and drill are being carried on day by day for No 12 G.S. at Capt PATON and Lt O'NEIL with a test subdivision left in the PROVEN. Complimentary orders from G.O.C. 61st Corps on the work of the division while in the Corps, including constructive work on horse standings etc.	
	25.		Instruction in limber line method of carrying weights.	
	29.		Capt WINTER returned to duty with the ambulance. Lts ELWOOD and R.A. MOSEN. U.S.A. report for duty.	
	30.		The division is still standing by. The time is being employed in lectures, drills and route marches. Football encouraged when possible. Winter clothing complete. Scale has been issued. Weather colder, with 2am at intervals. Under the leave allotment recently allowed most of the 10 months men have been home on leave. Two of the ambulance cars has been fitted with warming apparatus. This is successful, but the pipes need a protective wire covering.	

J.W. Emptione
Lieut. Colonel
O.C. 6 F.A.

2449 Wt. W14957/Mgo 750,000 1/16 J.B.C. & A. Forms/C.2118/12.

Army Form C. 2118.

WAR DIARY
or
INTELLIGENCE SUMMARY
(Erase heading not required.)

Place	Date 1917	Hour	Summary of Events and Information	Remarks and references to Appendices
ANNEZIN	Nov. 1	8 PM	Half the unit proceeded to Div. HQ. and went through the gas chamber	
	2		Remainder went through gas chamber	
	4		Packing up	
PECQUERE	5		Handed over to a holding party of the 1/N Midland FA (46th Divn) and marched with 6th Brigade group to PECQUERE via LILLERS - HAM EN ARTOIS - ISBERQUES. Q fine day, left 9 A.M. Arrived 1:50 PM. Capt KNOX marched with the S. Staffs on the and the following day. Billets satisfactory	
S. SYLVESTRE CAPELLE [Sheet 27 P17.d.]	6		Marched as per margin via HAZEBROOK. Drizzle, but warm. Units in isolated farms. Barns and tents purchased shew for latter which was a success.	
Sheet 27 E.19.a.0.8	7		Marched to a farm near HOUTKERQUE, via STEENVOORDE and DROOLANDT. Weather showery but warm. Barn and tents purchased shew as before.	
	9		The unit was bathed. Lecture on prevention of shock. Rain and mud.	
	10		Rain and mud.	
	11		Gas helmets inspected. Route march. 1st Lt O'NEIL rejoined from C.C.S. Capt WOOD sent in relief.	

Army Form C. 2118.

WAR DIARY
or
INTELLIGENCE SUMMARY

(Erase heading not required.)

Instructions regarding War Diaries and Intelligence Summaries are contained in F. S. Regs., Part II. and the Staff Manual respectively. Title Pages will be prepared in manuscript.

No. 5

Place	Date	Hour	Summary of Events and Information	Remarks and references to Appendices
Sheet 27. E19.a.0.8 near HOUTKERK.	1917 Nov. 12		All cars except 2 Fords and a Sunbeam reported to OC MAC at DUHALLOW. Capt CHATFIELD returned from 1st R.Berks. Capt PATON to VIIth Divn. Route march. Rain and mud. Issue of waterproof capes completed. Lt O'NEIL to temp. duty B. Siege Park	
	13		Route march.	
	15		Court martial on Dr Cassidy. Adjourned to 15th.	
	16		" " " " 19th.	
	18		Weather has improved. Route marches and recreational training continued. Unit was bathed.	
	19		Inspection of arm. rations. All cars returned from MDS and went for inspection to 13 Corps Supply Column. Orders to hand over Napier car in exchange for Daimler. Spare horse shoes are being completed up to 4 per horse.	
	20		Lt O'NEIL rejoined. Inspection of gas apparatus boots clothing etc. A marked deterioration is noticed in the leather now used for repairs. Some of the field boots issued this year have already worn out. Heavy rain and wind during the night.	
	23		Orders received to entrain at PROVEN for 3rd Army area tomorrow	

Army Form C. 2118.

WAR DIARY
or
INTELLIGENCE SUMMARY

(Erase heading not required.)

Instructions regarding War Diaries and Intelligence Summaries are contained in F. S. Regs., Part II. and the Staff Manual respectively. Title Pages will be prepared in manuscript.

Place	Date 1917	Hour	Summary of Events and Information	Remarks and references to Appendices
IN THE TRAIN	Nov 24		Reveille 3:15. Marched to PROVEN siding. Started entraining 9 AM. Finished 4:45. Strength: Officers 9, OR 220, Horses 48, Vehicles 4 wheeled 11, 2 wheeled 8, cycles 2. Cpl Brewster & D.R.L.S. Capt SOMERVILLE MC joined at the station and 1st/1st WOOD Regt. for 38th Divn. Proceeded via BERGUES, HAZEBROUK, S. POL, ARRAS.	
ROCQUIGNY	25		Detrained in pouring rain at MIRAUMONT 11.30 PM last night. Two lorries provided for blankets and a few of the personnel. Marched in rain and virtual wind to miquiraly named billet via ACHIET-BAPAUME-LE TRANSLOY. Arrived 7 AM. (20 Kilos) all village a ruin — accomodated in huts.	
"	26		Moved to Nissen huts and tents on the BUS-ROCQUIGNY road. Heavy rain.	
	27		Division moved into the line opposite MOEUVRES. Ambulance trains in ROCQUIGNY. Sent 3 cars to Walking Wounded Post HERMIES and 2 NCOs and 18 OR to the MDS of the 62nd Divn. HAVRINCOURT.	
LECHELLE	28		Moved at 9 AM to a hutted site at LECHELLE. This provides good accomodation for patients but has been allowed to fall into neglect. Put in a good days work improving the site.	
BARASTRE	29		Moved as per margin. Capt WINTER returned off leave. Capt KNOX and 50 bearers reported to OC 100 FA who is evacuating the line. The bearers of the three FAs are working in reliefs. One evacuating from regimental aid posts to Foot and	

2449 Wt. W14957/M90 750,000 1/16 J.B.C. & A. Forms/C.2118/12.

Army Form C. 2118.

WAR DIARY
or
INTELLIGENCE SUMMARY

(Erase heading not required.)

Place	Date 1917	Hour	Summary of Events and Information	Remarks and references to Appendices
BARASTRE	Nov. 30	8 PM	West of canal to leave post. One team to ADS DEMICOURT, and one in rest. Capt KNOX with remaining bearers reported at HERMIES at 9 A.M. 1st Lt MOSER and a tent subdivision proceeded on temporary duty to 48 CCS at YTRES. The ambulance is at present closed.	ga Kempthorne Lt Col OC 6 FA

2449 Wt. W14957/M90 750,000 1/16 J.B.C. & A. Forms/C.2118/12.

Army Form C. 2118.

WAR DIARY
or
INTELLIGENCE SUMMARY

(Erase heading not required.)

No. 6 FIELD AMBULANCE

Instructions regarding War Diaries and Intelligence Summaries are contained in F. S. Regs., Part II. and the Staff Manual respectively. Title Pages will be prepared in manuscript.

Place	Date 1917	Hour PM	Summary of Events and Information	Remarks and references to Appendices
BARASTRE	Dec 1	8	Visited 100 F.A. Dressing station at HERMIES. Bearers at work in the extreme forward area. Capt. SOMERVILLE to temporary duty with 100 F.A. Two remaining cargo cars sent to 100 F.A. for duty. Orders received 6 P.M. to despatch 3 horse ambulance wagons to same. About £200 of salvage has been collected and despatched to Salvage Dump. A limber has been received and one forage cart handed in to ordnance in exchange	
	2		Capt. WINTER and Lt. O'NEIL to temporary duty No. 5 F.A. M.D.S. Battle casualties:-	
			91028 Pte DUNFORD T R — Killed	
			80446 Pte CANN A S — Wounded	
			29009 Pte LEWIS T E — "	
			35478 Pte O'REILLY T J — "	
			95804 Pte GARLAND N — "	
			5181 Pte FRASER J — "	
	3		Ford Car to 100 F.A.	
	4		Pte DUNFORD buried at HERMIES J.29.b.5.8 Sheet 57c	
	5		Lt. O'NEIL to temporary duty Divisional School LEALVILLERS	
	6		Bearers returned to HQ. Capt. WINTER Rejoined	

2449 Wt. W14957/M90 750,000 1/16 J.B.C. & A. Forms/C.2118/12.

WAR DIARY
or
INTELLIGENCE SUMMARY

(Erase heading not required.)

Army Form C. 2118.

No. 6 FIELD AMBULANCE. Intelligence Regs, Part II. Title Pages

Place	Date 1917	Hour	Summary of Events and Information	Remarks and references to Appendices
BARASTRE	Dec 7	8 PM	Report by Capts. CHATFIELD and KNOX Bearer Officers. The second division took over the front from the 59th division on Nov 29th. The portion of line extended roughly from MOEUVRES on the left to the edge of BOURLON WOOD on the right. The evacuation of wounded was under the charge of Lt.Col. NEWMAN M.C., O.C. 100 F.A., with Bearer parties and officers from all three ambulances of the division. The area of operations was roughly divided by the CANAL DU NORD (still under construction) into right and left sectors. The left sector consisted of the front line (German) branches of the Hindenburg System, and the right sector of the reserve system of the same three trenches ran more or less at right angles to our own front line. Bearer relay posts, seven in number, of which six were in the front Hindenburg trench between where that trench cuts the BAPAUME-CAMBRAI road at right angles and what it meets the Sunken road about K.8.5.1 - were established as far back as DEMICOURT. Where no 1 post (the seventh) was situated at the southern edge of the village. An ambulance car was constantly in readiness at this post to take stretcher cases back to the A.D.S. at HERMIES. In post no 2 that was 4 squads of bearers and in Pots 3 and 4 relays of two squads in each. A short distance in front of no 4 post the HEINE WEG trench ran up to LOCK 6 and cases from LOCK 6 were evacuated through this relay post to and so back. The 3 posts in the Hindenburg line in front of the trench having to deal with cases from the left sector only, no squad in each post was thought sufficient. The evacuation of the left sector was thus a straight carry down the Hindenburg front line trench from the R.A. Post (Situated about	Ref Map 57C

2449 Wt. W14957/M90 750,000 1/16 J.B.C. & A. Forms/C.2118/12.

Army Form C. 2118.

WAR DIARY
or
INTELLIGENCE SUMMARY

(Erase heading not required.)

No. 6 FIELD AMBULANCE.

Instructions regarding War Diaries and Intelligence Summaries are contained in F. S. Regs., Part II. and the Staff Manual respectively. Title Pages will be prepared in manuscript.

Place	Date	Hour	Summary of Events and Information	Remarks and references to Appendices
			30 yards beyond the BAPAUME-CAMBRAI road) to Post 2, and thence by the sunken road or across country to DEMICOURT- Post no. 1. Later on Post no. 1 at DEMICOURT was given up and cases were carried from Post no. 2 to CHINESE WALL K14 c 3.0 and it was near this point that one bearer squad sustained 1 killed and 2 wounded. The evacuation of the right sector was regulated from LOCK 6 on the canal and thence via HEINZ WEG to Post 4. In front of LOCK 6 were 3 advanced bearer posts (1) at KANGAROO ALLEY on the south side of the CAMBRAI ROAD (E 28 b. 4.2.) where seven or eight squads were kept (2) 9mm. equally to the north side of the road where three squads were stationed (3) The chateau of the SUCRERIE where were three squads. All these posts evacuated to LOCK 6 from the two RAP's at the SUCRERIE, one RAP at E 29 6 4 2 and one about E 28 b 90. All these bearer posts and aid posts and the intervening trenches were under constant and heavy shell fire. The SUCRERIE was especially bad. There was ample accommodation and security inside, which was an advantage, as at times it was completely isolated by shell fire. The carry from LOCK 6 was very long and dangerous. In LOCK 6 there was accommodation for 12 or more stretcher cases in a tunnel and in a long chamber were other three RAP's. The carry down HEINE WEG was comparatively short and by trench all the way to the Hindenburg front line trench and Post 4 relay. The remainder of the bearers of the right sector were accommodated at LOCK 6. The original scheme of bearer relays was to have the bearers of one ambulance in each sector and one in reserve- Changing every 24 hours. On Nov 29th the bearers of 100 F.A. were evacuating the right sector and no 5. the left sector on the night of 29-30 Capt CHATFIELD received orders to proceed with 50 bearers to LOCK 6 in relief	

WAR DIARY
or
INTELLIGENCE SUMMARY

(Erase heading not required.)

Army Form C. 2118.

No. 6 FIELD AMBULANCE.

Place	Date	Hour	Summary of Events and Information	Remarks and references to Appendices

of the Bearers of 100 F.A. Capt KNOX to follow early next morning with 30 bearers, and the relief to be complete by 9 A.M. On relief 100 F.A. Bearers were to take over the left sector and rear evacuations while No. 5 went back to rest.

Capt CHATFIELD reached Lock 6 about 10 P.M. and relieved the Bearers of 100 F.A. in the posts in front of this point with the exception of those in the SUCRERIE. These Bearers of No.6 were kept busy all night as there had been a fair number of casualties. No. 100 F.A. continued to clear the SUCRERIE.

Next morning about 7 A.M. the enemy attacked heavily on the right and all available bearers were working at full pressure. Capt KNOX's party were delayed at DEMICOURT by lack of guides, the usual routes being under heavy barrage. On arrival at No. 2 Post they had immediately to set about clearing the first 4 relay posts which were becoming congested, and later, information being received that the left sector and post were not being cleared, two squads from no. 6 and one from no. 5 under L/C PETRIE (6 F.A.) were directed to this point and kept busy till late into the night.

The party did not reach Lock 6 till late at night and the relief of 100 F.A. was only completed by the following morning. A party of the 2nd H.L.I. assisted the bearers during the night.

On the morning of Dec 1st the Bearers of 6 F.A. took over the R. Sector, 100 F.A. the Left, and 5 F.A. went back to rest. On Dec 2nd No 6 F.A., on relief by no 5 F.A., took over the L. Sector. About 4.30 PM the sector was heavily attacked. The enemy were repulsed with great loss by the 2 H.L.I. and a company of the 2nd S. Staffs. Our casualties were heavy, including about 60 stretcher cases. R.A.P.'s were cleared by 2.30 A.M. without help from the infantry. The cases coming from the right sector had also to be cleared from Post 4 backwards—

Army Form C. 2118.

WAR DIARY
or
INTELLIGENCE SUMMARY

(Erase heading not required.)

Place	Date	Hour	Summary of Events and Information	Remarks and references to Appendices
			During this time the route from Post 2 to CHINESE WALL was in operation, which increased somewhat the length of the carry. On Dec 2nd No 6 FA Bearers went back for 24 hours rest at HERMIES. On Dec 3rd they took over the right sector. On night of Dec 3-4 orders were received to withdraw as the Division was evacuating its position to take up one further back in accordance with a general withdrawal of the Corps. HERMIES now became the advanced dressing station and also forward bearer post. Relays were left at the two buccaneers above and below LOCNY, DEMICOURT, and CHINESE WALL. 6 FA was now evacuating the whole line. The night passed off quietly. They remained in the line till the morning of the 6th when No 5 took over. The position was then not clear, but RAP's had been established at K8b.5.5, K14d.5.4 and K7c. During the whole operations the aid posts were never allowed to become congested.	

Instructions regarding War Diaries and Intelligence Summaries are contained in F. S. Regs., Part II. and the Staff Manual respectively. Title Pages will be prepared in manuscript.

WAR DIARY
or
INTELLIGENCE SUMMARY

(Erase heading not required.)

Army Form C. 2118.

Place	Date	Hour	Summary of Events and Information	Remarks and references to Appendices

2nd Division
Nov. 30 1917.

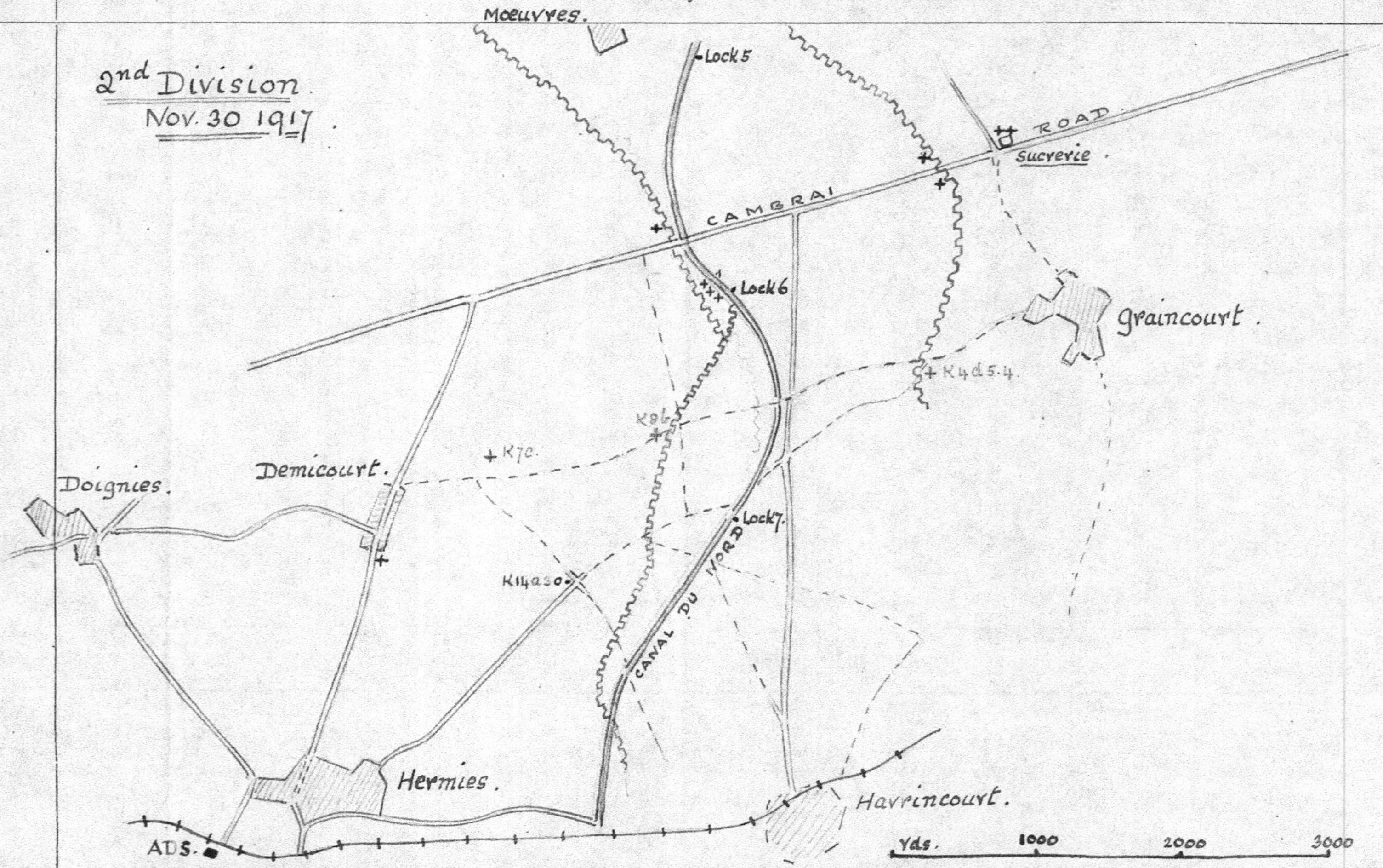
Moeuvres.
Lock 5
ROAD
Sucrerie
CAMBRAI
Lock 6
Graincourt.
+ K4d5.4
K9b
+ K7c.
Demicourt.
Doignies.
Lock 7.
K14a5o.
CANAL DU NORD
Hermies.
Havrincourt.
ADS.
Yds. 1000 2000 3000

G.A. Kempthorne
Lt Col
OC 6 FA

2449 Wt. W14957/M90 750,000 1/16 J.B.C. & A. Forms/C.2118/12.

Army Form C. 2118.

WAR DIARY
or
INTELLIGENCE SUMMARY

(Erase heading not required.)

Place	Date 1917	Hour PM	Summary of Events and Information	Remarks and references to Appendices
BARASTRE	Dec 9	9	The ambulance opened for light cases of sickness in the division	
	12		Capt SOMERVILLE returned to HQ	
	13		Capt WINTER to temporary charge RE	
	14		Capt SOMERVILLE MC to 2nd H.L.I. Capt J McA HILL rejoined the ambulance	
			Beavers went up to report to OC 100 HA at HERMIES	
N14 a	15		Moved into camp near the BARAQUE. Handed over to 148 RFA. 1st Lt MOSER rejoined. Snow and intense cold	
BEAULENCOURT N11.	17		Took over rest Station from 2/1 Highland F.A. opened as divisional rest Stn	
	18		Remaining 189 O.R. 2 Officers	
	19		Capt MILLER DSO MC joined. Remaining 251 O.R. Officers 2	
	22		Remaining 298 O.R. Officers 2	
	24		Remaining 322 O.R. Officers 4. Capt KNOX placed on the sick List.	
	25		Christmas day	

Army Form C. 2118.

WAR DIARY
or
INTELLIGENCE SUMMARY

(Erase heading not required.)

 No 6

Instructions regarding War Diaries and Intelligence Summaries are contained in F. S. Regs., Part II. and the Staff Manual respectively. Title Pages will be prepared in manuscript.

Place	Date 1917	Hour	Summary of Events and Information	Remarks and references to Appendices
Mill Central	DEC 27	9 pm	Remaining Officers 3. OR. 349	
	28.		" " 4 " 334	
	29.		" " 4 " 338	
	30.		" " 2 " 332	
			A working party sent up the line for making regimental arm posts	
			Capt Knox returned to duty.	
			Admitted during 1917 - British 11325	
			Canadians 50	
			S.Africans 20	
			Indians 4	
			Australians 120	
			Germans 48	
			600	
			12167	
			Transfers. 273	
			Officers	

2ND DIVISION
MEDICAL

NO. 6 FIELD AMBULANCE

JAN-DEC 1918

War Diary

No 6 Field Ambce

Vol XLII

No. 6 FIELD AMBULANCE.
No.
Date

No. 6 FIELD AMBULANCE.
No.
Date

COMMITTEE FOR THE MEDICAL HISTORY OF THE WAR
Date -4 MAR. 1918

YA 39

Jan. 1918
20

Army Form C. 2118.

WAR DIARY
or
INTELLIGENCE SUMMARY

(Erase heading not required.)

Instructions regarding War Diaries and Intelligence Summaries are contained in F.S. Regs., Part II. and the Staff Manual respectively. Title Pages will be prepared in manuscript.

Place	Date 1918	Hour PM	Summary of Events and Information	Remarks and references to Appendices
BEAULEN-COURT. M11.	Jan 1	8.	Lt MOSER to temp. duty 13th Essex. Remaining in hospital Offs 4. OR 334	gak
	2		Remaining - Offs 6. OR 327.	gak
	3		" " 5 " 330.	gak
	4		" " 3 " 325.	gak
	5		" " 2 " 328. 5 Reinforcements from Base. Lt MOSER rejoined.	gak
	6		" " 2 " 315. Three officers, transport, and tent subdivision 53rd #A 17th division reported for duty at the hospital which is now open for sick from the 2nd & 17th divisions. The division came out of the 17th took over. the line and	gak
	7		Remaining Officers 4. OR. 306.	
	8		" " 3 OR 344	gak
	9		" " 5 OR 388 Lt MOSER to sanitary course ARRAS Capt KNOX to temporary duty with 17th R.F.	gak

Army Form C.2118.

WAR DIARY
or
INTELLIGENCE SUMMARY
(Erase heading not required.)

Instructions regarding War Diaries and Intelligence Summaries are contained in F.S. Regs., Part II. and the Staff Manual respectively. Title Pages will be prepared in manuscript.

Place	Date 1919	Hour	Summary of Events and Information	Remarks and references to Appendices
	Jan 10	8 PM	Remaining Officers 3. O.R 390.	gak
	11.		Capt HILL to temporary duty with 10th DCLI.	gak
	13.		Remaining Officers 4. O.R. 369. Assumed duties of a/Adms. Handed over command to Capt JW MCKINNEY	gak galenthorpe Lt Col
			Awarded Military medals for recent operations 669 a.Sgt T A MARLBOROUGH (Bar) 62948 A.L.C. J M PETRIE 98329 Pte A. ANDERSON 1703 Pte W. BREEDS. M/20548 Dvr J H UPTON ASC MT	
			Took over command from Lt-Col G.A. Kimpthorne D.S.O.	James K. J.W. McKinney Capt- Rank
	14.		Remaining Officers 2. O.R 354.	James K.
	15		Remaining Officers 1 O.R. 401.	James K.

Army Form C. 2118.

WAR DIARY
or
INTELLIGENCE SUMMARY.

(Erase heading not required.)

Place	Date 1918	Hour 8 PM	Summary of Events and Information	Remarks and references to Appendices
BEAULEN- COURT N 11 Central Sheet 57C	16		G.O.C. Division inspected Camp. Remaining Officers 1 O.R. 339	Summer
	17		Capt D.N. Knox proceeded to 17th H.A.G. for duty	Summer
			Lt. Col. G.A. KEMPTHORNE D.S.O. received orders to proceed to ETAPLES for duty. Remaining Officers 1 O.R. 361	Summer
	18		Lt. Col. G.A. KEMPTHORNE proceeded as above Officers – O.R 374 Party of 16 O.R returned from temporary duty from 48 C.C.S	Summer
	19		Officers 2 O.R. 409 remaining	Summer
	20		Officer 1 O.R. 386 "	Summer
	21		Lieut MOSER to V Corps School Temporary duty Remaining Officer 1 O.R 414	Summer
	22		Officers 2 O.R 377	Summer
	23		" 3 " 374	Summer
	24		" 5 " 374	Summer
	25		D.M.S. Third Army inspected Regt. Station – Officers 6 O.R 377	Summer
	26		Capt A.G. WINTER to 21 C.C.S. Temporary duty " 5 " 388	Summer

Army Form C. 2118.

WAR DIARY
or
INTELLIGENCE SUMMARY.

(Erase heading not required.)

Instructions regarding War Diaries and Intelligence Summaries are contained in F. S. Regs., Part II. and the Staff Manual respectively. Title pages will be prepared in manuscript.

Place	Date	Hour	Summary of Events and Information	Remarks and references to Appendices
BEAUENCOURT	27	8 P.M.	Remaining Officers 5 O.R. 378	June 27
	28	"	" " 5 " 380	June 28
	29	"	" " 6 " 375	June 29
	30	"	" " 5 " 381	June 30
	31	"	" " 5 " 381	June 31

James W. McKinney
Capt. R.A.M.C.
A/O.C. 6th Field Ambulance

1/2/18.

No. 6. F.A.

COMMITTEE FOR THE
MEDICAL HISTORY OF THE WAR
Date —8 APR. 1918

Army Form C. 2118.

WAR DIARY
or
INTELLIGENCE SUMMARY

(Erase heading not required.)

No. 6 FIELD AMBULANCE

=War=Diary=

=Nº 6 Field Ambce.=

=February=1918=

Vol XLI

Army Form C. 2118.

WAR DIARY
or
INTELLIGENCE SUMMARY.
(Erase heading not required.)

Instructions regarding War Diaries and Intelligence Summaries are contained in F. S. Regs., Part II. and the Staff Manual respectively. Title pages will be prepared in manuscript.

No 6
FIELD AMBULANCE

Place	Date	Hour	Summary of Events and Information	Remarks and references to Appendices
BEAULENCOURT N 11 Central 57 c	July 1.7.18	8 P.M.	Remaining Officers 6. OR 393	form 4t
	2		" " 6 " 369	fumer
	3		" " 6 " 390	fumer
	4		" " 4 " 376	fumer
	5		" " 6 " 367	fumer
	6		" " 7 " 348	fumer
	7		" " 6 " 344. Working party 10 OR to 46 BAS for busy. 1st Lt W J Mehyer U.S.M.C arrived for duty.	fumer
	8		Remaining Officers 4 OR 368 Working party 40 OR to 5 F A -	fumer
	9		" " 3 " 354 Lt. MOSER rejoined from V Corps School	fumer
	10		" " 3 " 341	fumer
	11		" " 4 " 354 Lt MOSER to 24th R Fus. T Reilly Capt J M°A Hill Posted to 10th D & L.I	fumer
	12		Remaining Officers 5 O.R. 346 Capt W B MARBURY MORE U.S.A Arrived for Sudy -	fumer

Army Form C. 2118.

WAR DIARY
or
INTELLIGENCE SUMMARY.

(Erase heading not required.)

No. 6 FIELD AMBULANCE.

Place	Date 19 2-18	Hour 8 PM	Summary of Events and Information	Remarks and references to Appendices
BEAUMENCOURT	13		Capt CHATFIELD to 2.H.L.I. T. duty. Remaining Officers 3 O.R. 331	Weekly.
	14		Officers Remaining Officers 5 O.R. 340	June 15
	15		" " 5 " 343	June 15
	16		" " 5 " 355	June 15
	17		" " 3 " 369	June 15
	18		62948 L/Cpl PETRIES wounded slightly in left hand at 5 F.A. A.I.O.S. Remaining Officers 4 O.R. 355.	June 15
	19		" " 4 " 360	June 15
	20		Capt WINTER transferred from T.O. 21 C.C.S. to T. duty 1 R.BERKS Remaining Officers 3 O.R. 369	June 15
	21		Handed over command to 1/Capt K.W. MACKENZIE M.b. Remaining Officers 3 O.R. 361. James W Mackenney Major R.A.M.C.	June 15
	22		Lt. Col. K.W. MACKENZIE assumed duties O/C No 6 F.A.	now.
	23		Inspection of Rest Station by DMS III Army. Horns Tents & Rooms 2 Dis/formed. Bivouaced sites & floors for eleven nits Carts Reat RT— Lt. McGREGOR MORE USA. returned from Course at BUS. Lt. O'NEILL " " Proceeded on leave to U.K.	now.

Army Form C. 2118.

WAR DIARY
or
INTELLIGENCE SUMMARY

(Erase heading not required.)

Instructions regarding War Diaries and Intelligence Summaries are contained in F.S. Regs., Part II. and the Staff Manual respectively. Title Pages will be prepared in manuscript.

Place	Date	Hour	Summary of Events and Information	Remarks and references to Appendices
BEAUVENCOURT	24		Capt. WINTER RAINE & MARBURN more additional hospital sick.	---
	25.		Routine	---
	26.		Capt. McKINNEY proceeded on leave. Erection of tents proceeding.	---
	27		1 N.C.O. & 30 men arrived from 52 F.A. for fatigue duty.	---
	28.		First officers ward opened - additional accommodation for sick.	---

M. MacKenzie
Lt. Col. Raine

WO 95/41
140/902

COMMITTEE FOR THE
MEDICAL HISTORY OF THE WAR
Date -6 JUN.1918

CONFIDENTIAL

War Diary

No. 6
Field Ambulance

Month of March 1918
Vol. XLIV

March/18

Army Form C. 2118.

WAR DIARY
or
INTELLIGENCE SUMMARY

(Erase heading not required.)

No. 6 FIELD AMBULANCE

Instructions regarding War Diaries and Intelligence Summaries are contained in F.S. Regs., Part II. and the Staff Manual respectively. Title Pages will be prepared in manuscript.

Place	Date	Hour	Summary of Events and Information	Remarks and references to Appendices
BEAUVAL COURT	March	1st	Capts WINTER & MARBURY discharged to duty. Lieut Finlay joined from tempy Estabt Q. Rest Stn.	
		2nd	Lt. MOSER rejoined from tempy duty to sunset. Langroftor NCOs proto 2 N.G. Battn.	
		3rd	Capt. WINTER Quico posted R.E. In Def.	
		4th	1 NCO & 20 men attached to No 5 Fd Ambc. (dressing aid posts in the line) Capts MILLER & McKINNEY authorised 7 days leave of abs.	
		5th	Capt. CHATFIELD returned from tempy duty to 2TF. Huts for officers & other ranks started.	
		6th	Majr Mills R.C.H.C. proceeded on leave.	
		7th	Preparation continuing to open a Confolesc. Stn.	
		8th	Arrangements made for Syphilis C.R.S.	
		9th	Opened as C.R.S. 12 noon - 550 patients taken over.	
		10th	} routine.	
		11th	}	
		12th	Entire Working parks, 1 Driver & Orderly proved - Ministers gas shells.	
		13th	Capt. MARBURY sent to XIII Army School of Sanitation. 2 NCOs & 40 men sent as learners to No 2a. Fd in the line.	
		14th	Capt. CHATFIELD Revue Cent to No 2a. Fd. to work & learn & Capt MARBURY recalled.	
		15th	MAJOR McKINNEY Mathers from leave.	
		16th	Capt. CHATFIELD admitted (sick) - (Eyes)	

Army Form C. 2118.

WAR DIARY
or
INTELLIGENCE SUMMARY

(Erase heading not required.)

No. 6 FIELD AMBULANCE

Place	Date	Hour	Summary of Events and Information	Remarks and references to Appendices
BEAUENCOURT March	17.		Lt. MOSER proceeded in relief of Capt. CHATFIELD.	
	18.		Sergt WALTON admitted sick; 1 Dr. 10 O.R.s + 1 Officer also joined with the unit.	
		22	O.R. joined but remained with the unit.	
	19.		Lt. A.T. SMITH MO.R. reported for duty.	
	20.		Lt. MOSER + Reserve came back from the line. Capt. MARROW in team.	
	21.		Commencement of Enemy attack. Lt. MOSER 35 stretcher bearers sent to LECHELLE, No. 1 No. 2 men sent to 56 C.O.S EDGEHILL. Patients in C.R.S handed over to 53 F.A. Orders to dress; all possible.	
	22		C.R.S finally handed over to 53 F.A. - patients clearing out. C.M.D.S - 149 (R.N) F.A took over at night. Capt MILLER went up to Trams.	
Nr LESARS	23.		F.A. moved out at 11 a.m. took up position in Albert-Bapaume Road at M. 20. d. 5.2. prepared to open as Div M.D.S.	
BEAUMONT HAMEL	24.		Passed through a few wounded. Cars sent up to help MAJOR MILLER who had been successional through VILLERS AU FLOS, BEAULENCOURT, LEBARQUE. Cars insufficient to deal with all wounded coming down and some 12 cars has the lift at BEAULENCOURT - dumped + infantry in sight. Long distances + available C.O.'s layout due for shortage. Cars did not come up to F.A. Road LESARS until after the M.T.D.S had moved; but evacuation under the difficult circumstances was satisfactory.	

WAR DIARY or INTELLIGENCE SUMMARY

(Erase heading not required.)

Army Form C. 2118.

Place	Date	Hour	Summary of Events and Information	Remarks and references to Appendices
BEAUMONT HAMEL	Nov 24	4.pm.	Ambulance moved from LE SARS to AVELUY. Met them ½ way & ordered to BEAUMONT HAMEL. Arrived 11pm	
LOUVENCOURT		25	Lt. Col. MACKENZIE made touch with Bdes. in the line at COURCELETTE, formed late & Capt. LANE & horse ambces. & learns at PYS, fall back with the infantry via MIRAUMONT, GRANDCOURT, BEAUCOURT. Evacuated all possible wounded — many of 51st Divn. met late in afternoon & our own M.Os. arriving. Sent back some of 51st Divn.	
			MAJOR MILLER & his bearers reports late in the day at LOUVENCOURT. Lt SMITH sent up as M.O. to Composite Battn at PUCHONVILLERS	
ARQUEVRES	"	26	Lt. Col MACKENZIE & Major ARMSTRONG (No 29) established a small M.D.S. at BEAUSSART, Bearers to MARTI LANE ('100 yd) and Capt. CHATFIELD works with our Cars. M.A.C. (Clear) from MAILLY-MAILLET forward evacuating 300-400 during the evening, including many of New Zealand troops.	
			No 6 F.A. moves to ARQUEVRES.	
ARQUEVRES	"	27	Capt. CHATFIELD and bearers and Lt. SMITH returned. Division out of the line.	
ARQUEVRES		28	Warned for the forward evacuation in front of Div. taking up line AVELUY WOOD — HAMEL	

Army Form C. 2118.

WAR DIARY
or
INTELLIGENCE SUMMARY

(Erase heading not required.)

Instructions regarding War Diaries and Intelligence Summaries are contained in F.S. Regs., Part II. and the Staff Manual respectively. Title Pages will be prepared in manuscript.

Place	Date	Hour	Summary of Events and Information	Remarks and references to Appendices
HERDUVILLE	MARCH 29		Ambulance moved at 6 a.m. to HERDUVILLE. Transport to R.E. dump CLAIRFAYE (near VARENNES) Major MILLER D.T.A. He, & Capt. CHATFIELD Sent in by cars with learns to take over the line. A.D.S. near ENGELBELMER - posts at MARTINSART and LE MESNIL. M.D.S. + H.Q. at HERDUVILLE - Good accommodation. 4 MHC + 2 lorries working here for M.D.S., 4 cars clearing forward section, to M.D.S.	None
"	30.		No difficulties in evacuation. Rain. M.D.S. shelled afternoon. 4 K. and 30 w. in village.	None
"	31.		Showery. Evacuation straight. Average of 70 patients per hour passed through. Notification received that 4 of the cases seen among personnel has died at base hospital.	None

Notice of change
Lt Col Plumc
O.C. no 6 F.A.

Army Form C. 2118.

WAR DIARY
or
INTELLIGENCE SUMMARY.
(Erase heading not required.)

CONFIDENTIAL

Instructions regarding War Diaries and Intelligence Summaries are contained in F. S. Regs., Part II. and the Staff Manual respectively. Title pages will be prepared in manuscript.

WAR DIARY
No 6 FIELD AMBCE.
April 1918
Vol. XLIV

160/2909

COMMITTEE FOR THE
MEDICAL HISTORY OF THE WAR
Date -6 JUN. 1918

No. 6
FIELD AMBULANCE.

CONFIDENTIAL

Army Form C. 2118.

WAR DIARY
or
INTELLIGENCE SUMMARY.
(Erase heading not required.)

No 6

Hour, Date, Place	Summary of Events and Information	Remarks and references to Appendices
HEDAUVILLE April 1st 8.00	Capt W.B. MARBURY rejoined from leave. Village shelled – 4 K. + 30 W. but no R.A. personnel.	
" 2nd	Party of 38" Div. looked round to view to taking over.	
CLAIR FAYE " 3rd	M.O's & horses handed over to 150" F.A. 63" (R.N.) Div. F.A. moved to CLAIRFAYE	
FAMECHON " 4th	Marched @ 5.15am to FAMECHON	
IVERGNY " 5th	" " " IVERGNY	
CANETTEMONT " 6th	" " " CANETTEMONT	
" 7th	New draft 26 reinforcements arrived. More front men from base hospitals.	
" 8th	Internal administration, kit inspection, bathing, Co.	
" 9th	S.	
OPPY " 10	Marched to OPPY.	
POMMERA " 11	" " POMMERA.	
SAULTY " 12	" " SAULTY	
" 13	R.S.M. MACKENZIE attached & tasting over him to O.C. 9" (Guards) F.A. Capt MARBURY & Lieut MOSER & leaving Sergts went up to reconnoitre the lines.	

WAR DIARY
or
INTELLIGENCE SUMMARY.

(Erase heading not required.)

Army Form C. 2118.

No 6
FIELD AMBULANCE

Hour, Date, Place	Summary of Events and Information	Remarks and references to Appendices
BLAIRVILLE April 14 8pm	F.A. moved to BLAIRVILLE. Transferred numerous at R.A.P. to Sud Roar H.Qrs. to Capt Mule McKINNEY. Regt Holden at BRETENCOURT.	—
15.	Capt. CHATFIELD proceed on special leave at BLAIRVILLE	—
16.	Raid on 12th KINGS Regt. Regt Aid post visited and prob. Squads stood up.	—
17.	Lt. O'NEILL & more R.S.A. returned from 2 B.W.R Barth. Lt. SMITH proceeded to 52 W. Yp. on tempr duty. Cellars inspected & villag. emergence R.O.S, work on dug out for officers.	—
18.	—	—
19.	Res slated work in cellars, & Ravin Lane, timbering up of dump and water tolumn.	—
20.	—	—
21.	M. O'NEILL went up to 2 H.L.I. trenches for one night drawing a road & town.	—
22.	—	—
23.	Sgt. UNWIN Evacuated Sick to No 5 F.A	—

Army Form C. 2118.

WAR DIARY
or
INTELLIGENCE SUMMARY.
(Erase heading not required.)

Instructions regarding War Diaries and Intelligence Summaries are contained in F.S. Regs., Part II. and the Staff Manual respectively. Title pages will be prepared in manuscript.

No. 8

Hour, Date, Place	Summary of Events and Information	Remarks and references to Appendices
MARVILLE April 24" 8TH	Sgt UNWIN struck off Strength. Car contains two personnel leHain completed.	—
25	CAPT K. PRETTY posted to M.G. 2a Fm Club. M. O'NEILL to rank up to 2nd R.T.	—
26	Lieut J.H. GRAFF M.G.R. USA. arrived fm 110 2a F. temp B Chief.	— —
27	—	
28	CAPT. HARBORD proceeded in tran/fr to 42nd Div. Simenson E. F.	— — —
29	LT. COL. K.W. MACKENZIE awarded D.S.O.	
30		

M.W.Mackenzie
Lt. Col. RMMC

= WAR = DIARY =
= N° 6 = FIELD = AMB CE =
= MAY — 1918 =
= Vol — XLV =

Army Form C. 2118.

WAR DIARY
or
INTELLIGENCE SUMMARY.
(Erase heading not required.)

No. 6 FIELD AMBULANCE.

Hour, Date, Place	Summary of Events and Information	Remarks and references to Appendices
BLAIRVILLE. MAY 1		
2.	Military Medals awarded to Pte TAYLOR & TEAR for good work during raid on 1st King's Regt. Clayton Evacuating Section from abandoned VI Corps laundry at BOISLEUX AU MONT	
3. 4. 5. 6.	} routine.	
7.	Camp shelled, hut containing 1st KRRC hit, 2 killed.	
8.		
9.	Capt. CONDON U.S.A. Sanfam 308th Inf: reported for instruction	
10.	O.C. 90th F.A. came round & taking over.	
11.	Advanced Party 90th F.A. arrived. Heavy Gas shelling in valley in front of BLAIRVILLE in afternoon. Masks worn 1 hour. Genl. HART SNNBT 6th VBDe. Severely wounded in village and admitted.	
12.	Handed over to 90th F.A. Unit moved to BARLY. Billets for 150 men remainder (Own and Bivouacs.	
BARLY 13.		
14.	Training commenced.	
15.	Capt. K. PRETTY, 2 NCO's & 17 men (off: for 48 Coys FREVENT	
16.	Bath.	
17.	Capt. CHATFIELD returned from leave.	

WAR DIARY
or
~~INTELLIGENCE~~ SUMMARY.
(Erase heading not required.)

Army Form C. 2118.

Hour, Date, Place	Summary of Events and Information	Remarks and references to Appendices
BARLY MAY 18		—
19		—
20	G.O.C. 2ⁿᵈ Div. inspected Transport and billets of the unit & found them satisfactory.	—
21		—
22		—
23	Baths.	—
23	Inspection of the unit, with 6ᵗʰ Inf. Bde. by Genl. HALDANE	—
24	⎫	—
25	⎬ Routine training.	—
26	⎬	—
27	⎬	—
28	⎭	—
29	Unit passed through gas chamber.	—
30		—
31	Baths. Camels passed through gas chamber.	—

Mouralingzi
W.O. Kane.

WAR DIARY

\# No 6 FIELD AMBULANCE \#

= FOR =

╪ JUNE — 1918 ╪

╪ VOL XLVI ╪

No. 6
FIELD AMBULANCE

Army Form C. 2118.

WAR DIARY
or
INTELLIGENCE SUMMARY

(Erase heading not required.)

No. 6 FIELD AMBULANCE

Instructions regarding War Diaries and Intelligence Summaries are contained in F.S. Regs., Part II. and the Staff Manual respectively. Title pages will be prepared in manuscript.

Hour, Date, Place	Summary of Events and Information	Remarks and references to Appendices
BARLY	June	
	1	
	2 } routine	
	3	
	4	
	5 C. O.C. 2nd Div inspected transport and billets.	
	6	
LA CAUCHIE	7 The F.A. moved to LA CAUCHIE and took over D.R.S. from No.4. F.A.	
	8 Lt. MOSER returned from leave & 1 July to 2nd S. Staffs. Regt.	
	9 Lt. O'NEILL was struck off the Strength on being posted to 24th R17.	
	9 Lt. K.A. ANDERSON MOBC joined the Ambulance.	
	10 Orderlie's Rooms to form M.I. rooms at POMMIER & HUMBERCAMP	
	11 } Beginnings of Influenza epidemic. Major McKinney Sick	
	12	
	13 Fresh site for F.A. prospected at WARLINCOURT to some	
	14 Advanced party sent to WARLINCOURT to clear huts &c.	
	15	
	16	
WARLINCOURT	17 F.A. moved to WARLINCOURT and opened a D.R.S. - 150 beds.	
	18 } work started on huts and Officers ward.	
	19	
	20 Lt. ANDERSON lent to 23rd R.F. on Temp/y duty.	
	21	
	22	
	23 Lt. MOSER and Capt CHATFIELD sick	
	24 Lt ANDERSON admitted sick	

WAR DIARY or INTELLIGENCE SUMMARY

Army Form C. 2118.

(Erase heading not required.)

Hour, Date, Place	Summary of Events and Information	Remarks and references to Appendices
WARLINCOURT June 25		
26	⎱ Construction of huts and expansion of hospital.	
27	⎰	
28		
29	Lt. ANDERSON on temp. duty to 10th D.C.L.I.	
30	Accommodation now 300. Hospital full owing, 75% of cases being influenza.	

No. 8 FIELD AMBULANCE.

Kinnearkenzie
Lt.Cr. Kame
O.C. No 6 F.A.

Vol 45
Med/3131

= War Diary =
= Nº 6 Field Ambulance =
= For =
= July 1918 =
= Vol = XLVIII =

No. 6
FIELD AMBULANCE.
July 1918

COMMITTEE FOR
MEDICAL HISTORY
Date

Army Form C. 2118.

WAR DIARY
or
INTELLIGENCE SUMMARY.
(Erase heading not required.)

Instructions regarding War Diaries and Intelligence Summaries are contained in F. S. Regs., Part II. and the Staff Manual respectively. Title pages will be prepared in manuscript.

Hour, Date, Place	Summary of Events and Information	Remarks and references to Appendices
WARLINCOURT. July 1.		
2		
3		
4		
5	Lt. ANDERSON M.R.C. USA. proceeded to 10th Bn. for duty.	
6	" " " posted to 10th Bn.	
7	Lt. MOSER proceeds on leave to U.K.	
8		
9		
10		
11	Lt. Col. MACKENZIE proceeded on leave to U.K. Major McKINNEY took over Command of the unit.	
12		
13		
14		
15		
16		
17	Lt. CASE M.R.C arrived from S.F.A. for temporary duty.	
18	Major MILLER, Lt. NELSON M.R.C. and 30 O.R. took over 32nd Div Rest Stn with 200 cases at WARLUZEL	
19		
20		
21		
22	Major MILLER's party informed heavy smoke shelling partly in charge of sta.	

Army Form C. 2118.

WAR DIARY
or
INTELLIGENCE SUMMARY.
(Erase heading not required.)

Instructions regarding War Diaries and Intelligence Summaries are contained in F.S. Regs., Part II. and the Staff Manual respectively. Title pages will be prepared in manuscript.

Hour, Date, Place	Summary of Events and Information	Remarks and references to Appendices
WARLINCOURT July 23.	Lt. Moser returned from U.K.	Summer
24	Lt. Moser proceeded to Central Officers Depôt of the Am. Ex. Force for duty. Lt. Case returned S.K.4	Summer
25		Summer
26	Lt. Col Mackenzie returned from U.K. and resumed command of unit	James Wingfield Major R.A.M.C.
27	Sto. at WARLUZEL has handed over to No. 113 F.A.	Minor
28	Epidemic of Influenza has nearly died out	Minor Minor Minor Minor
29		
30		
31		

Wingfield
Lt. Col. R.A.M.C.
O.C. No 6 F.A.

No. 6
FIELD AMBULANCE.

WO 46
140/3200.

COMMITTEE FOR THE
MEDICAL HISTORY OF THE WAR
Date 5 OCT 1918

CONFIDENTIAL

WAR DIARY

No. 6
FIELD AMBULANCE.
No.....
Date.....

AUGUST 1918
Vol XLIX

29
Aug 1918

Army Form C. 2118.

WAR DIARY
or
INTELLIGENCE SUMMARY.
(Erase heading not required.)

Instructions regarding War Diaries and Intelligence Summaries are contained in F. S. Regs., Part II. and the Staff Manual respectively. Title pages will be prepared in manuscript.

Hour, Date, Place	Summary of Events and Information	Remarks and references to Appendices
WARLINCOURT Aug. 1.	Routine	
2.	"	
3.	"	
4.	Took over Medical Chant. 2nd Div Recept.n Camp	
5.		
6.		
7.		
8.	"B" mess reclassified	
9.		
10.		
11.	Major Malone left on 1 months leave.	
12.	Lt. C.S. CANTOUGH MORS reported for duty	
13.	Lt. A.S. SMITH MORS posted to 2nd Div, Bords M Pol.	
14.		
15.	Lt. NELSON MORS to 35th Bdo. R.F.A. for temporary duty.	
16.		
17.	S/Mr. Wilkinson left for home establishment	
18.	2/Sgt. DRUMMOND left for 2/Lt. m. Mid. Eg. on promotion.	
19.		
20.	Major MILLER R.E. M.C. and Capt. CHATFIELD went up the line to BIENVILLERS, in reserve.	
21.	Officer i/c Div. in MORCLAIN TUNEL + COURCELLES	
22.	1 N.C.O. and 18 O.R. additional braves cond. M.O.	
23.	BEDMONIER & SAD. GIVES tiluer hincuan for C.R.E. arrived.	

Army Form C. 2118.

WAR DIARY
or
INTELLIGENCE SUMMARY.
(Erase heading not required.)

Hour, Date, Place	Summary of Events and Information	Remarks and references to Appendices
WARLINCOURT. Aug. 25.	Opened as A.R.S. Division in line relieved.	—
26	Work in Wds carried on.	—
27	Accommodation increased to 500.	—
28		—
29	Lt. NELSON ACRC admitted to hospital sick.	—
30		—
31	Patients in C.C.S. 450.	—

Wournedhurs
M.A. Rame
w.a. no? 2.

Vol 47
14/32-9

= WAR DIARY =
= No 6 FIELD AMBULANCE =
+ FOR +
* SEPTEMBER * 1918 +
+ VOL - L +

COMMITTEE FOR THE
MEDICAL HISTORY OF THE WAR
Date 9 NOV. 191...

Army Form C. 2118.

WAR DIARY
or
INTELLIGENCE SUMMARY.
(Erase heading not required.)

Instructions regarding War Diaries and Intelligence Summaries are contained in F.S. Regs., Part II. and the Staff Manual respectively. Title pages will be prepared in manuscript.

Hour, Date, Place	Summary of Events and Information	Remarks and references to Appendices
WARLINCOURT-LEZ-PAS SEPT 1	Routine	summer
2	CAPT PRETTY rejoined from 43 C.C.S	summer
3	Routine	summer
4	"	summer
5	"	summer
6	"	summer
ERVILLERS 7	Moved to ERVILLERS. 1st Lt E G NELSON MRCVSA posted to 1st Kings L'POOL. 1st Lt S BARONE from 1st KINGS B.O.R reinforcements joined	summer
8	Company Established ADS at MORCHIES over bearers under Major MILLER took over line	summer
9	Routine	summer
10	Moved to billet hutted. 1R additional horses sent up. C.O wounded at Vicey	summer
11	Lt BARONE evacuated M.D.N. No 89 680 Pte MARSH W.T & 46307 Pte Wounded No 89 680 Pte MARSH W.T & 46307 Pte EDWARDS E.H killed in action. 340131 Pte MITCHELL R.A Died of Wounds in S.F.A. CAPT PRETTY and J.O.R to inspect wounded pad at BEAUMETZ	summer
MORY-VRAUCOURT ROAD B39 d 38 (57d) 12	J.O.R Evacuated joined.	summer

Army Form C. 2118.

WAR DIARY
or
INTELLIGENCE SUMMARY.
(Erase heading not required.)

Instructions regarding War Diaries and Intelligence Summaries are contained in F.S. Regs., Part II. and the Staff Manual respectively. Title pages will be prepared in manuscript.

Hour, Date, Place	Summary of Events and Information	Remarks and references to Appendices
MORY-VRAUCOURT Rd Sep/13	O/R NCO & 9 Men gassed. remaining with unit. Major McKinney returned from leave	turned.
14	Sgt Craig proceeded to England as candidate for a Commission	turned.
15	ROUTINE	turned.
16	"	turned.
17	C.O. Officers & Bearers returned from line which was taken over by Guards & 3rd Div	turned.
18	15 O.R. returned from 43 C.C.S.	turned.
19	1st L/Cs. Cantough & 1 Roy. Bearers for temporary duty	turned.
20	Lt. Col. K.W. Mackenzie admitted sick to 6 Stay HPL (ANAPHYLAXIS) Major J.W. McKinney took over command	turned.
21	ROUTINE	turned.
22	"	turned.
23	"	turned.
24	"	turned.
25	"	turned.

Army Form C. 2118.

WAR DIARY
or
INTELLIGENCE SUMMARY.
(Erase heading not required.)

Instructions regarding War Diaries and Intelligence Summaries are contained in F. S. Regs., Part II. and the Staff Manual respectively. Title pages will be prepared in manuscript.

Hour, Date, Place	Summary of Events and Information	Remarks and references to Appendices
MORY-VRAUCOURT Rd Sept 26.	BEARERS under Major MILLER and Capt CHATFIELD proceeded to DEMICOURT for work under Major ELLIS 5FA in charge of BW BEARERS ADS finally 20 O.R. to same place. CAPT. K.PRETTY to 43 CCS. on duty	women women
BEUGNY-VAUX Rd 19 d 4.5 (57c) 27	Unit moved to see in margin	
MOEUVRES DEMICOURT Rd K 1 c 50 (57c) 28	Amb moved to see in margin, HQ bombed by aircraft. Two NCO's slightly wounded at duty. 1 O.R. evacuated wounded	women women women A
29	Routine	
30	2 O.R. evacuated wounded.	

James W. Whitney
Major R.A.M.C.
A/OC 6th Field Ambulance

War-Diary

No 6 Field Ambulance

Month of October 1918

Vol - LI

Army Form C. 2118.

WAR DIARY
or
INTELLIGENCE SUMMARY.
(Erase heading not required.)

No. 8 FIELD AMBULANCE.

Instructions regarding War Diaries and Intelligence Summaries are contained in F. S. Regs., Part II. and the Staff Manual respectively. Title pages will be prepared in manuscript.

Hour, Date, Place	Summary of Events and Information	Remarks and references to Appendices
NEAR DEMICOURT 20.00 hrs 1 Oct 1918	Routine	J.W. McK.
2	"	JWMcK
3	1 NCO & 4 MEN TO 46 C.C.S. T Duty.	JWMcK
4	1 O.R. to 2" Div Train T Duty. Capt Pretty from 46 CCS.	JWMcK
5	Capt PRETTY proceeded on leave to U.K. Pretty returned from 46 C.C.S. Capt F.R. LE BLANC, RAMC. SR.	JWMcK
	Arrived from Base. 1 N.C.O & 1 MAN wounded at Duty.	
6	Routine	JWMcK
7	Moved to position in Margin. Capt J.H. McR. arrived from 1st R Fus for T Duty. 1st to C.S.	JWMcK
Etrack Beaucourt 8	Cantough to 17th R Fus + Duty. Routine	JWMcK
9	BEARERS & A.D.S party returned to HQ. Lt Col R.W. MacKenzie Returned from Hospital and Resumed Command.	JWMcK

James W McKenney
Major RAMC

Army Form C. 2118.

WAR DIARY
or
INTELLIGENCE SUMMARY.
(Erase heading not required.)

Instructions regarding War Diaries and Intelligence Summaries are contained in F.S. Regs., Part II. and the Staff Manual, respectively. Title pages will be prepared in manuscript.

No. 8 FIELD AMBULANCE

Hour, Date, Place		Summary of Events and Information	Remarks and references to Appendices
DENICOURT	Oct. 10th	Ptes. GOSDEN and BROOKS awarded M.M. for gallantry and devotion in the recent fighting.	—
	11	} Clearing up surrounding country. Much salvage collected.	—
	12		—
FORENVILLE	13.	F.A. marched to FORENVILLE. Brigade on arrival C.Q.M/Sergt. MULLETT for leave.	—
	14.	Devoted to clearing up the area, collecting and burying dead. Collecting salvage.	—
	15.	As above. a/Q.M.S. A. STAFF, appointed Sergt. Major.	—
	16.		—
	17.	7 Reinforcements arrived.	—
	18.		—
	19.		—
	20.	Capt. LILLOWE went to 100 F.A. in transfer duty.	—
	21.		—
ST. HILAIRE	22.	F.A. moved to ST. HILAIRE. Lt. Col. K.W. MACKENZIE A.D.M.S. took charge of the Divisional trains, and took over A.D.S. at ST. PYTHON from Guards Div. 5th Bde. Went into the line. Capt. NOIR Mc Comb C. A.D.S. part.	—
ST. PYTHON	23.	Attack by 5th Bde on HARRIES River and village of VERTAIN and ROMERIES. Entirely successful. ESCARMAIN obstacle. A.D.S. was moved up to VERTAIN in the afternoon. F.A. and learnt moved to ST. PYTHON. Capt. PRETTY rejoining from leave; was posted to M.D.S. No. 5 F.A. for transfer duty.	—

Army Form C. 2118.

WAR DIARY
or
INTELLIGENCE = SUMMARY.
(Erase heading not required.)

Instructions regarding War Diaries and Intelligence Summaries are contained in F.S. Regs., Part II. and the Staff Manual respectively. Title pages will be prepared in manuscript.

No. 8
NEW MINISTRY

Hour, Date, Place		Summary of Events and Information	Remarks and references to Appendices
VERTAIN	Oct. 24th	Attack of 99th Infy Bde on ECAILLON R. WLY of RUESNES and VALENCIENNES—LEQUESNOY Railway — Strong opposn/ M. A.D.S. moved to CAPELLE, forward post pushed down to RUESNES. F.A. moved to VERTAIN.	Min.
	Oct. 25.	A.D.S. site explored in RUESNES. No further attack on Div. front.	Min.
	26	—	Min.
	27th	3rd Div. took over whole Corps front. (VI Corps) Bearers returned to F.A.	Min.
	28th	H. Col. MACKENZIE returned & H.Q.rs open	Min.
	29	2nd Div. took over VI Corps front from 3rd Div. 5th & 6th Bdes. in the line. CAPT MOIR MO. H. Col. MACKENZIE & A.D.S. Parts. established A.D.P. in RUESNES. Bearers under Capt. CHATFIELD at A.D.P. with squads @ 6th Bde. Gas + shelling of village.	Min.
	30	Capt. CHATFIELD went to No 5 M.Q.S. Comps. & Capt. PRETTY took over command of No 6 F.A. bearers.	Min.
ESCARMAIN	31	F.A. moved to ESCARMAIN	Min. Min.

M.Wachurst
Cot. Rawe
O.C No 6 F.A.

War Diary

No. 6 Field Ambulance

Month of November 1918

Vol. LII

Army Form C. 2118.

WAR DIARY
or
INTELLIGENCE SUMMARY.
(Erase heading not required.)

Instructions regarding War Diaries and Intelligence Summaries are contained in F.S. Regs., Part II. and the Staff Manual respectively. Title pages will be prepared in manuscript.

Hour, Date, Place		Summary of Events and Information	Remarks and references to Appendices
ESCARMAIN	Nov. 1.	Heavy shelling of A.D.S. Ruesnes. Pte Mills wounded.	None
ST. HILAIRE	2.	The Ambulance moved to St Hilaire. Lt Col. MacKenzie handed over A.D.S. to No 9 F.A. Guards Div. and A.D.S. pack moved back.	None
"	3.	Capt. Le Blanc rejoined. Capt. Chatfield on leave. Cpl. Price awarded M.M.	None
"	4.	Capt. Le Blanc to 1st Kings for temp. duty.	None
"	5.	Capt. Noir on temp. duty at C.R.S.	None
"	6.	Major Miller FSc. MC from France.	None
ESCARMAIN	7.		None
"	8.	Ambulance moved to Escarmain - Brigaded 99th Inf Bde.	None
"	9.		None
"	10.		None
"	11.	Hostilities ceased at 11 a.m.	None
"	12.	Major Miller & Capt. Chatfield rejoined. Congratulatory cards from the General, 2nd Div.	None
"	13.	Inspection & M.G.C. 2nd Div.	None
PREUX AU SART	14.	Amb. moved to Preux au Sart. Brigaded c 6th Inf Bde.	None
"	15.	Equipment & vehicles for forward march. Col. Buckland received CBE's card & congratulation.	None
MECQUIGNIES	16.	Amb. moved to Mecquignies.	None

Army Form C. 2118.

WAR DIARY
or
INTELLIGENCE SUMMARY.
(Erase heading not required.)

Instructions regarding War Diaries and Intelligence Summaries are contained in F.S. Regs., Part II. and the Staff Manual respectively. Title pages will be prepared in manuscript.

Hour, Date, Place		Summary of Events and Information	Remarks and references to Appendices
	Nov. 17		
MAUBEUGE	18	Aubks moved to MAUBEUGE.	
	19		
FAUROEULX	20	Aubks crossed frontier into BELGIUM. to FAUROEULX.	
	21		
	22		
	23		
ANDERLUES	24	Aubks moved to ANDERLUES.	
NONTIGNIES SUR SAMBRE	25	Aubks moved via CHARLEROI to MONTIGNIES SUR SAMBRE	
	26	Capt. H.Q. LANGDALE-SMITH Rance (?) reported for duty.	
	27		
SART ST LAURENT	28	Aubks moved to SART ST LAURENT	
MALONNE	29	" " MALONNE	
		Curé Welcoms & Burgomasters and Communal officials + head of Pensionnat St. BERTHUIN, being the first British troops to enter the town.	
	30	Capt. PRETTY Rance posted to 2d/4th R.7. for duty.	

Montgomery
Major R. Rance

WR 50
140/3481

No. 6
FIELD AMBULANCE.
No.
Date

WAR DIARY
FOR
DECEMBER 1918
VOL LIII

No. 6 F.A.

COMMITTEE FOR THE
MEDICAL HISTORY OF THE WAR
6 MAR 1919
Date

WAR DIARY
or
INTELLIGENCE SUMMARY.
(Erase heading not required.)

Army Form C. 2118

No. 6 FIELD AMBULANCE

Hour, Date, Place		Summary of Events and Information	Remarks and references to Appendices
MALONNE	8 PM 1st Dec	Capt Langdale-Smith to Second Army R.T.O.W. Camp Temp duty.	Sunset.
	2	Routine	Sunset.
	3	Major W.A. Miller. D.S.O. M.C. to England for demobilisation	Sunset
	4	Moved as per margin	Sunset
SCLAYN	5	"	Sunset
HUY	6	"	Sunset
OUFFET		Capt F.R. LeBlanc to 1st Kings	
	7	1st Lt K. Fargo from 5th Fd Amb.	Sunset
ROUVREUX-LES-AYWAILLE	8	Moved as per margin	Sunset
VERT BUISSON	9	"	Sunset
ANDRIMONT	10	Resid.	Sunset
ELSENBORN TRUPPEN LAGER.	11	Crossed the German Belgian frontier to Camp in margin	Sunset
WITTERATH	12	Moved as per margin	Sunset

WAR DIARY
INTELLIGENCE SUMMARY
(Erase heading not required.)

Army Form C. 2118.

No. 6 FIELD AMBULANCE.

Hour, Date, Place	Summary of Events and Information	Remarks and references to Appendices
B THUM Dec 13th	Moved as per margin	sunset
DÜREN " 14	Moved to final Area Unit in Civilian Billets	sunset
15	Capt S.H. Nathan D.C.M. loaned for duty	sunset
16	Routine	sunset
17	Routine	sunset
18	Capt LeBlanc reported from 1st Kings. Capt A.J. Winter arrived for Temp Duty. Capt LeBlanc + 19° O.R to 17° C.C.S for Temp Duty.	sunset
19	Lt.Col Mackenzie to A.K on leave. Major J.W. McKinney took over command	sunset
20	Routine	sunset
21	Opened a M.R.S in KOIRING HAUS new billet— Moved to DURENER HOF Lt Cantough to 17 R F for Duty. Lt. Fargo to 1st Kings for Duty	sunset

Army Form C. 2118

WAR DIARY
or
INTELLIGENCE SUMMARY.
(Erase heading not required.)

Instructions regarding War Diaries and Intelligence Summaries are contained in F. S. Regs., Part II. and the Staff Manual respectively. Title pages will be prepared in manuscript.

No. 6
FIELD AMBULANCE

Hour, Date, Place	Summary of Events and Information	Remarks and references to Appendices
DÜREN Dec 22"	Routine	sunset
23	"	sunset
24	"	sunset
25	Xmas Dinner & Concert.	sunset
26	PTE SAUL proceeded into unoccupied Germany as Batman to Lt FUDSS R.A.M.C Guards Div under orders of P.D.M.S VI CORPS.	sunset
27	Routine	sunset
28	Capt F.R. LeBLANC to No1 Stationary Hospital	sunset
29	Capt J. ROBERTSON arrived fr burg & posted to 17CCS fr Temp duty. Lt W.S. KMYRE M.R.C.M.S.A. and 11 O.R. R.A.M.C. arrived	sunset
30	Lt MYRE to 17th R.F Temp duty, 1 NCO & 6 Men Remainders & Coalminers left for England.	sunset
31	Routine	sunset

James W. McKim
Maj. R.A.M.C
O/C 6" Fld Amb

BEF
2 Div Troops

6 FLD AMB

1919 JAN to 1919 AUG

Box 1012

2nd DN Vol 5
140/3524

Box 1012

= War Diary =
= FOR =
= JANUARY 1919 =
Vol. LIV

No. 6
FIELD AMBULANCE
No. JANY
Date 1918

No. 6 F. A.

Jan. 1919

CONFIDENTIAL

Army Form C. 2118.

WAR DIARY
No. 6 or FIELD AMBULANCE
INTELLIGENCE SUMMARY

(Erase heading not required.)

Instructions regarding War Diaries and Intelligence Summaries are contained in F.S. Regs., Part II. and the Staff Manual respectively. Title pages will be prepared in manuscript.

No. 6 FIELD AMBULANCE.

No..............
Date............

Hour, Date, Place	Summary of Events and Information	Remarks and references to Appendices
DÜREN Jan. 1.		
2.		
3.	Lt. MYRE returned from 17 C.C.S. Lt. F.L. McGAHEY MRC reported	
4.	3 O.R. demobilised.	
5.	Major CHATFIELD went on Special duty, to collect prisoners of war into Germany. Capt. J. ROBERTSON proceed to England for demobilisation.	
6.	Lt. McGAHEY to 17 C.C.S. Lt. MYRE to 10 C.C.S. on temporary duty.	
7.		
8.		
9.		
10.	6 men demobilised. Pte. SML returned from special duty Berlin.	
11.		
12.		
13.	R.M.S. 2nd Army. Major Genl. GUISE MOORES inspected the unit.	
14.	G.O.C. 2nd Div. inspected. 5 men demobilised.	
15.	Lt. McGAHEY returned from C.C.S.	
16.		
17.	A.C.2. R.W. MACKENZIE returned from leave.	
18.		
19.	Lt. McGAHEY proceeded on temp. duty to 2nd Div. Reached 2nd Div.	
20.	Major CHATFIELD returned from temp. duty. Capt. C.E. CATHCART arrived from temp. duty from no. 25 Genl. A.	
21.	15 men demobilised. Major MILLER DSO. MC awarded bar to the M.C. Major CHATFIELD awarded M.C.	

CONFIDENTIAL

Army Form C. 2118.

WAR DIARY
or
INTELLIGENCE SUMMARY.
(Erase heading not required.)

No. 6 FIELD AMBULANCE.

No. ....
Date ....

Instructions regarding War Diaries and Intelligence Summaries are contained in F.S. Regs, Part II. and the Staff Manual respectively. Title pages will be prepared in manuscript.

Hour, Date, Place	Summary of Events and Information	Remarks and references to Appendices
DÜREN Jan. 22	Capt. CATHCART evacuated to 17 CCS sick (influenza.)	
23		
24		
25	Rev. HEWITT evacuated 17 CCS pneumonia.	
26	D. NYRE returned from 10th Batt.	
27		
28	W. McGHEY posted to Medical Coy, 2 Div. British Army of Rhine.	
29	1 O.R. (overseas) demobilised.	
30		
31		

Nouriahurst
Lt. Col. RAMC

"War = Diary."
"N° 6 Field Ambce."
February 1919
Vol. LV

Army Form C. 2118.

WAR DIARY
or
INTELLIGENCE SUMMARY.
(Erase heading not required.)

No 6 FIELD AMBULANCE

Instructions regarding War Diaries and Intelligence Summaries are contained in F.S. Regs., Part II. and the Staff Manual respectively. Title pages will be prepared in manuscript.

Hour, Date, Place	Summary of Events and Information	Remarks and references to Appendices
DÜREN Feb.		
1		
2	Lt. O. KITTELSON M.R.C. joined for duty	Mem.
3		Mem.
4	2 h.c.os demobilised.	Mem.
5		Mem.
6		Mem.
7	Lt. KITTELSON sent to 3rd S. Staffs on Temp'y duty.	Mem.
8		Mem.
9		Mem.
10	Capt. WINTER sent A.T.S. Staff on Temp'y duty	Mem.
	Lt. KITTELSON posted M.O. to 3rd Batt. R.F.A.	Mem.
11		Mem.
12	Ambulance moved by rail and road to MONHEIM	Mem.
	took over from 1st N.Z. F.A.	Mem.
	Handed over Eilz at DÜREN & holding party 142 F.A.	Mem.
13		Mem.
14		Mem.
15	Lt. NYRE rejoined from 17th R.F. Capt. WINTER from S. Staff	Mem.
16	Maj. MCKINNEY Went on leave.	Mem.
	Rev. S. R. HEWITT C.F. died of pneumonia in 17 C.C.S.	Mem.
17	Lt. NYRE posted to 42nd D.A.C.	Mem.
18		Mem.
19		Mem.
20	D.D.M.S. 2nd Corps. (Col. POE) inspected hospital.	Mem.
21		
22		
23		
24		
25		
26		
27		
28		

MONHEIM

War Diary

No 6 Field Ambulance

March 1919

Vol LVI

Army Form C. 2118.

WAR DIARY
or
INTELLIGENCE SUMMARY.
(Erase heading not required.)

Instructions regarding War Diaries and Intelligence Summaries are contained in F.S. Regs., Part II. and the Staff Manual respectively. Title pages will be prepared in manuscript.

Hour, Date, Place		Summary of Events and Information	Remarks and references to Appendices
MONHEIM MAR	1 8 PM	G.O.C. 6th Inf Bde inspected unit & Billets -	furnes
	2		furnes
	3		furnes
	4		furnes
	5	1 MT A.S.C. demobilised.	furnes
	6		furnes
	7	Maj Chatfield inverted to Capt on reorganisation of unit	furnes
	8	Rev W.L. Hannan (RC) Chaplain joined from 11th Div	furnes
	9	Parig rejoined from 14 CCS	furnes
	10		furnes
	11		furnes
	12		furnes
	13		furnes
	14	Maj Genl Pereira G.O.C. 2nd Div addressed the unit previous to his departure from Div	furnes
	15	Maj McKinney returned from leave	furnes
	16		furnes
	17		furnes
	18		furnes
	19		furnes
	20		furnes
	21	Capt Lansdale-Smith returned from leave. 12 O.R. reinforcements arrived	furnes
	22		furnes
	23		furnes
	24		furnes

Army Form C. 2118.

WAR DIARY
or
INTELLIGENCE SUMMARY.
(Erase heading not required.)

Instructions regarding War Diaries and Intelligence Summaries are contained in F.S. Regs., Part II. and the Staff Manual respectively. Title pages will be prepared in manuscript.

Hour, Date, Place		Summary of Events and Information	Remarks and references to Appendices
MONHEIM MAR 25 20 hours		Lt. Col. K.W. MACKENZIE DSO MC relinquished Command of Unit. proceeded to ENGLAND for demobilisation. Major J.W. McKINNEY assumed Command.	lumsk
	26		
	27	5 O.R. R.A.M.C. demobilised	lumsk
	28	Capt LANGDALE-SMITH 53" Rifle Brigade for duty	lumsk
	29		lumsk
	30		lumsk
	31		lumsk

James W. McKinney
Major R.A.M.C.
A/OC 6 Fd. Amb.
Rifle Division

3/H/19.

[No. 8 FIELD AMBULANCE]

= WAR · DIARY =

= APRIL · 1919 = (Eighth Division Rhine Army)

= Vol. LVII =

April 1919

Army Form C. 2118.

WAR DIARY
or
INTELLIGENCE SUMMARY.
(Erase heading not required.)

Instructions regarding War Diaries and Intelligence Summaries are contained in F. S. Regs., Part II. and the Staff Manual respectively. Title pages will be prepared in manuscript.

Hour, Date, Place			Summary of Events and Information	Remarks and references to Appendices
MONHEIM	April	1	Routine	Sunset.
		2	"	Sunset.
		3	"	Sunset.
		4	Lt Col H HARDING RAMC from 135 F.A took over command	Sunset.
		5	Routine	Sunset.
		6	"	Sunset.
		7	Advance party to New Barracks at CASTER	Sunset.
		8	Routine	Sunset.
		9	Unit moved to marginally named Military rail -	Sunset.
		10	Lt Col H HARDING proceeded to ENGLAND under orders for INDIA	Sunset.
CASTER		11	Routine	Sunset.
		12	"	Sunset.
		13	"	Sunset.
		14	"	Sunset.
		15	"	Sunset.
		16	"	Sunset.

WAR DIARY
OF
INTELLIGENCE SUMMARY.
(Erase heading not required.)

Army Form C. 2118.

Instructions regarding War Diaries and Intelligence Summaries are contained in F.S. Regs., Part II. and the Staff Manual respectively. Title pages will be prepared in manuscript.

Hour, Date, Place		Summary of Events and Information	Remarks and references to Appendices
CASTER	April 17	Capt H.T. CHATFIELD M.C. to 20th K.R.R.C. for Duty.	Summet
	18	Capt. C.H. BRYAN from 20th K.R.R.C.	Summet
	19	Raining	Summet
	20	Capt. O/C Col H.C.D. RANKIN R.A.M.C. from 4 F.A. took over Command of Unit.	James W. Mortimer Major R.A.M.C.
	21.	Took over Command from Maj. Jas. T. Kinney R.A.M.C.	HCDR
	24.	Capt. A.S. LOUIE R.A.M.C. posted for duty to this Unit. Capt. D.E. CARTER Y.C. Reported to 20th K.R.R.C. Capt. Carter Y.C. taken on the strength from 65 Labour Coys.	HCDR
	25.	Capt. Carter to 51st R.B. for temporary duty. Capt. C.H. Bryan to 2nd Bn. H.G.C. for duty.	HCDR

1919.

Army Form C. 2118.

WAR DIARY
or
INTELLIGENCE SUMMARY.
(Erase heading not required.)

Instructions regarding War Diaries and Intelligence Summaries are contained in F.S. Regs., Part II. and the Staff Manual respectively. Title pages will be prepared in manuscript.

Hour, Date, Place	Summary of Events and Information	Remarks and references to Appendices
KASTER. April 30.	Unit inspected by B.E.C. before dinner - Brig. Ge. West. Sir R.D. Whigham. The Unit has been taking in sick from the 3rd Light Brigade, and seeking cases from the Division. Accommodation for patients is poor, consists of a small village hall & tent tentage. CRE is going to build huts, a bath house & a dressing station. The site for these have been chosen. Brick for the personnel and Good. Training is proceeding in accordance with a syllabus.	

McLauchlin
Lieut RAMC
OC 6 Field Ambulance.

War Diary.

No 6 Field Ambulance

May, 1919.

Vol. LVIII

Army Form C. 2118.

WAR DIARY
or
INTELLIGENCE SUMMARY.

(Erase heading not required.)

No. 3 FIELD AMBULANCE

Instructions regarding War Diaries and Intelligence Summaries are contained in F.S. Regs., Part II. and the Staff Manual respectively. Title pages will be prepared in manuscript.

Hour, Date, Place		Summary of Events and Information	Remarks and references to Appendices
CASTER	MAY 8.PM 1	Routine	France
	2		France
	3		France
	4	Lt Col Rankin proceeded on leave to UK.	France
	5	Routine	France
	6		France
	7		France
	8		France
	9	Capt Winter to 20th KRRC for duty	France
	10	Routine	France
	11		France
	12		France
	13		France
	14	10 O.R. Infantry attached for duty with Ease. H.T.	France
	15		France
	16		France
	17		France
	18	Demobilisation R.A.M.C. O.R. at rate of 3 per team	France

WAR DIARY
or
INTELLIGENCE SUMMARY.
(Erase heading not required.)

Army Form C. 2118.

Hour, Date, Place		Summary of Events and Information	Remarks and references to Appendices
CASTER	May 19	Routine	
	20	Capt CARTER from temporary duty 51st RR. Lt Col RANKIN returned from leave and resumed command.	Stored Kennedy map scheme.
	24.	3 to O.R. Infantry attached for duty with R.A.M.C. with a view to transfer. 1 N.C.O. + 9 Ptes. transferred from 100 Field Ambulance.	KCST
	25.	15 t.R. Infantry attached with a view to transfer t to RAMC. Capt D.C. Coate. R.C. proceeded to England on separation of contract.	KCST
	26.	Rev. W.R. Newman C.F. proceeded to England on leave. Commenced training attached infantrymen.	KCST

Army Form C. 2118.

No. 8
FIELD AMBULANCE

WAR DIARY
INTELLIGENCE SUMMARY.
(Erase heading not required.)

1919

Instructions regarding War Diaries and Intelligence Summaries are contained in F.S. Regs., Part II. and the Staff Manual respectively. Title pages will be prepared in manuscript.

Hour, Date, Place	Summary of Events and Information	Remarks and references to Appendices
CASTER. May 27.	Four A attached Infantry proceeded to 33 Sanitary Section for training.	HOSR
31.	Rev. W. B. Fyfe C.F. joined for temporary duty.	HOSR
	During the month reinforcements & released men have proceeded steadily with a view to bringing the unit down to 50% of War Establishment. 39 O.Rs. RAMC were sent to Infantry to replace casualties. The training of the Infantry k replace them is now occupying most of the time. This consists of lectures, demonstrations, stretcher drill, care & carriage of sick. Turnround & most of the Infantry cas been to learn & show promise of turning out well. The unit continues to treat scattered cases of the Division.	H.O.S Rankin. LtCol RAMC OC 6 Field Ambulance

7/9
3208

No 6 Field Ambulance

June 1919

MEDITERRANEAN EXPEDITIONARY FORCE

WAR DIARIES

OF

1st LOWLAND FIELD AMBULANCE.

52nd (LOWLAND) DIVISION.

8th CORPS - HELLES

June 1915 - MARCH 1916.

1919.

Army Form C. 2118.

28 MAR 1920

WAR DIARY
INTELLIGENCE SUMMARY.
(Erase heading not required.)

Hour, Date, Place	Summary of Events and Information	Remarks and references to Appendices
KASTER. June 1.	Unit taking in Scabies cases of the Division and Sick 1/B	MCR
2.	Third Lipur Brigade and Divisional Artillery.	
	Capt. H. Bailey M.O.R.C. U.S.A. rejoined from leave.	MCR
	NCOs and 6 men from M.T. Coy. posted for duty.	
3.	Birthday of H.M. King George V. Special Parade at 10 AM	MCR
	at which three cheers for the King were given. Remainder	
	of day was observed as a holiday.	
5.	1 NCO 16 ORs R.A.S.C. M.T. left for Demobilization.	MCR
6.	S/Lieut. Staff proceeded on leave to Malta.	MCR
7.	Capt. H.S. Bailey U.S.A. left to rejoin A.E.F.	MCR

1919.

Army Form C. 2118.

WAR DIARY
INTELLIGENCE SUMMARY.
(Erase heading not required.)

Instructions regarding War Diaries and Intelligence Summaries are contained in F.S. Regs., Part II. and the Staff Manual respectively. Title pages will be prepared in manuscript.

Hour, Date, Place	Summary of Events and Information	Remarks and references to Appendices
KASTER. June 13.	T.R. to Appointed with Rose Wronter.	
" 16.	Allotment from O.C. 5Rs per day for demobilization.	
HUCKELHOVEN. " 18.	Unit moved to HUCKELHOVEN. Baggage dump & Front and Scabies patients remained at KASTER.	
BOCKLEMUND. " 19.	Unit continued move to BOCKLEMUND. Advance Party, FANCO & C. were proceeded to take over billets at HOHENBERG from 140 Field Ambulance.	
" 20.	Move cancelled. Unit remained stationary. Not admitting patients except Scabies patients at KASTER.	

1919.

Army Form C. 2118.

WAR DIARY
INTELLIGENCE SUMMARY.
(Erase heading not required.)

Hour, Date, Place	Summary of Events and Information	Remarks and references to Appendices
BOCKLEMUND. June 23.	1 O.R. proceeded to U.K. on leave.	WCSR
" 26	1 O.R. returned from _____	
	1 O.R. returned from Hospital.	WCSR
	3 O.Rs returned from leave to U.K.	WCSR
" 28.	Peace was signed this day.	WCSR
" 29.	Received orders to return to KASTER.	
" 30.	Unit marched from BOCKLEMUND to KASTER and took up the billets. Advance party withdrawn from HOHENBERG.	WCSR
KASTER.	During the week 26 R.A.M.C. were demobilized, leaving 7 for demobilization next week. Unit will then be down to 30% R.A.M.C. personnel.	

WCBlanken
I/CS. RAMC

[signature] RAMC

No 6 Field Ambulance

July 1919

Army Form C. 2118.

WAR DIARY
INTELLIGENCE SUMMARY.
(Erase heading not required.)

1919.

Instructions regarding War Diaries and Intelligence Summaries are contained in F.S. Regs., Part II. and the Staff Manual respectively. Title pages will be prepared in manuscript.

Hour, Date, Place	Summary of Events and Information	Remarks and references to Appendices
KASTER. July 1.	Unit inspected by G.O.C. Light Division.	MOIR.
" 8.	Lt. Colonel Holden proceeded on leave to U.K.	MOIR
HILDEN.	Unit moved from KASTER to HILDEN. Transport by road, personnel by train.	
OHLIGS. " 9.	Unit moved by road from HILDEN to OHLIGS taking over Field Ambulance site from 27 Field Ambulance Rowland Division. Personnel billeted in large hall. Field Ambulance site is small hutted hospital complete with latrines and delouser. Used for Scabies and other skin diseases. One ward is set apart for light medical cases, the remainder will be used as a skin hospital.	MOIR
" 18.	Staff Sergt. Thompson joined for duty from 83 Gen. Hospital.	

1919.

Army Form C. 2118.

WAR DIARY
INTELLIGENCE SUMMARY.
(Erase heading not required.)

Hour, Date, Place		Summary of Events and Information	Remarks and references to Appendices
OFFICES. July.	19.	Staff. Sergt. Jenkins proceeded Home Establishment.	WCSR
"	23.	Observed as holiday to celebrate the Signing of Peace.	WCSR
"	27.	Capt. Bryan RAMC joined for duty.	WCSR
"	30.	ADMS held Conference of Medical Officers of Division at 6 Field Ambulance.	WCSR
"	31.	Attended D.M.S. Conference at 64 CCS. During the month 7 ORs RAMC proceeded to demobilization, being the last of the 1915 men with the Unit. The Unit continues to treat the Scabies cases of the Division, & collects Sick from 2" & 3" Light Brigades and 246 Bde. R.F.A.	

RCSBowker
Lt.Col RAMC
Commanding No. 1 Field Ambulance

N. C. Field Ambulance.

1919.

Army Form C. 2118.

WAR DIARY
INTELLIGENCE SUMMARY.
(Erase heading not required.)

Instructions regarding War Diaries and Intelligence Summaries are contained in F.S. Regs., Part II. and the Staff Manual respectively. Title pages will be prepared in manuscript.

Hour, Date, Place	Summary of Events and Information	Remarks and references to Appendices
OHLIGS. August 1.	Unit reviews at OHLIGS, admitting sick & OR's 2ⁿᵈ & 3ʳᵈ Light Brigades, and treating Scabies cases of the Division.	HQR
" 5.	G.O.C. Light Division inspected Hospital & men.	HQR
" 9.	Capt. Or. Mr. Holder RAMC returned from leave.	HQR
" 16.	D.M.S. Rhine Army accompanied by Sir Potts Heyer inspected the Unit.	HQR
" 23.	Col. Bliss, AMS acting D.M.S. Rhine Army, accompanied by D.A.D.M.S. Sanitation inspected the Unit.	HQR

2

1919

Army Form C. 2118.

WAR DIARY
INTELLIGENCE SUMMARY.
(Erase heading not required.)

Hour, Date, Place	Summary of Events and Information	Remarks and references to Appendices
O.H.I.G.S. August 31.	During the month work proceeded on normal lines. Two O.Rs were demobilized on Compassionate grounds and 40 O.Rs proceeded on leave to U.K. General health of unit is excellent. 1 Off. & 94 O.Rs were admitted suffering from Scabies. Venereal disposal & Scabies continue to be the causes of the largest no. of hospital admissions. McLauken Lt Col RAMC O.C. 6 Field Ambulance	

2 DIVISION. TROOPS.

6 FIELD AMBULANCE.

1914 AUG TO 1919 AUG.

1338